Southern Fried

Southern Fried

Going Whole Hog in a State of Wonder

Rex Nelson

The Butler Center for Arkansas Studies
Central Arkansas Library System
100 Rock Street
Little Rock, Arkansas 72201

www.butlercenter.org

First edition: October 2016
ISBN 978-1-935106-98-2

Manager: Rod Lorenzen
Cover design: H. K. Stewart
Book design: Mike Keckhaver
Copyeditor: Ali Welky

Library of Congress Cataloging-in-Publication Data

Names: Nelson, Rex. author.
Title: Southern fried : going whole hog in a state of wonder / Rex Nelson.
Other titles: *Arkansas Democrat Gazette*.
Description: First edition. | Little Rock, Arkansas : Butler Center Books, [2016] | Includes bibliographical references and index.
Identifiers: LCCN 2016040377 | ISBN 9781935106982 (pbk. : alk. paper)
Subjects: LCSH: Arkansas--Description and travel. | Arkansas--Social life and customs.
Classification: LCC F411.5 .N45 2016 | DDC 976.7--dc23 LC record available at https://lccn.loc.gov/2016040377

All photographs in this book were taken by Mary Osteen and are used here with the permission of the Arkansas Department of Parks and Tourism.

Butler Center Books, the publishing division of the Butler Center for Arkansas Studies, was made possible by the generosity of Dora Johnson Ragsdale and John G. Ragsdale Jr.

Printed in the United States of America

This book is printed on archival-quality paper that meets requirements of the American National Standard for Information Sciences, Permanence of Paper, Printed Library Materials, ANSI Z39.48-1984.

To Austin and Evan, our sons who were born and raised in this state. I hope they love it as much as I do.

TABLE OF CONTENTS

Voices Columns

Arkansas Places

Arkansas People

ACKNOWLEDGMENTS

Thanks to Walter Hussman Jr. and Paul Greenberg, who welcomed me back aboard as an *Arkansas Democrat-Gazette* columnist in 2009 when I returned to the private sector following a 13-year detour into government service. I last worked full time in journalism in 1996, but the weekly column allows me to keep a finger in the newspaper world I still love. No writer could ever ask for more freedom than Walter and Paul have given me. I appreciate the *Democrat-Gazette* for giving copyright permission for these columns to be published in book form.

Thanks to Rod Lorenzen, Bobby Roberts, Nate Coulter, David Stricklin, Ali Welky and Mike Keckhaver at the Central Arkansas Library System and the Butler Center for believing in this project and seeing it through to completion.

Thanks to my wife, Melissa, for putting up with the countless nights when I was late getting home because I had a column to write after finishing my real job for the day.

Speaking of a real job, thanks to George Makris Jr., Steve Massanelli and Marty Casteel at Simmons Bank for letting me continue to write while also serving as the director of corporate community relations for this growing Arkansas-based company.

Finally, thanks to the readers of the column in all parts of Arkansas who keep my energy level high with their emails, letters and phone calls to comment on what I've written.

Note: The pieces appear here as they did in the *Arkansas Democrat-Gazette* but with minor editorial adjustments.

PREFACE

On September 2, 1965, I turned age six.

Rather than being one of the youngest people in my class at school, I would be one of the oldest. In other words, I would wait a year to start the first grade.

It was my father's decision. A former coach, he loved to tell people: "We decided to redshirt him in kindergarten."

Instead of attending kindergarten a second consecutive year, though, I would travel the state of Arkansas with my father as he sold athletic supplies to high schools and colleges. It was a magical nine months for me.

Looking back, I realize now that he was doing it as much for himself as he was for me. On February 29, 1964, my nine-year-old brother had been killed in an accident at Pine Bluff while my parents were in the town to take him to a Ouachita Baptist University basketball game. Less than two years after that tragedy, I suspect my father decided that it would be good therapy to have his surviving son with him on the road as he traveled the state. He was 41 years old at the time, 15 years younger than I am as I write these words.

I was young, but the memories of that year remain vivid.

I can remember waiting in line at a small café at Delight to buy a hamburger.

I can remember stopping at Caddo Gap to wade in the Caddo River.

I can remember watching a deer run across the school campus at Magazine.

I can remember eating a whole trout for the first time at Tommy's Restaurant in Conway.

While the weather was still warm that September, I was allowed to jump into the pool at the Holiday Inn before supper.

I was in heaven.

We sat in gyms built by the Works Progress Administration (WPA) during the Depression, watched high school basketball games, shared pieces of pie in country restaurants and listened to KAAY-AM on the car radio.

It was during that 1965-66 school year that I learned to love traveling Arkansas.

I've had the privilege of writing millions of words through the years about Arkansas. I left a full-time career in journalism in 1996 to work in the governor's office. What I thought would be a short detour into government turned out to be a 13-year adventure. When I returned to the private sector in 2009, I contacted my former employers at the *Arkansas Democrat-Gazette* to see if they might be interested in having me write a weekly column. Since I had spent nine years in the governor's office and four years in a presidential administration, I'm sure they figured that I would write about politics. But I came to the conclusion that there already was so much political writing on the *Voices* page of the newspaper that I simply would be yet another voice with nothing to distinguish me from those other columnists. That's when I decided to make Arkansas—its places, its colorful characters, its fascinating history, its food, its music, its events—my niche.

Arkansas is a hard place to explain to outsiders. We're mostly Southern but also a bit Midwestern and a tad Southwestern. The Ozarks are different from the pine woods of the Gulf Coastal Plain, the Delta different from the Ouachitas. Invariably, though, those who take the time to get off the main roads and get to know the real Arkansas are entranced by the place.

Thanks for going on a statewide journey with me in these pages. Maybe we can stop to wade in the Caddo River and eat a piece of pie along the way.

Arkansas Places

The Arkansas Delta has surprises around every corner for visitors.

July 8, 2009
The Delta

It's not yet 6 a.m. as I pull out of my driveway in Little Rock, the state's largest city. It promises to be another hot day, but at this hour the temperature is still low enough for an open window to suffice. The vehicle's air conditioning can stay off a few more minutes. While others head north and west to the state's lakes and mountains, I choose to head east on this day. The drive will be through the verdant, alluring, sometimes mystical Arkansas Delta.

Never does the Delta seem more like the Delta of legend than on a scorching summer day. It's the place described by author and historian James C. Cobb of the University of Georgia as "the most Southern place on earth." Cobb was writing about the Mississippi Delta, but he could just as easily have been referring to the Arkansas Delta. In many ways, the Arkansas Delta is forgotten by the scholars and historians who focus on Mississippi. But the Arkansas Delta is larger, has an even richer musical heritage, has better barbecue and even grows more cotton than Mississippi.

Heading east on Interstate 40 toward Memphis, it does not take long to realize I'm already in what qualifies as east Arkansas. Even just past the Galloway exit suffices, in fact, as the row crops become evident on my right and majestic cypress trees poke out of stagnant water on my left. I battle the rows of large trucks crowding the interstate, thinking of favorite eating stops along the way: Nick's at Carlisle, Murry's near Hazen (formerly of DeValls Bluff) and Craig's at DeValls Bluff. I cross the White River on a bumpy stretch of road and mercifully leave the interstate at the Biscoe exit.

I breathe a sigh of relief. There are no truck stops, no convenience stories, no fast food restaurants, no businesses of any kind at this exit. There are just the fields of soybeans, milo and cotton; a pecan orchard and a couple of well-kept country homes stand nearby. If I headed north on Arkansas 33, I would reach Beulah in a couple of miles. When I sang about the Beulah Land in church, I didn't realize there was a Beulah in Prairie County. A trip farther north will take you past Horn Lake and Spring Lake. These White River oxbows once attracted fishermen from as far away as Memphis and Little Rock. Those were the days before huge U.S. Army Corps of Engineers impoundments covered much of the state.

On this morning, however, I turn south on Arkansas 33 and drive into Biscoe. At the intersection of U.S. 70 and the Old Memphis Highway, there's my favorite vegetable stand in Arkansas. It's not yet open at this early hour, but the return trip will necessitate a stop to buy locally grown tomatoes, bell peppers and cucumbers for that night's salad. I do stop just down the road at Martin's Grocery for two sausage biscuits and a cup of coffee to be consumed in the car. It's just before 7 a.m., but Martin's is open and I'm not the only customer. Heading east on U.S. 70, I pass the country version of a salvage yard on my left that has a hand-painted sign advertising "Taters" for sale. I'm not sure how junkyard taters will taste and decide to wait on another trip to make the purchase.

Crossing the Cache River at Brasfield, I look to my right and mourn the loss of the restaurant that once floated atop that muddy water. The Riverfront Bait Shop and Restaurant—known locally as W. O.'s—was a unique place. Customers would order supper in the bait shop—right there next to the live minnows—and then walk down a steep hill to the barge. Some of the best catfish and steaks in east Arkansas would then be brought down to you. I can't help but wish someone would buy a new barge and resurrect that place.

Continuing east on U.S. 70, I'm in the bottoms between the Cache River and the Bayou DeView. I skirt the south part of the Arkansas Game and Fish Commission's Dagmar Wildlife Management Area. I'm also in the northern part of the largest remaining tract of the Big Woods. At 550,000 acres, this is the largest corridor of bottomland hardwood forest remaining in the Delta north of Louisiana's Atchafalaya River. It's here that the ivory-billed woodpecker reportedly was rediscovered in 2004, drawing international attention to east Arkansas and making Gene's Barbecue in Brinkley a hangout for media crews from the likes of *60 Minutes* and National Public Radio.

Leaving those bottoms, I make a sharp right on Arkansas 17. After a few miles, I turn left on Arkansas 241. This is the shortcut from Little Rock to Helena-West Helena. As always, I drive a bit too fast on 241, one of the straightest, flattest roads in the state. On the right, I pass a modern duck club with a road sign proclaiming the entry as Duck Road. Then, I'm surrounded by fields. On return trips at dusk, this is the stretch where the bugs hitting the window in summer sound like a heavy rain. When the highway intersects with U.S. 49, I take a right and head south.

I pass the turn to Monroe, a destination in the winter for some of the world's best duck hunting, along Piney Creek. Hopefully, the Game and Fish Commission has eradicated the invasive snakehead fish from that creek. Continuing through the four-way stop at the U.S. 79 intersection, I reach the turnoff to the Louisiana Purchase Historic State Park, which conserves a rare headwater swamp along Little Cypress Creek. It contains the granite monument that marks the starting point for the original survey of lands added to the United States through the Louisiana Purchase.

I have reached my destination. Walking along the modern boardwalk through the tupelo swamp as the morning sun rises higher, I think about what a remarkable state this is and how many colorful characters call it home.

Elk can often be found in the Boxley Valley of the Arkansas Ozarks.

August 9, 2009
Ozark Weekend

It's the first day of August, and the rain is coming down steadily atop Mount Sherman in Newton County. Following the wettest July on record for some parts of Arkansas, the month of August dawns wet as well. I look down into the valley that houses the Horseshoe Canyon Ranch, filled with guests anxious for the rain to stop so they can ride horses, take part in rock climbing expeditions and play disc golf.

The rain lets up soon enough, and I head out for a day of exploring a sparsely populated section of the Arkansas Ozarks. I drive west on Arkansas 74 and then south on Arkansas 43, passing areas known to house a large portion of the state's elk herd. Elk once roamed much of what's now Arkansas, but the majestic creatures had disappeared by the 1840s. The U.S. Forest Service stocked 11 elk in Franklin County in 1933, and the herd increased to an estimated 200 elk before disappearing in the 1950s. The elk were the victims of widespread illegal hunting and the loss of suitable habitat. A second restoration effort was begun by the Arkansas Game and Fish Commission in 1981. By 1985, 112 elk had been stocked near the Buffalo National River. There are now an estimated 500 elk roaming parts of Newton, Searcy, Boone, Carroll and Madison counties.

Elk often can be seen at Boxley Valley, Erbie and Carver and in the Gene Rush Wildlife Management Area of Newton County. No elk are spotted this day, but the scenery is worth the drive as low clouds envelop the tops of the mountains. At the intersection of Arkansas 74 with Arkansas 21, you could head south into Johnson County or north into Madison County. I choose to drive north, having heard about the quality of the doughnuts and the coffee at the café on the square in Kingston. It's also a chance to visit the renovated building that housed the Bank of Kingston, now a branch of the First National Bank of Green Forest. The building, constructed in the early 1900s, has been meticulously restored. It features old safes, original tellers' windows, an ornate tile floor and a pressed-tin ceiling.

The Bank of Kingston also has a spot in Arkansas' political history. That's because Jim and Susan McDougal bought the bank in late 1980, about the time that Gov. Bill Clinton was defeated by Frank White in Clinton's first gubernatorial reelection bid. Two years earlier, the McDougals had convinced Bill and Hillary Clinton to join them in purchasing 230 acres along a remote stretch of the White River in north Arkansas. Susan McDougal christened that property Whitewater.

The McDougals renamed the Bank of Kingston as Madison Bank & Trust. It would be wiped out by a bad loan in 1982, but the couple later would buy Woodruff Savings & Loan in Augusta and rename it Madison Guaranty Savings & Loan.

There are no hints of the Whitewater affair on this August Saturday morning in Kingston. The bank is quiet, and the doughnuts next door are as good as advertised. I leave Kingston, continuing north on Arkansas 21. I cross the Kings River, reach the intersection of U.S. 412 and take a right. I enter Carroll County and stop in Osage at another building that's on the National Register of Historic Places, the former home of the Stamps General Store. Built in 1901, this building now houses the Osage Clayworks. Newt Lale has been a potter for almost three decades. The pottery is fired in the store, which seems to attract a steady flow of customers despite its remote location.

One definition of *lagniappe* is "an extra or unexpected gift or benefit." There's definitely lagniappe at Osage on this Saturday morning as gospel music flows from under the pavilion across the street and smoke billows from a giant portable smoker. It turns out there's a gospel singing and a chicken "dinner on the ground" to benefit the restoration of the Possum Trot Church. I wander across the street to grab lunch—just $5 per plate—and listen to the music. The Possum Trot Church is on an unpaved road in a remote part of Carroll County, alongside a branch of Possum Trot Creek. The building, constructed in the early 1900s, served as both a church and a school. The church was nondenominational but required men and women to sit on opposite sides. The building also was used for gospel singings and family reunions.

Earlier this year, the Historic Preservation Alliance of Arkansas placed the Possum Trot Church—also known as the Pleasant Grove School House—on its "Six to Save" list of Arkansas' most endangered historic places. A new roof is desperately needed to prevent water damage. The gospel music stops for a blessing. Following the prayer, I buy two chicken dinners. The lady behind the serving table asks for $10. I give her a $20 bill and tell her to keep the change as a donation for the restoration. Morning has turned into afternoon, and I'm feeling blessed to have discovered this section of the Arkansas Ozarks. After lunch, I cross Osage Creek and follow Arkansas 103 back into Newton County. The sun breaks through the clouds, illuminating the mountains. It's as green as spring in this wetter-than-normal summer.

August 22, 2009
Where Does the South End?

Does the South end before you leave Arkansas? The question has always fascinated me. If you want to stir up a hornet's nest, do as I recently did in a post on my Southern Fried blog at www. rexnelsonsouthernfried.com and contend that Fayetteville is actually in the Midwest. As a native of south Arkansas, I've long felt that northwest Arkansas has far more in common with Kansas, Oklahoma and Missouri than it does with Louisiana, Mississippi and even east Texas.

There's no doubt that Little Rock is a Southern city. As a young newspaper reporter living in Washington, D.C., in the 1980s, I would chuckle whenever I would hear natives of Philadelphia, New York and Boston describe Washington as a Southern city. This south Arkansas product wanted to scream: "Washington is a Northeastern city! You want to go to a Southern city? Go to Little Rock, Jackson or Birmingham. Those are Southern cities. Atlanta doesn't count. Too many Yankees. And Miami is a Latin American city."

Little Rock and most counties south and east of the state's largest city are in the South. There's no doubt that the folks in Forrest City think differently, act differently and live differently than residents of Rogers or Bentonville. So, does the South end in Clarksville? Ozark? Alma?

Texas Monthly once published a feature story on where the South ends in Texas. The editors decreed that the South ended at the farthest spot west with a Confederate memorial on the courthouse lawn. Using those criteria would kill my theory about northwest Arkansas being in the Midwest since there's a Confederate memorial on the Bentonville square.

No one, though, can deny that Washington and Benton counties have changed significantly during the past four decades. Could it perhaps be said that they were once in the South and migrated culturally to the Midwest?

Dave Edmark of Fayetteville, a former newspaperman who

now works for the University of Arkansas, says this: "Fayetteville is in the South, the Midwest and the Southwest all at once, part of each of them and indicative of none of them. There are also small traces of the Northeast and West Coast here too; all welcome parts of the mix even if somewhere under the radar. People from the three predominant regions mentioned above have been coming here for decades and settling in with those already here as native born or long-time immigrants."

Edmark contends that the folks who move to northwest Arkansas fall into two categories. There are the ones who "look around and see most of the culture is not exactly like it was back home, wherever that was. They hoped for a carbon copy of life back home and didn't find it here. They complain a lot and generally flee within a few years." The second group consists of the people who "look around and see, in addition to some of their original home's culture, an intriguing blend of other regional cultures that appears to co-exist and thrive rather well within one municipality. They stay for a long time and become part of a local melting pot that is largely indifferent to where one is from, much less where one's ancestors lived."

One of the things that makes Arkansas fascinating is the vast cultural change that can occur with just a short drive. Leave Little Rock and head west to Perryville. You'll find yourself in a mountain culture. Drive just a few miles east to Scott, however, and there's no doubt you're in the Delta. It was much the same when I grew up in Clark County. If you headed out of Arkadelphia and drove a few miles east to Dalark, there was no doubt you were in the Deep South—a predominantly African American population, row crops, nearby oxbow lakes along the Ouachita River with alligators in them. If you headed west out of Arkadelphia to Amity, you found yourself in a mountain culture—the population was all white, many of the residents worked in timber mills and people floated the Caddo River to catch smallmouth bass.

The original blog post was written in defense of the University of Arkansas football team still playing games in Little Rock. Then-Gov.

Mike Huckabee took the Little Rock side in what became known as the Great Stadium Debate because he grew up in a far corner of southwest Arkansas and understood that this state's flagship university risked regionalizing itself without a Little Rock football presence. He knew the issue was about more than how much money the athletic department could earn per game. Hopefully, athletic director Jeff Long has learned how unique the state is. A school in the Southeastern Conference should continue to play at least a couple of home games in the South. And Fayetteville isn't the South. That's not necessarily a bad thing, mind you.

Back to Dave Edmark: "If you're in Fayetteville and looking for the real South, you'll probably have to drive at least as far as Little Rock to find it. For that matter, if you want to find the real Midwest, you'll have to drive about as far the opposite direction and head to Kansas City. If you want to find the real Southwest, start in Tulsa and keep going. It's all easily accessible to us from Fayetteville and makes us a bit separate from everyone else. Nobody has ever really claimed us."

It's part of what makes Arkansas special and makes this debate fun. So we ask again: Where does the South really end?

June 26, 2010
Temple Beth El

I almost feel like an intruder as I enter Temple Beth El in Helena-West Helena. It's quiet here.

In one corner of the parking lot, two men are washing a car on this sultry afternoon. Inside, the building is dark. Katie Harrington, director of the Delta Cultural Center (DCC), unlocks the door. The DCC, an arm of the Department of Arkansas Heritage, now operates Beth El as an assembly center. At some point, part of the building will be used to tell the story of the Jewish experience in Arkansas. It's a fascinating one.

According to the Encyclopedia of Southern Jewish Communities, a project of the Goldring/Woldenberg Institute of Southern Jewish

When the Delta's economy was booming, Jews were a significant part of the population, having come down the Mississippi River from St. Louis and up the river from New Orleans. Pictured here is Temple Beth El in Helena-West Helena.

Life, Jews first settled in Helena in the early 1840s. In 1846, a Torah was borrowed from Congregation B'nai Israel in Cincinnati to use for the high holidays. An official congregation was organized in 1867 when 65 Jews formed Congregation Beth El (House of God). Eight years later, the congregation purchased land for a Jewish cemetery. Helena's first Jews worshiped in the homes of members. They later met in a rented storage room on Ohio Street and then in a former church.

The city's first synagogue was constructed in 1880. The building we're entering on this day was built in 1916 and still features the original organ, purchased for $4,000 by the congregation's Ladies Benevolent Association. That association earlier had raised money to add indoor toilets to the original synagogue in 1904 and to pay for a new roof the following year.

"In addition to serving Jews in Helena, Beth El was a regional congregation that attracted Jews from such smaller towns as Marianna, Marvell, Trenton and West Helena," according to the Encyclopedia of Southern Jewish Communities, which went on, "In 1904, Jews in Marianna asked whether Beth El's rabbi could lead services there once a month; the temple board agreed as long as they became dues-paying members of Beth El, which they did. This regional nature of the congregation is apparent in the window memorials in the main sanctuary. One was donated by the Jewish citizens of Marianna, one by those in Marvell and another by a member who lived in Marks, Miss."

When the Delta was booming economically, there was a significant Jewish population. Jews had come up the Mississippi River from New Orleans and down the river from St. Louis. Many initially worked as traveling peddlers. A number of these Jewish immigrants went on to become successful merchants and planters. The 1870 census showed that most of the Jews in Helena had been born in Prussia and other parts of what would become Germany. By 1880, Jews dominated the retail trade in Helena. There were 22 Jewish-owned businesses in the city in 1909.

Men such as Pete Goldsmith, Harry Grauman and Joseph Solomon also became leaders in the state's cotton industry. Helena even had a Jewish mayor, Aaron Meyers, from 1878 to 1880. Jacob Fink, whose father had come to Helena in 1862 and opened a mercantile store, was later mayor. Jacob Trieber, whose family settled in Helena in 1868, became the first Jew ever appointed as a federal judge when President William McKinley nominated him in 1900. Trieber served until 1927 in the Eastern District of Arkansas. Born in Prussia in 1853, he sometimes presided over more than 1,000 cases a year as a judge and issued nationally important rulings in areas ranging from antitrust to prohibition.

By 1927, the year Trieber died and the year of the great flood along the Mississippi River, there were at least 400 Jews living in Helena. As the Delta declined during the decades that followed, so did the Jewish population. One Jew who did remain was prominent attorney David Solomon, whose grandfather first settled in Phillips County in the 1860s. David and Miriam Solomon's three sons left Helena and moved to the East Coast. One became director of the American Jewish Historical Society. Another became the dean of the law school at Rutgers University–Camden.

25

In 1967, when Beth El celebrated its 100th anniversary, the congregation had 68 families with 109 members, not including children. Four years ago, with only about 20 members remaining, the synagogue was closed and the temple was donated to the state. Many of the building's artifacts were shipped to Bentonville to help out Congregation Etz Chaim, which is thriving as Walmart employees and vendors move to northwest Arkansas from across the country.

In a story in December 2009 for the Jewish news service Jewish Telegraphic Agency (JTA), Ben Harris told of a Friday night gathering at the home of Miriam and David Solomon:

"Six elderly Jews—nearly all in their 90s—took their seats in the Solomons' living room as David, a Harvard-trained lawyer and dapper Southern gentleman, led a short, mostly English service. When it was over, cocktails were mixed—'a libation,' he called it—and the group passed around a tray of cheese straws, a local specialty."

Since Beth El was donated to the state, the remaining Jews in the area have gathered for services in private homes just as those first Jewish settlers had done in the 1800s. Jewish life has come full circle in east Arkansas. Harris notes that there's a quote from Isaiah near the entrance of Beth El: "Thy gates shall be open continually." With the temple in the hands of the Delta Cultural Center, visitors will have a place for the next generations to come to learn about the Jewish experience in Arkansas.

As Miriam Solomon told Harris, "Why wouldn't I be proud? As long as that temple stands, there will be a Jewish presence in Helena."

Miriam Solomon died in July 2011 at age 92, and David Solomon celebrated his 100th birthday in July 2016.

July 24, 2010
The Greenville Bridge

Tuesday, September 17, 1940, was quite a day for residents of southeast Arkansas and the Mississippi Delta.

People came from miles around for the dedication of the $4.5

The modern bridge linking Mississippi and Arkansas near Lake Village replaced a span that lasted for seven decades despite being hit from above by planes and below by barges.

million bridge over the Mississippi River between Lake Village and Greenville, Mississippi.

At the bridge's tollhouse south of Greenville, more than 5,000 people gathered. They came not only from Delta communities but also from Memphis, Little Rock, Jackson and New Orleans. Marvin Pope, who represented the City of Memphis that day, told those gathered at the tollhouse: "The bridge is not merely a span from one bank to another but a pathway of progress."

Next week, almost 70 years after that bridge was dedicated, a new span will open. Dedication ceremonies are Monday with the bridge opening two days later for U.S. 82 traffic. The 1940 bridge has been considered a navigational hazard for years. It crosses the Mississippi River just south of a sharp bend, making it difficult for towboats to complete their turns and straighten up in time to clear the bridge. Numerous barges have rammed into the bridge through the decades.

According to a Mississippi Department of Transportation website set up to track the progress of construction: "The Greenville Bridge has weathered the wrath of the Mississippi River and ever-increasing volumes of highway and river traffic. Since 1972, it has sustained more barge collisions than any other bridge on the Mississippi. In the 1950s, an airplane from the nearby Greenville Air Force Base crashed into the bridge. Though the 1940 Greenville Bridge remains structurally as sound as ever, the bridge is considered functionally obsolete by modern standards."

As those who drove across the 1940 bridge can attest, its traffic lanes are narrow and there's no shoulder. Even a simple flat tire could force officials to close the bridge. The new bridge will have four lanes for traffic rather than two, with plenty of outside shoulder space.

The new bridge was a long time coming. In 1994, the State of Mississippi issued an engineering study that explored a four-lane crossing for U.S. 82. That study outlined three alternatives. Two alternatives called for building new bridges and tearing down the old bridge. The third alternative called for keeping the old bridge and building a new bridge next to it, as had been done at Natchez, Mississippi. It was determined that the new bridge should be built half a mile down the river from the 1940 bridge, with the old bridge being removed.

In 1995, a cable-stayed design was chosen. By the end of 1999, studies had concluded and engineers had drawn their plans. But it would take another decade before the massive project was completed. Interestingly, the new bridge was designed by Howard Needles Tammen & Bergendoff of Kansas City, the same firm that designed the 1940 Greenville Bridge. That firm earlier had designed bridges over the Mississippi River at Vicksburg in 1930, Natchez in 1937, and Cape Girardeau, Missouri, in 1926.

Work on the main span began in December 2001 and wound up costing almost $110 million. Still, there was much more to be done. The Arkansas approach is 1.25 miles long, consisting of a four-lane road and a four-lane bridge over the flood zone. Work began in March 2006 and cost almost $66 million. The Mississippi approach is 1.8 miles long, also consisting of a four-lane road and a four-lane bridge over the flood zone. Work began in April 2006 and cost almost $86 million.

Getting the 1940 bridge had been a challenge, too. Greenville was thriving in the 1930s, proud of its title as the Queen City of the Delta. Mayor Milton C. Smith understood that further growth was being hindered by the lack of a bridge. In 1936, a group known as the Arkansas-Mississippi-Alabama U.S. 82 Association was formed with the goal being the construction of a bridge connecting Greenville and Lake Village. The United States was in the midst of the Great Depression, and funds were limited for major public works projects.

Smith and John A. Fox, secretary of the Washington County Chamber of Commerce, dedicated themselves to finding the money. They spent weeks at a time in Washington. At the 1940 dedication ceremony, W. R. French, president of the U.S. 82 Association, said: "Two years ago, the bridge was a fond hope, a dying dream. But with loyal cooperation between the people of Arkansas and Mississippi, the dream came true."

During the past decade, people have posted their memories of the 1940 bridge on the greenvillebridge.com website. Leslie Brown of Warren wrote in 2002, "Every time I pass over the Greenville Bridge, I feel the history and work that poured into it. This is especially true to me since my great-grandfather, Jim Bryant, painted the bridge many years ago....It is a piece of history that will not be forgotten."

Robert Nelson of Little Rock wrote in 2002, "The Greenville Bridge was fascinating to me as a boy and soon-to-be structural engineer. I had no idea of its stature among major truss bridges. Just knew that in height and span it was the most impressive bridge I had ever seen by far. It seemed incredible that we could see, from my sister's home miles away in Lake Village, the blinking warning lights on top of it. My mother frequently would comment, 'It looks so delicate.' My brother-in-law, John Fish, finally replied, 'You wouldn't think it was so delicate if you had seen what happened to that airplane that crashed into it.'"

That crash occurred in 1951. The 1940 bridge was hit from above by planes, from atop the span by cars and trucks and from below by barges. The old bridge provided seven decades of service.

August 14, 2010
Wine Country

The view from the parking lot of St. Mary's Church at Altus is nothing short of spectacular as the sun sets on this Friday. In a state filled with nice views, this is one of the best. After all, Altus comes from the Latin word for high.

Built in 1902, the Roman basilica-style Catholic church is also worth a visit, with its paintings and ornate goldleaf work. The church, which is on the National Register of Historic Places, has been restored in recent years. In November 1879, Father Beatus Maria Ziswyler of Little Rock organized the church to serve the growing number of Swiss and German immigrants who settled near Altus after finding the countryside similar to their homelands. The original frame building was constructed in 1881 at a cost of $1,000. The present facility was built of stone quarried in the area.

Jacob Post had immigrated to the United States in 1872 from Baden-Baden in Germany. His efforts to grow grapes in Illinois had failed, but he was told by Catholic monks that Arkansas had a climate suited for grapes. Those monks established St. Benedict's Colony near Paris (now Subiaco Abbey) in 1877. Post moved to the area in 1880.

Coal mining had begun there in 1873. A year later, a passenger train depot was built at Altus to serve the Little Rock and Fort Smith Railroad. Work on the railroad and in the mines attracted the Swiss and German immigrants. These immigrants were accustomed to having wine with their meals, giving Post an outlet for his products. He sold his wine to coal miners, railroad workers and other immigrants. What's now the Arkansas wine country was born.

Johann Andreas Wiederkehr and his family came from Switzerland in 1880, the same year Post arrived. Wiederkehr

German and Swiss immigrants gave the area around Altus a strong winemaking tradition, attracting visitors to the region.

chose St. Mary's Mountain as his home and carved a wine cellar from a hillside. That cellar was later converted into the Weinkeller Restaurant as part of the Wiederkehr Village complex. Wiederkehr Wine Cellars is now run by third- and fourth-generation members of the family, who publicize the fact that the company helped pioneer the American wine industry. Wiederkehr is U.S. bonded winery No. 8.

With the start of Prohibition in 1920, wine production was limited to sacramental wine for Catholics. Many of the vineyards went untended until Prohibition ended in 1933. Five years later, a group of growers that included members of the Post family formed the Altus Cooperative Winery. It was renamed Post Winery in the 1940s. When Matt Post's children joined the business in the 1980s, it took on its current name of Post Familie Vineyards.

Meanwhile, another branch of the family consisting of Eugene Post and sons Eugene Jr., Michael and Robert developed and expanded the Mount Bethel Winery. In 1935, a daughter-in-law of Jacob Post had acquired a federal bonded winery permit to manufacture and sell wine. After her death, her grandson Eugene began learning all he could about making wine so he could continue the family tradition. In 1956, after graduating from the University of Arkansas with a degree in chemistry, Eugene opened a winery in the underground cellars his grandmother had used. He purchased the family homestead and vineyards from his mother and named it Mount Bethel in honor of a Presbyterian church and school that had been located on Pond Creek Mountain.

The last passenger train departed Altus on May 15, 1936. Four years later, the last major coal mine closed. But the wine industry lived on. In 1984, almost 12,000 acres near Altus received the federal designation of American Viticultural Area, and the Altus Grape Festival was revived as an annual event. In 2001, Paris Hilton and Nicole Richie showed up to film the reality television series *The Simple Life*. That show featured two socialites who proved to be incompetent when it came to working on a farm.

Perhaps more important than the short visit of Hilton and Richie, however, had been the 1998 arrival of Audrey House. She was born in Oklahoma in 1976 and lived there until 1989, when she moved to Little Rock. House graduated from Pulaski Academy in 1994 before heading to the University of Oklahoma. The 20 acres she bought from Al Wiederkehr in 1998 formed the basis for Chateau Aux Arc, which promotes itself as the largest planter of Cynthiana grapes in the world and the largest U.S. planter of chardonnay grapes outside of California.

Living at first in tents, House and some friends developed the land. She purchased another 30 acres in 2000 and opened her winery in July 2001. In 2005, she opened a 5,400-square-foot tasting room with views of the surrounding vineyards. Chateau Aux Arc is now a vital part of the Altus wine scene that has long included Wiederkehr Wine Cellars, Post Familie Vineyards and Mount Bethel Winery. Add Robert Cowie's operation just west of Paris, and you have all the elements of the Arkansas wine country. Cowie Wine Cellars became bonded in August 1967 and has added the Winery Bed & Breakfast and the Arkansas Historic Wine Museum to its operations through the years.

After dinner at the Weinkeller on that Friday night, I drove to downtown Altus where things were quiet. It dawned on me that Arkansas should do more to promote its wine country. The state should place larger signs on Interstate 40. Efforts to attract investors who could build a boutique hotel at Altus should be intensified. With the exception of the three rooms at the St. Mary's Mountain Country Inn, there's nowhere for overnight guests to stay other than RV parks. They must head west to Ozark, east to Clarksville or south to Paris.

With a boutique hotel containing a fine restaurant, affluent couples would have a reason to stay for several days rather than several hours. Those German and Swiss immigrants gave Arkansas a tradition on which we could further capitalize if only we would choose to do so.

October 2, 2010
Hope Watermelons

October has arrived, and the late-summer Hope Watermelon Festival is becoming a distant memory. But the big watermelons—the *really* big ones—sometimes stay in the fields until late fall.

My biology teacher at Arkadelphia High School was Lloyd Bright, scion of Hope's famous watermelon-growing Bright family. He would regale us with stories of spending the night in the fields with giant watermelons, making sure they stayed warm as cooler fall temperatures kicked in. Bright and a handful of other southwest Arkansas farmers still attempt to grow record-setting melons. The world-record melon was, in fact, produced by my former teacher five years ago. Now 67 and retired from the public schools, Bright operates a family farm at Hope that has produced six world champion watermelons through the years.

On August 18, the *New York Times* led its weekly Dining section with a lengthy story about Hope watermelons. Kim Severson wrote that for a watermelon producer to have a commercially viable operation, a farm must grow melons with thick rinds and uniform shape. That allows the melons to ship well.

The Hope Watermelon Festival attracts melon fans of all ages.

"It has to be small enough so people pushing grocery carts in big-city stores will buy it," Severson wrote. "And it can't have seeds."

Bright told the visiting reporter, "When I was growing up, the guys were always talking big melons."

Indeed, Carolina Cross melons can add three to four pounds a day. Bright sells his huge melons for $75 to $80 each, and you can buy seeds from him. While market conditions have changed dramatically during the past several decades, I hope there will always be a place for those really big melons around Hope. It is, quite simply, a part of the culture.

"The articles were unusual in that they were negative in regard to large watermelons," Bright told me after reading the *New York Times* spread. "I'm not sure why she is so opposed to large watermelons grown for competitive events. Maybe she will come back sometime when the big melons are ripe and available for tasting."

On January 17, 2001, President Bill Clinton made his final out-of-state trip before leaving the White House, coming home to Arkansas to address a joint session of the legislature. Prior to his address in the House chamber, Clinton dropped by the office of Gov.

Mike Huckabee for a short visit. Huckabee and Clinton had both been born in Hope. Though they differed on many issues, they had similar political instincts.

During his decade as governor, Huckabee kept a large Bowie knife in a glass case. I had never seen anyone actually open the case until the president popped it open that day and picked up the knife, no doubt startling the Secret Service agents in the room.

"It doesn't matter what Huckabee and I accomplish in life, we'll always rate third at best in Hope behind watermelons and Bowie knives," Clinton said.

If Clinton and Huckabee take a back seat to watermelons in Hope, they can blame it on C. M. "Pod" Rogers Jr., the circulation director at the *Hope Star* for many years and later one of the newspaper's owners. Rogers, who died in 1998, traveled the country, appearing on national television shows and anywhere else he could spread the gospel of Hope's big melons.

During the 1984 Republican National Convention in Dallas, I helped Rogers carry a watermelon into the lobby of the Hyatt Regency Hotel at 4 a.m. in the hopes that Willard Scott would put him on NBC's *Today* show. Rogers yelled at Scott as the famed weatherman walked to the temporary *Today* set in the hotel lobby. Scott walked over and admired the melon. In the final hour of the show, Rogers again found himself on national television.

In the 1920s, the Hope Chamber of Commerce would hold a one-day festival each year to celebrate the local watermelon crop. Slices would be served to the passengers on the trains that passed through Hempstead County. A watermelon queen would be crowned, and a parade would be held. By 1931, however, the Great Depression had forced an end to the festival.

In 1975, Hope celebrated its centennial. Rogers saw what a success that celebration had been and decided to organize a new Hope Watermelon Festival in 1977. The city hasn't missed a watermelon festival since. It's now a four-day event that brings almost 50,000 people to town each August.

It's in September and October, though, when the really big watermelons are harvested. I've been watching the news closely in recent weeks to see if my former biology teacher has a monster melon lurking in his fields.

April 2, 2011
Bucket List

The assignment was fairly straightforward: Come up with a list of things you must do at least once in your life to be considered a well-rounded Arkansan.

That was the task given to the readers of my Southern Fried blog at www.rexnelsonsouthernfried.com. The items on the list could be festivals a person should attend, restaurants that should be visited and activities in which people must engage in order to earn their Arkansas bonafides.

You're invited to add your own suggestions to what we're calling the Natural State Bucket List. Here's a partial list of what we've come up with so far:

- Float the Buffalo River.
- Dig for diamonds at Crater of Diamonds State Park near Murfreesboro.
- Eat an entire hubcap cheeseburger at the original Cotham's in Scott.
- Search for the Gurdon Light late one night.
- Have an all-you-can-eat dinner of catfish straight from the lower White River at the Georgetown One Stop.
- Fish for trout early one morning on the upper White River when the fog is thick.
- Watch the sun rise from a duck blind on the Grand Prairie.
- Spend a night at the Arlington Hotel in Hot Springs and the Crescent Hotel in Eureka Springs.
- Attend a Battle of the Ravine one fall Saturday afternoon between Ouachita and Henderson in Arkadelphia.
- Eat barbecue at Craig's in DeValls Bluff.

- Attend the Hope Watermelon Festival and buy cold slices of watermelon for all of your friends.
- Eat a watermelon from Hope and Cave City on the same afternoon before beginning a debate on which one is better.
- Listen to live music one Saturday night on the courthouse lawn at Mountain View.
- Go to the infield at Oaklawn on Arkansas Derby day and then eat an Oaklawn burger at a table under a crab apple tree.
- Descend deep below the ground at Blanchard Springs Caverns to cool off on a hot summer day.
- Show up for an Arkansas Travelers game at Dickey-Stephens Park in North Little Rock when there's either midget wrestling or it's clunker car night.
- Watch the toad races in downtown Conway during Toad Suck Daze.
- Drive all the way from Helena to Fayetteville, staying off the interstate highways, in order to get a feel for the state.
- Attend the blues festival in Helena. On the way home, walk into the swamp to see the Louisiana Purchase monument.
- Walk around Dyess and imagine what it was like when Johnny Cash was a boy.
- Have a steak with some political power brokers in the back room at Doe's in Little Rock.
- Drive the length of Arkansas Highway 7 from the Louisiana border in the south to Bull Shoals Lake in the north.
- Take U.S. Highway 71 rather than Interstate 49 from Alma to Fayetteville just for old time's sake. Get out and stretch your legs atop Mount Gaylor.
- Drive the Pig Trail to Fayetteville when the leaves are changing colors in the fall.
- Attend the all-tomato luncheon during the Bradley County Pink Tomato Festival at Warren.
- Attend the Gillett Coon Supper and actually eat the coon.
- If you're a man, attend the Slovak Oyster Supper. No women

allowed. Buy some raffle tickets while there.

- Make it a point to be in the Hardin pecan grove on the third Thursday in August for the Grady Fish Fry. Dance to the prison band.
- Walk through a cotton field in Mississippi County when the cotton is ready to pick.
- Listen to live music one Friday night at George's Majestic Lounge on Dickson Street in Fayetteville.
- Eat a steak for dinner at Josie's in Waldenburg following a Saturday afternoon Arkansas State football game.
- Wait in line for a seat at the Venesian Inn in Tontitown following a Razorback football game.
- Visit the Lakeport Plantation near Lake Village and then have supper at the Cow Pen just before driving over the new Mississippi River Bridge.
- Head to Wye Mountain west of Little Rock when the jonquils are in bloom.
- Sit in a deer stand on a frosty November morning in the middle of the pine woods of Dallas County.
- Try to eat a full tamale spread at McClard's in Hot Springs.
- Drive across the dike at DeGray Lake just as the sun is setting.
- Hike to the top of Pinnacle Mountain.
- Visit the Museum of Automobiles atop Petit Jean Mountain before heading over to the state park to hike.
- Pick pecans from a Delta pecan orchard on a November afternoon.
- Have your photo taken on the Arkansas-Texas line in downtown Texarkana.
- Hang out in downtown Hot Springs on St. Patrick's Day and attend the World's Shortest St. Patrick's Day Parade.
- Float around in Skinny Dip Cove on Lake Hamilton on a summer Sunday afternoon.
- Fish for smallmouth bass from a canoe on the Kings River.
- Listen to the bagpipes during the Scottish Festival at Lyon

College in Batesville.

- Attend both the spring and fall craft fairs at War Eagle.
- Eat a turkey leg at the Arkansas State Fair.
- Talk a farmer into letting you ride in the combine in a rice field outside Weiner on the first cool day in October.
- Attend a high school football game one fall Friday night at Nashville.
- Attend a high school basketball game one winter Friday night at Valley Springs.
- Take a slow walk through Mount Holly Cemetery in Little Rock.
- Watch the Memphis fireworks on the Sunday before Memorial Day from a sandbar on the Arkansas side of the Mississippi River.
- Sit on the east side of Mount Nebo and watch the sun rise over the Arkansas River Valley.
- Buy some wine at Altus and then visit the monastery at Subiaco.
- Watch the cardboard-boat races at Greers Ferry Lake and then have dinner at the Red Apple Inn.
- Fish for crappie in a south Arkansas oxbow lake during the day and go frog gigging on the same lake that night.
- Drink some spring water at the Mountain Valley headquarters in Hot Springs.
- Watch Sonny Payne do his *King Biscuit Time* radio show on Cherry Street in Helena.
- Buy a stack of books at That Bookstore in Blytheville.

June 8, 2011
Camp Meeting

The official start of summer approaches, and for some Arkansans that means it's almost camp meeting time. It's a tradition that dates back to 1821, 15 years before Arkansas became a state.

The first of the big religious camp meetings reached Arkansas that year. The 19th-century camp meeting movement had begun early

39

in the century in Kentucky when a large group of Baptists, Methodists and Presbyterians met for two weeks in late August. Camp meetings generally lasted one or two weeks. Whole families would stay in tents, attracted by the preaching, personal testimonies, Bible study, fellowship, music and food.

Among the camp meetings that have survived in Arkansas through the decades are those at Salem in Saline County, at the Davidson Campground near Hollywood in Clark County and at Ben Few in Dallas County.

The Ben Few Campground is two miles west of Princeton. The first camp meeting at Ben Few was organized in 1898 by Rev. Benjamin Asbury Few.

The Salem Camp Meeting near Benton is held each June. People no longer stay in tents or cabins at Salem, and there are only evening services. Still, the crowds come each year.

The marker in front of the Salem United Methodist Church states, "In the early days of Saline County's history, the settlers would gather here after the crops had been laid by for rest, relaxation and to give thanks to the Lord. The early camp meetings were held under brush arbors lighted by pine knots and included daily preaching and singing services. The Salem Camp Meetings were first organized soon after 1830. Annual meetings have been held continuously on this hallowed spot since 1867. During its history, many renowned ministers of Methodism have inspired those attending with their great preaching."

The early camp meetings in Arkansas usually were held early in the fall after crops had been harvested. Once public school attendance became common, the meetings were moved to the summer.

The granddaddy of the remaining Arkansas camp meetings is the one at the Davidson Campground. The campground is just off Arkansas Highway 26, about 12 miles west of Arkadelphia. Music groups will perform each night beginning at 6:30 p.m.

There are almost 100 wooden cabins on the grounds, and many families spend the 10-day camp meeting in recreational vehicles.

There are up to 600 people staying on the grounds at any time.

The campground bears the name of the site's donor, Jerry Davidson. Services are held under a shed in the center of the campground. The first shed was built by W. B. Pullen and his wife in the 1800s. A new shed was completed in time for the 1911 camp meeting. Lighting was provided by burning pine that was set atop four-foot scaffolds at each of the four corners. This method of lighting the shed gave way to oil lamps and later to generators in the 1920s. Electricity for the campground is now provided by the South Central Arkansas Electric Cooperative.

The numerous springs in the area were among the initial attractions of the site. An 1888 story in the *Southern Standard* at Arkadelphia (a newspaper that gave me my first job in journalism in 1976 but no longer exists) described it this way: "Mr. J. J. Davidson donated five acres of land to be used exclusively for a Methodist campground, and anyone has a privilege of building a tent on the grounds. It was named Davidson's Camp Ground as a compliment to the generous donor, Uncle Jerry Davidson. It is a beautiful place for a campground, situated in a lovely grove of trees and surrounded by 15 to 20 mineral springs."

For years, campers obtained their drinking water from a spring about 50 yards from the shed. An electric pump was installed in the 1950s. In the 1960s, deep wells were dug.

The largest of the annual Davidson gatherings is believed to have been the 1925 camp meeting when an estimated 8,000 people showed up on a Sunday to hear W. G. Hogg from Texas preach. The full meeting has been called off only once. That occurred in 1905 when Terre Noire Creek overflowed its banks and inundated the campground.

Here's how the Davidson Campground website (www.davidsoncampground.com) describes the annual gathering: "While children enjoy bicycle riding and water balloons to stay cool, adults relax on the front porch swings of their cabins. Youth can be found playing volleyball, ping pong and basketball throughout the day. Cool drinks and handdipped ice cream cones are always close by at the camp's commissary....While rest and relaxation is a major activity of the camp meeting, spiritual revival is the focus of the encampment. Visitors are always welcomed and encouraged to bring their RVs. Albeit a Methodist campground, all Christian denominations are welcome and campers represent many faiths."

You can bet that people from several denominations will descend each July on the Davidson Campground. It's one of the few places that continues an Arkansas tradition that's almost two centuries old.

September 7, 2011
Atop Petit Jean

It's quiet atop Petit Jean Mountain as summer nears its conclusion.

Former governor Winthrop Rockefeller died of pancreatic cancer in February 1973. That same year, 188 acres that had been part of the Rockefeller ranch on Petit Jean became the home of the Winrock International Livestock Research and Training Center. The center's goal was to improve animal agriculture, in part by utilizing the expertise that had been developed as Rockefeller raised Santa Gertrudis cattle on the mountain.

In 1985, the research and training center merged with two organizations—the Agricultural Development Council and the International Agricultural Development Service—that had been founded by Winthrop's older brother, John D. Rockefeller III. The three organizations became Winrock International. With worldwide operations, Winrock International needed its headquarters to be in a metropolitan area near a commercial airport. It moved to the Riverdale area of Little Rock in 2004. The 188 acres on Petit Jean then reverted to the Winthrop Rockefeller Charitable Trust.

Wanting to use the property to its fullest potential, the board of the trust provided the University of Arkansas System with $53 million to fund a master plan for capital improvements, operations and educational programs. The plan called for the adaptive reuse of 30,000 square feet of existing space, the construction of additional

42

Fifteen years after the Civilian Conservation Corps left Petit Jean Mountain, Winthrop Rockefeller arrived.

lodging facilities and extensive landscaping.

The result was the nonprofit Winthrop Rockefeller Institute, which was established in 2005 and has its own board. One member of that board is fittingly Lisenne Rockefeller of Little Rock, the widow of Winthrop Paul Rockefeller, the former lieutenant governor who died of cancer in the summer of 2006. During its first six years, the institute's program areas have ranged from agriculture to the environment to economic development to the arts.

I never make the drive up the mountain on Arkansas Highway 154 without thinking of Winthrop Rockefeller, perhaps my favorite 20th-century Arkansas figure. The New York native, who arrived in our state in 1953 and helped transform Arkansas during the next two decades, made things possible that otherwise would have taken much longer. What an unlikely savior. He was, however, good for Arkansas. Arkansas, in turn, was good for him.

Here's how a profile in *Time* magazine put it in December 1966: "Win Rockefeller, at 54, needs Arkansas as much as it needs him. Indeed, his brothers David, 51, president of New York's Chase Manhattan Bank, and Nelson, 58, governor of New York, both use the same words to describe his incentives: 'Win found himself in

Arkansas.' Adds David: 'It was just what he wanted and needed.'"

The man known by aides simply as WR began buying land atop Petit Jean within months of moving to Arkansas. He was determined to develop one of the nation's premier cattle ranches while also building a place that could host influential visitors from around the world. He eventually would buy 927 acres, build an elaborate home, add six lakes to the property, install an irrigation system that pumped water up the mountain and construct a mountaintop airfield that would handle his private jet.

People long have been attracted to Petit Jean. There's evidence dating back almost 10,000 years of Native Americans living on the mountain. There are about 100 documented archaeological sites on Petit Jean, including the state's largest known concentration of rock art on outcrops and in rock shelters. Petit Jean was mentioned by explorer Thomas Nuttall in 1819 and government surveyor Henry Downs in 1821.

"Benefiting from the offers of cheap railroad land, a German-American Lutheran colony called Wittenberg arose on the mountain in the mid-1880s, and Petit Jean claimed 100 family farms by 1900," Donald Higgins writes in the online Encyclopedia of Arkansas History & Culture. "For perhaps 75 years, small farm agriculture and orchards flourished on Petit Jean Mountain. By the late 1920s, however, a crash in cotton prices, droughts, blight and insect infestations—combined with poor soil management practices—took a toll on family farms. Petit Jean's population decreased, making land available for other uses."

In 1920, the YMCA took over land on the eastern end of the mountain that previously had been used to grow apples. That plot is now an Episcopal facility known as Camp Mitchell. There's also a Lutheran camp on the mountain. Efforts to create a national park on Petit Jean had begun in 1907. While those efforts were unsuccessful, Petit Jean did give birth to the state parks system. When officials of the Fort Smith Lumber Co. decided it would be too expensive to log the canyon and Seven Hollows areas, a physician named

Thomas William Hardison began an effort to deed the land to the federal government for a national park. In 1921, Stephen Mather, the director of the National Park Service, decided the parcel was too small to be a national park. Hardison then turned his attention to the Arkansas Legislature, and legislators decided to develop the area as a state park.

Petit Jean State Park was established in 1923. From 1933 to 1938, members of the Civilian Conservation Corps (CCC) built roads, buildings, lakes and trails in the park. The CCC facilities, now listed on the National Register of Historic Places, remain a tourism draw. Fifteen years after the CCC left the mountain, Winthrop Rockefeller arrived. Petit Jean would never be the same.

January 18, 2012
Terrible Ted in Nashville

Ramon Wilson vividly recalls the day in August 1938 when Floyd Hamilton and Huron "Terrible Ted" Walters came to Howard County and robbed Wilson's father at the Nashville Coca-Cola Bottling Co. Wilson was 15 at the time.

Wilson, now 88, sits in his office wearing a Nashville Scrappers windbreaker on a Friday afternoon and recounts the robbery as his son Kenneth and daughter Elizabeth listen. Last June, his company celebrated 100 years of bottling Coca-Cola. The Wilson family has owned the company that entire time.

On August 12, 1938, four years after the ambush of former partners Bonnie Parker and Clyde Barrow, Hamilton and Walters drove to Nashville to rob the First National Bank. Word that they might be in the area had resulted in armed men being stationed on the bank's roof. Hamilton and Walters headed instead to the bottling plant.

Hamilton, who had been a driver for Bonnie and Clyde, had joined Walters on a crime spree that stretched from Chicago to Dallas. Forrest Wilson, Ramon Wilson's father, was in his office that day discussing a Boy Scout project with the city's water superintendent,

H. B. Carruth, when the criminals entered with their guns drawn.

According to Ramon Wilson, Hamilton said, "We want your money, and we mean business."

Forrest Wilson was ordered to open the safe. Fortunately, the delivery trucks had not yet returned to the plant, and the robbers got away with just $67.36.

"My dad pulled out the checks that were in the safe and said, 'You won't need these,'" Ramon Wilson says. Hamilton and Walters had entered through the rear door. They left the engine running on their 1937 two-door blue Ford, which they had stolen from a deputy sheriff at Marion. The exchange in the office happened so quickly and quietly that bottling company employees outside the office didn't realize what was happening.

The Associated Press story that ran in newspapers across the state the next day began this way: "Officers from two states, aided by bloodhounds, pressed a search late today along the densely wooded southern Arkansas-Oklahoma border for two men believed to be Floyd Hamilton and Ted Walters, southwestern desperadoes. A detachment of Arkansas State Police routed the pair from an automobile near King, Ark., with a burst of machine gun fire this afternoon. Assistant Supt. Cliff Atkinson reported that after firing on the car, the two men escaped in thick underbrush."

The cash drawer that had been taken from the bottling company was found the next day near Ben Lomond. After the getaway car was hit by bullets, the two robbers stole a car from a casket salesman named H. T. Fewell. Hamilton and Walters later caught a freight train to Texarkana and another train to Dallas. They were captured soon after arriving in Dallas on August 21, 1938.

Years later, Ramon Wilson learned that Hamilton was still alive in Dallas. He stopped along with his wife, Nelda, to visit the man who had robbed his father. Hamilton said the robbery in Nashville had been his last. Hamilton was convicted of several crimes and sent to federal prisons at Leavenworth in Kansas and Alcatraz in California. He escaped Alcatraz in April 1943 but returned after two days because of cold water and biting crabs. In 1979, Ramon, Nelda, Kenneth and Elizabeth Wilson visited the cell at Alcatraz where Hamilton had been held decades earlier.

The 1938 robbery is just one part of the colorful history of a company that has its roots in W. W. Wilson's move to Nashville in 1902 from Clark County. In 1910, W. W. Wilson and his son Forrest purchased Hill Brothers Wholesale Grocery on Main Street in Nashville. An employee named Hence Wilder bottled soft drinks in the back of the business, using a hand-cranked spring stopper carbonation machine. He could fill 75 bottles a day.

In 1911, the Wilsons obtained from the Bellingrath family of Pine Bluff the rights to bottle Coca-Cola and sell it in five southwest Arkansas counties. Known by then as the Nashville Bottling Works, the company moved in 1916 from the grocery building to a larger location. In 1917, 19,236 cases of soft drinks were sold. Sales fell to 18,151 cases a year later due to sugar rationing in World War I, but Wilson family members devised a barter system by which they would trade drinks for raw materials.

Ramon Wilson became a full-time employee in 1942. He served in the Marines in 1944 and 1945 and was part of the invasion of Iwo Jima. After the war, he helped oversee the expansion of the company with the purchase of the Mena Coca-Cola Bottling Co. in 1953 and a plant expansion at Nashville in 1962. Forrest Wilson died in 1967, and Ramon Wilson succeeded his father as company president. Kenneth Wilson joined the company in 1977.

The company moved into its current 35,000-square-foot facility in 1981. The inside walls are covered with artifacts. It's a Coca-Cola museum, a Howard County history museum and a Wilson family museum all in one. Kenneth Wilson was named company president in 1988, becoming the fourth generation of the Wilson family to operate the business, which began distributing Dr Pepper that same year. A decade later, the company was honored for the highest per capita Dr Pepper sales in the world, having quadrupled sales in those 10 years.

Nashville is a proud town. Its residents take pride in their high school football team, and they take pride in a bottling company that's among the oldest family-owned businesses in Arkansas.

January 25, 2012
A Coke in Fort Smith

In Arkansas, as is the case across the South, we like Coca-Cola. In fact, we often use Coke as a generic term for a soft drink, something that's unheard of in other sections of the country. Coca-Cola is also the lead product for some of the oldest businesses in the state.

Fort Smith has as colorful a history as any city in this part of the country. Given its role as a gateway to the Indian Territory and the American West, Fort Smith has been an important part of the region since the first American troops arrived at Belle Point in November 1817 and began building a fort.

Fort Smith is the home of several of Arkansas' longest-running businesses. One of them can be found at 3600 Phoenix Ave. It's the Coca-Cola Bottling Co. of Fort Smith.

Yes, another Coke bottler. Last week in this column, the spotlight was on the Nashville Coca-Cola Bottling Co., which has been run by four generations of the Wilson family. That company obtained the rights in 1911 to bottle Coca-Cola and sell it in a five-county area of southwest Arkansas.

There must be something about corporate loyalty to Coke. That's because the Coca-Cola Bottling Co. of Fort Smith acquired bottling rights even earlier than the Wilsons, in 1903 to be exact. The Fort Smith plant first served as a subbottler for M. W. Fleming of Little Rock. The men who purchased those rights 109 years ago were J. W. and Robert Meek. The company remains in the hands of the Meek family to this day.

Coca-Cola was introduced in Atlanta in 1886 by John S. Pemberton. He spent $46 on advertising that year and sold 25 gallons of syrup. In 1894, Coca-Cola was first sold in a bottle in Vicksburg, Mississippi. Far to the west in Fort Smith in 1895, half-brothers J. W.

and Robert Meek purchased the D. J. Young Bottling Co. Four years later, they built a three-story building at the intersection of South Second Street and Rogers Avenue to house the companies known as J. W. & Robert Meek Manufacturing Confectioners and the Fort Smith Steam Bottling Works.

Records in Atlanta show that 190 gallons of Coca-Cola syrup were shipped to Fort Smith in 1903 for a territory that ran 50 miles in any direction from the city. In 1907, the Meek family paid Fleming $1,500 for the exclusive right to bottle Coca-Cola in a territory that included all of western Arkansas from Scott County north to the Missouri border, stretching to Boone County in the east.

By 1915, four salesmen were on the road for the bottling company. That's the same year a patent was secured by the Root Glass Co. for what became Coke's internationally recognized contour-shaped green bottle. Coca-Cola was still using its original slogan from 1886: "Delicious & Refreshing."

"The first trucks were purchased about 1915," Carolyn Meek Nelson wrote in a history of the Coca-Cola Bottling Co. of Fort Smith. "Before that time, all Fort Smith deliveries were by horse-drawn vehicles, with deliveries to towns outside Fort Smith being made by rail. Rail shipments were made in barrels of 18 dozen bottles and cases of three and six dozen bottles....Fletcher Bell, the father of former Van Buren Mayor Gene Bell, was at one time a truck driver for Coca-Cola. He recalled that when his truck was to go up a fairly steep hill, he had to go in reverse gear because the truck did not have a fuel pump and gasoline would not flow to the engine."

The Coca-Cola Bottling Co. of Fort Smith was incorporated in 1916 with Robert Meek as president and J. W. Meek as vice president. In January 1917, the company purchased the Muskogee, Oklahoma, territory.

By 1929, Coca-Cola was using the slogan "The Pause That Refreshes." That slogan was in place until 1965, when "Things Go Better with Coke" was introduced. Just four years later, it was replaced by "It's The Real Thing."

49

A number of drinks other than Coke were bottled by the Fort Smith plant through the years. It began bottling Ward's Orange Crush in 1919, something called Green River in 1920, Delaware Punch in 1922 and Grape-Ola in 1928. There was competition. Double Cola— which these days is headquartered in Chattanooga, Tennessee, and is most popular in the Evansville, Indiana, area—operated a plant at 3737 Grand Ave. in Fort Smith in the 1940s. That drink came in 12-ounce bottles, almost twice the size of Coca-Cola's 6.5-ounce bottles.

The Coca-Cola headquarters in Atlanta introduced other drinks through the years. There were Tab and Fresca in the 1960s, followed by Mr. Pibb in the 1970s. Diet Coke came along in 1983.

The so-called "New Coke" debacle occurred in 1985 but was followed within months by the reintroduction of what was known as "Classic Coke." In 2003, the Fort Smith company issued a special bottle to commemorate its 100th anniversary as a Coke bottler.

Through it all, people named Meek were in charge of the Fort Smith Coca-Cola Bottling Co. A fourth generation of the Meek family is now running things. Roger Meek Jr., a great-grandson of J. W. Meek, and Robert Meek III, a grandson of Robert Meek Sr., serve as managing partners.

A longtime employee of the Coca-Cola Bottling Co. of Fort Smith, Fred Kirkpatrick, kept extensive records of the company's history and also saved Coke memorabilia. Due to his efforts through the decades, the Coca-Cola museum housed inside the Fort Smith facility is among the best collections of its kind in the country. In 1998, a commemorative Coca-Cola bottle was produced in Fort Smith to recognize Kirkpatrick's 60 years of service to the company.

When west Arkansas residents buy a Coke, they're purchasing a product from a truly historic Arkansas business.

June 27, 2012

Historic Washington

The sun was already high in the June sky by the time Paul Austin, who is the executive director of the Arkansas Humanities Council, and I arrived at Historic Washington State Park. In a small field in the middle of one of this state's most historic communities, tarps helped keep the early summer sun off the professional archaeologists and volunteers who were hard at work.

This field was the commercial district of Washington in the 1830s. What we now think of as the cotton country of the Arkansas Delta was mostly mosquito-infested swamps and impenetrable forests of bottomland hardwoods in those days. The cotton plantations were farther to the southwest, with Camden and Washington as centers of trade.

We're greeted by Tom Green of Fayetteville, director of the Arkansas Archeological Survey, the finest organization of its type in the country. In 1967, the Arkansas Legislature created the survey, making this the first state to have a coordinated research and public service organization of this kind. The survey is responsible for

Washington in Hempstead County is among the most important historical and cultural assets in this part of the country.

studying archaeological sites, managing information about those sites and sharing that information with the public.

Longtime state representative John Bethel of Des Arc was interested in archaeology. As early as 1959, he sponsored legislation to create an archaeological laboratory on the University of Arkansas campus. Bethel also sponsored a 1959 bill protecting archaeological sites on state land. The work of the survey has been complemented through the years by the efforts of the Arkansas Archeological Society, which was formed in 1960.

In 1964, a series of weekend events began under the direction of University of Arkansas Museum archaeologists and society members. The Arkansas Archeological Survey partnered with the society in 1967 on these events. By 1972, what had begun as weekend excavations expanded into a 16-day training program held at various sites across the state. It's the oldest and best program of its type in the country.

The archaeologists were in Washington for a second consecutive summer, carefully removing everything, from nails and pieces of pottery to coins. Meanwhile, life went on in this part of southwest Arkansas. A large lumber truck rumbled down the sunken gravel road that once was part of the Southwest Trail, the network of routes that linked St. Louis with northeast Texas. The trail entered the state at Hix's Ferry across the Current River in Randolph County and exited the state southwest of Washington along the Red River.

The first big wave of immigration to Texas took place in the 1820s. After 1817, an estimated four-fifths of the new arrivals in Texas came via the Southwest Trail. Sam Houston, Davy Crockett and Jim Bowie were among those who passed through Washington on their way to Texas. Washington later was a mustering point for troops marching south to fight the Mexican War.

Prior to 1820, Elijah Stuart had built a log house on a sandy hill at the site of what would become Washington. The house served as an inn and tavern. Stuart's Tavern was designated as the first permanent seat of government in Hempstead County in 1824. A courthouse and

Presbyterian church were built in 1836. The *Washington Telegraph* began in 1840 and was the oldest weekly newspaper west of the Mississippi River when it ceased publication in 1946.

A new courthouse was constructed in 1874, and the businesses that were at the site being excavated this summer began to move. A major economic blow came in the 1870s when the Cairo & Fulton Railroad bypassed Washington. A depot was built at what's now Hope, and that city was incorporated in April 1875. Devastating fires struck Washington in July 1875 and January 1883, furthering its demise as a center of commerce. As early as 1879, some were advocating that the Hempstead County seat be moved to Hope, though the change didn't take place until 1939.

The Arkansas Legislature appropriated $5,000 in 1929 to help restore the 1836 courthouse. The United Daughters of the Confederacy played a key role in pushing for those funds and supplemented them with private contributions. In 1958, the Pioneer Washington Restoration Foundation was organized to raise money and plan the preservation of Washington's historic homes and commercial properties.

During the administration of Gov. Dale Bumpers, when the state parks system was in an expansion mode, the Pioneer Washington group donated buildings and antiques to the state. On July 1, 1973, Old Washington Historic State Park opened. During my years working in the administration of Gov. Mike Huckabee, I regularly was contacted by noted Arkansas preservationist Parker Westbrook. He would say, "It's not Old Washington. It's just Washington."

Westbrook got his wish in September 2006 when the state's Parks, Recreation and Travel Commission voted to change the name to Historic Washington State Park. The 101 acres in the park contain 54 buildings, 30 of which are historically significant. I've always been most impressed by the massive, gnarled trees at Washington. There are catalpa, magnolia, pecan and black walnut trees. Trees planted in the 1800s for their shade and nuts survive.

Just across the street from where the archaeological work is taking place, there's an enormous magnolia that reportedly was planted in 1839. In sight of that tree, eight professional archaeologists worked this month with volunteers from across the country. Some of them have been participating in the 16-day program since the 1970s. Under a pavilion, 86-year-old Anna Parks, who has been a volunteer since 1976, helped bag items.

The past enveloped us as we walked through Washington. It's among the most important historical and cultural assets in this part of the country.

July 4, 2012
Where Southern Forestry Began

U.S. Senator Dale Bumpers once declared that "forestry began in Crossett." While that's a bit of a stretch, there's no denying that many of the advancements in modern forestry occurred because of the work done by foresters for the old Crossett Lumber Co. and by U.S. Forest Service researchers stationed in south Arkansas.

I was reminded of Crossett's contributions to the advancement of Southern forestry during a recent trip to Ashley County to address the Crossett Rotary Club. For years, Crossett was a company town. In many respects, it still is, with its fortunes tied to the ups and downs of the timber industry.

On May 16, 1899, three businessmen from Davenport, Iowa—Edward Savage Crossett, Charles Gates and John Watzek—formed the Crossett Lumber Co. They had purchased 47,000 acres of land in south Arkansas and north Louisiana for $7 per acre from a Michigan investment firm. The Crossett Lumber Co. existed until the corporation and its 565,000 acres of timberland were sold to Georgia-Pacific in April 1962.

In October 2010, Georgia-Pacific announced that it would invest more than $250 million to upgrade an existing paper machine in Crossett with advanced technology and install associated equipment. About 1,300 people work at the Crossett paper mill. Bad news followed in September 2011, though, when Georgia-Pacific

54

Sen. Dale Bumpers once declared that "forestry began in Crossett."

announced it would shut down its plywood and stud mills at Crossett as the housing recession continued.

Ashley County is a far different place now than it was when the thick virgin forests were purchased by those three Iowa investors. As the forests of the Great Lakes region began to be depleted during the late 1800s and early 1900s, investors turned to the huge swath of pine forests that ran from east Texas to the panhandle of Florida. Along the Gulf Coast were virgin forests of longleaf and slash pines. Farther inland, loblolly and shortleaf pine trees dominated the landscape.

The Crossett investors spent almost $1 million starting the company before the first commercial timber was sold. Construction of the company's first pine mill began in 1899, and construction of a second mill commenced in 1905. By the time both mills were operating, the Crossett Lumber Co. was producing 84 million board feet of lumber annually. The Crossett Lumber Co. became a leader in Southern forestry, adding paper mills and chemical plants through the years in an effort to ensure there was minimal waste. Money also was spent on research and development projects, unusual in the early 1900s when timber companies had a cut-and-get-out philosophy in the South.

The Crossett Lumber Co. built a school and homes, incorporating the company town of Crossett in 1903. There was full electric service, something rare at the time in south Arkansas. A Methodist church was built in 1904, the city's newspaper began publishing in 1906 and telephone service was added in 1907. As part of its progressive philosophy, the company established a relationship with the Yale University School of Forestry. With the virgin timber running out across south Arkansas and north Louisiana, company officials knew they would either have to change their ways or go out of business.

In July 1930, the U.S. Forest Service's Southern Forest Experiment Station hired a University of Michigan forestry graduate named Russ Reynolds to help landowners develop sustainable forestry plans. In 1932, Reynolds was assigned to help the Ozark-Badger Lumber Co. at Wilmar in Drew County. He became familiar with the work of the Crossett Lumber Co, which was down to its final 25,000 acres of virgin timber. Reynolds moved to Crossett in August 1933 and began to work with a Civilian Conservation Corps crew to help the company inventory and mark its timber.

In the fall of 1933, Reynolds began to hunt for a site on the company's cutover land that would be suitable for an experimental forest. The 1,680-acre tract he decided on was seven miles south of Crossett and had been cut prior to 1920. The Crossett Lumber Co. agreed to give the Forest Service the land in exchange for the standing volume of timber and the promise that research would be conducted there for the next 50 years. The deed conveying the property to the federal government was dated August 2, 1934. The Crossett Experimental Forest, the first such tract in the South, was the home for decades of scientific research in areas such as forestry, wildlife, hydrology and soils. Several buildings on the site are now on the National Register of Historic Places.

Reynolds, who headed U.S. Forest Service efforts in Crossett for more than three decades, retired from federal service in 1969 but remained active in the industry as a practicing tree farmer. He later wrote that he came to Arkansas at a time when "clear-cutting of virgin pine timber came to a crashing halt because there was no more. It also marked the start of managing the second-growth stands at a time when no one knew how or why they should be managed."

Reynolds noted that once the Crossett Lumber Co. began to manage the second-growth forests, visitors from "around the country and the world came to Crossett to see the far-reaching developments." Crossett was living up to its moniker of the Forestry Capital of the South.

December 19, 2012
Hemingway in Piggott

It has been 16 years since Ruth Hawkins, an administrator at Arkansas State University (ASU), first stood in the yard of the Pfeiffer home atop Crowley's Ridge in Piggott. It was the day after Thanksgiving in 1996, and it was raining. I joined about 50,000 of my fellow Arkansans at War Memorial Stadium in Little Rock on that wet afternoon of November 29, 1996, to watch Louisiana State University defeat the Arkansas Razorbacks by a final score of 17-7. It was much quieter where Hawkins was standing in the northeast corner of the state.

At the time, Hawkins was leading an eight-county effort to attain National Scenic Byway status for the Arkansas segment of Crowley's Ridge, the unusual natural formation that extends more than 200 miles from just below Cape Girardeau, Missouri, to Helena. The ridge was named for Benjamin Crowley, the first European settler to reach what's now the Paragould area in about 1820. Hawkins needed an attraction in far north Arkansas, and she thought Piggott might provide fertile ground.

"Crowley's Ridge includes six state parks, one national forest and numerous small rural museums, county parks and recreation areas," Hawkins says. "The Delta Cultural Center and the King Biscuit Blues Festival in Helena anchor the southern end. Identifying a northern anchor for the ridge, however, was somewhat problematic. While efforts were under way to create a recreational lake as well

57

The public can now visit the Pfeiffer family home atop Crowley's Ridge in Piggott thanks to the efforts of Arkansas State University.

as to capitalize on Civil War history in Clay County, there were no already-developed major attractions."

Hawkins knew Piggott had potential. Famed Hollywood film director Elia Kazan (whose son later would write for the *Arkansas Gazette*) and writer Budd Schulberg decided in 1956 to film *A Face in the Crowd* at Piggott—the film debut of Andy Griffith and Lee Remick. Kazan and Schulberg were looking for a bucolic small town in the middle of the country, and Piggott fit the bill. Piggott also had gained a reputation in the late 1940s and the early 1950s as a place to get married. Most states had a three-day waiting period for marriage licenses in those days. Arkansas law allowed the waiting period to be waived, and Clay County took the position that all marriages were special cases. In 1950, there were 5,960 marriages in Piggott, more than twice the city's population.

Hawkins ultimately focused on the fact that Piggott had been the home of Paul and Mary Pfeiffer, who moved there from St. Louis in 1913. Paul Pfeiffer would acquire almost 63,000 acres in the area, making him one of the country's largest plantation owners. He set himself apart from many of the Delta planters by providing his sharecroppers and tenant farmers with quality homes. The Pfeiffers had the first electric refrigerator and stove in Piggott and later led the effort to provide electricity to the entire town.

In 1927, the couple's daughter, Pauline, became Ernest Hemingway's second wife. The marriage lasted until 1940, and during that time there were regular visits to Piggott. A barn adjacent to the home of Paul and Mary Pfeiffer was converted into a place for Hemingway to write. He wrote parts of *A Farewell to Arms* at Piggott. Hemingway disliked the humidity of an Arkansas summer, but he enjoyed bobwhite quail hunting in the fall and winter. In the February 1934 issue of *Esquire*, he wrote that one of the places he would rather be other than France was "Piggott, Arkansas, in the fall."

"As the 1996 inventory of potential attractions along Crowley's Ridge proceeded, the report came back to ASU that not only did the historic Pfeiffer home and barn still exist, but the house was for sale," Hawkins later wrote. "If nothing else, it sounded like a good prospect for a bed and breakfast along the new national scenic byway. Standing in the yard for the first time, even before extensive research indicated the true impact of the Pfeiffers on the development of northeast Arkansas and on Hemingway's life and writing, I became convinced that this property was more than a bed and breakfast. That day marked the beginning of ASU's Hemingway-Pfeiffer Museum and Educational Center."

The house might have been for sale, but the barn was not. The properties had been acquired by Tom and Beatrice Janes in 1950 following Mary Pfeiffer's death. The Janeses raised six children in the home and made only minor alterations. Beatrice Janes had the home and barn placed on the National Register of Historic Places in 1982. Beatrice Janes, a widow since 1976, had moved to North Carolina in 1996 to be with her daughter. The barn earlier had been deeded to her son, Bruce. After several meetings with Hawkins and other ASU officials, Bruce Janes decided to sell his property also.

Hawkins went to nearby Rector to meet with Sherland and Barbara Hamilton, longtime ASU supporters. She asked them to head a fundraising committee. After telling Hawkins they didn't like committees and didn't like asking other people for money, they agreed to donate $200,000 for the project. Sherland Hamilton said at the time: "We always knew we wanted to do something for ASU in our wills. This project gave us an opportunity to do something important now while we are both still here to see it."

The Arkansas Legislature appropriated $135,000, and the Arkansas Natural and Cultural Resources Council came through with another $280,000. The museum opened July 4, 1999. Hawkins has written a book on the Hemingway-Pfeiffer marriage titled *Unbelievable Happiness and Final Sorrow* (University of Arkansas Press, 2012).

"Hemingway's other wives spoke, but Pauline didn't, making her the least understood of the four women," says Hemingway scholar John Fenstermaker. "She never stopped loving Ernest, and the reverse is also true."

July 10, 2013
The Greers Ferry Water Garden

On October 3, the people of Heber Springs will mark the 50th anniversary of the dedication of Greers Ferry Dam. The highlight of the 1963 event was a visit from President John F. Kennedy. It would be one of Kennedy's final public appearances outside Washington prior to the fateful trip to Dallas the following month.

If Jerry Holmes, the first-term Cleburne County judge, has his way, some of the people marking the 50th anniversary will mention a grandiose idea that received a direct boost from the president on that fall day in 1963. Holmes, who was raised just north of Quitman in Cleburne County, has made it his personal mission to revive efforts to build an ornate water garden just below the dam.

Here's the story in a nutshell: Little Rock businessman Herbert Thomas Sr. was the founder of the Red Apple Inn and the surrounding community of Eden Isle on Greers Ferry Lake. He and his wife, Ruby, had fallen in love with the area years before the lake was constructed. In 1961, Thomas purchased 500 acres near Heber Springs to develop Eden Isle.

Thomas, who had been born in rural Ashley County in 1899, was among the state's leading 20th-century business figures. He formed an insurance company known as Mutual Assessment Co. in 1923. By 1925, there were more than 10,000 policyholders, many of whom were rural Arkansans. He later incorporated the First Pyramid Life Insurance Co. at Little Rock. Thomas served on the University of Arkansas Board of Trustees from 1943 to 1951 and was instrumental in the admission of the first black student, Silas Hunt, to the University of Arkansas Law School in 1948. Thomas also became involved in banking, acquiring City National Bank of Fort Smith in the 1950s and Citizens Bank of Booneville in 1963.

Thomas was a close friend of Senator J. William Fulbright, having headed Fulbright's first Senate campaign after convincing him to run for the office. In the early 1960s, Thomas arranged for a class of architecture students at the University of Arkansas to draw plans for a water garden below the dam being built on the Little Red River. He sent those plans to Fulbright in Washington and urged the senator to convince the U.S. Army Corps of Engineers to develop an attraction that had fountains, waterfalls, trees, shrubs, flowers and bridges. Thomas was convinced that such a garden would attract tens of thousands of additional tourists to Cleburne County each year.

During a visit to Italy, Thomas and his wife had been entranced by the Villa d'Este at Tivoli, a villa and garden constructed by monks in the 1500s. He vowed to use his political connections to get the Corps to build a Greers Ferry water garden as a pilot project. The generals at the Corps, however, had other ideas.

"I am sure I need not tell you that matters of aesthetics, especially a new idea in this field, rather startle the Engineers, and they will probably have to be reminded from time to time in order to get this project under way," Fulbright complained in a 1963 letter to Kenneth

O'Donnell, a special assistant to Kennedy. "The more I think of it, the more exciting I think this project is, as it could have application in many places in the country if we could prove its value by a pilot project."

After persuading Kennedy to attend the Greers Ferry dedication, Fulbright sat by the president aboard Air Force One on the flight to Arkansas. Fulbright showed Kennedy the drawings that the UA students had done. Kennedy reportedly liked what he saw and told Fulbright to contact the Corps. The sometimes acerbic Fulbright quickly replied that he had done so but had not received a positive response. An Army general who was listening to the conversation nodded in the direction of the president and said, "You're now talking to the man who could reopen it."

According to a 1964 *Arkansas Gazette* story, Kennedy told the general to have the Corps prepare a preliminary plan and cost estimate. Jerol Garrison wrote in that *Gazette* article: "After speaking at the dedication of the dam, Mr. Kennedy and his party left in a fleet of five helicopters for Little Rock. As his helicopter took off, the president arranged for it to separate from the others and fly over the site of the proposed water garden so he could get a better look at it."

The Little Rock District of the Corps of Engineers received orders from Washington on October 18, 1963, to draw up a plan for a water garden. The task was assigned to a 24-year-old staff member named William McCauley. Meanwhile, Thomas and Fulbright contacted the famous New York–based architect Edward Durell Stone, a Fayetteville native. Somehow, the two men convinced Stone to take what McCauley had done and come up with his own plan at no cost.

Following Kennedy's death, Fulbright kept pushing for the project. In 1965, it was assigned by the Lyndon Johnson administration to the National Park Service. Stone submitted extensive plans for the Greers Ferry water garden to the Park Service on June 13, 1966. The Park Service finally declared in 1972 that the project was outside its jurisdiction.

Several months ago, Holmes put together a small working group to discuss ways to increase tourism in the area. Billy Lindsey, known by trout fishermen for his long ownership of Lindsey's Resort on the Little Red River below the dam, first told Holmes of the water garden. Lindsey even had color drawings that had been under the front seat of his truck for years. Holmes worked with Chris Caldwell, a staff member for Senator John Boozman, to find the Stone plan, which had been gathering dust for decades in a Park Service storage facility in Colorado.

The Stone plan now sits on the county judge's desk in downtown Heber Springs. "The next step is getting somebody in Washington to get this off dead center again," Holmes says. "If President Kennedy had not been assassinated, I have no doubt the water garden would have been built. Can you imagine how that would have changed this part of the state? This could be a Crystal Bridges-type project for Arkansas. The 50th anniversary of the dedication is a good time to start pushing for it again."

There has been little progress on reviving this dream since this column was published.

July 31, 2013
Along the St. Francis

Headed east out of Wynne on U.S. Highway 64, you quickly come off Crowley's Ridge and are back in the heart of the Delta. On either side of the highway, the corn stands tall. In this era of high corn prices, there are parts of east Arkansas that resemble Iowa more than the cotton-dominated region that some of us once knew. There's still cotton grown here, just not as much of it as there once was. The blooms are evident from the highway, the crop having been helped by the previous week's rains. There has been enough rain, in fact, for there to be standing water in the fields, an unusual sight in late July.

Rice, soybeans and milo also grow here. A field next to the Parkin Archeological State Park is filled with sunflowers. It's hard to imagine this was once a giant forest of bottomland hardwoods.

Those hardwoods helped build Chicago, St. Louis, Memphis and other cities in the early decades of the previous century. They were cleared by the timber companies that entered the region, having now been replaced by the mile upon mile of row crops.

The St. Francis River runs muddy due to the rain. The St. Francis originates in the Missouri hills south of St. Louis and flows as a clear upland stream before slowing down near Poplar Bluff. The river forms the boundary between the Missouri Bootheel and Arkansas before entering the state for good near Childress in eastern Craighead County. It flows between the Mississippi River on the east and Crowley's Ridge on the west, finally emptying into the mighty Mississippi in the St. Francis National Forest just north of Helena.

The river is sluggish and filled with silt by the time it reaches Parkin in Cross County. William Parkin of Memphis was in charge of laying tracks for the St. Louis, Iron Mountain & Southern Railroad in 1887, and the new town that sprang up along the tracks was later named for him. Within a decade, Parkin was the center for lumber operations in the area. A couple of brothers from Pennsylvania formed what would become the Lansing Wheelbarrow Co. in 1890. That same year, George and Jake Mattox established the Northern Ohio Lumber Co.

In 1902, Henry Clay Coldren began the Parkin Cooperage Co. His business and the Mattox brothers' company merged in 1906 to become the Northern Ohio Cooperage & Lumber Co. By the 1920 census, Parkin had 1,378 residents, up from the 1,105 residents in the 1910 census. Families—both black and white—moved to Parkin to work in the lumber industry in the early 1900s, and the companies provided segregated schools for the children of those workers.

More than three-quarters of the Northern Ohio sawmill employees were black. The company constructed a wood-framed schoolhouse for black children in 1910, and it remained in service until 1948. That one-room schoolhouse has been restored and is on the grounds of the Parkin Archeological State Park. Also on the grounds is a cemetery that was used from 1909 to 1927. Blacks were buried in the northern half of the cemetery, and whites were buried in the southern half. Sawdust from the massive Northern Ohio mill was dumped here on a daily basis for years, and the area became known as Sawdust Hill.

Nature has never been a friend to this area. There were major floods along the St. Francis in 1912, 1913, 1927 and 1937, causing many residents to flee to tent camps on Crowley's Ridge. A tornado hit the town in 1928, scattering lumber from the Northern Ohio mill for miles. That was followed by the Great Depression and a series of droughts. By the late 1940s, both the Northern Ohio and the Lansing Wheelbarrow Co. were gone. The hardwood forests had been depleted, and cotton was king.

In a strange twist, the existence of the Sawdust Hill community protected what turned out to be one of the premier archaeological sites in North America. Because homes sat atop much of the Parkin site, it was protected from what archaeologists simply call "pot hunters." It also was protected from cotton farmers and their plows. The 17-acre Parkin site had housed a large community of Native Americans from about the year 1000 until at least 1550. It was surrounded by a moat and a log palisade wall for protection. A tall mound is still on the banks of the St. Francis River. The Parkin site has been designated a National Historic Landmark, one of only 10 such sites in Arkansas.

A number of scholars believe this was the village of Casqui, visited by the Hernando de Soto expedition in the summer of 1541. The Spanish explorers were in what's now Arkansas from 1541 to 1543. They reported that the chief known as Casqui and the residents of the community named for him walked to greet de Soto and then invited the Spaniards to stay in the village. The chief and dozens of residents were baptized as Christians during that visit. The Spaniards erected a big wooden cross atop the mound during what's believed to have been the first Christian service ever held in what's now Arkansas. [*In April 2016, archaeologists said they believed they had found the remains of a Christian cross erected at the Parkin site in 1541 by de Soto.*]

In 1965, the University of Arkansas conducted a field school at the Parkin site. A year later, the Arkansas Archeological Society held its annual training program at Parkin. A powerful state senator from Parkin, Clarence Bell, began working to bring a state park to the site. The park was authorized by the Arkansas Legislature in 1965, but no money was available until a decade later when land acquisition began. Park development started in 1991, and the current visitors' center was dedicated in 1994. The park operates under a partnership with the Arkansas Archeological Survey. A research station is housed in the visitors' center.

The state park is now the main attraction in the eastern part of Cross County, though old-timers also will tell you that it was after a show in Parkin that musician Carl Perkins overheard someone on the dance floor warn folks to stay away from his blue suede shoes. It's said that Perkins wrote down those words and then recorded "Blue Suede Shoes" in December 1955—more than 400 years after de Soto had made some history of his own in the area.

August 7, 2013
Deep in East Arkansas

As I walk through the front door of Martin's Grocery in Biscoe early on a Friday morning, I notice there's only one sausage biscuit left. I order it quickly before someone else can snatch it up. Then, I walk back to grab a cup of coffee. I used to be a regular here. During the almost four years that I worked for the Delta Regional Authority and made a weekly trip to DRA headquarters in Clarksdale, Mississippi, the morning stop at Martin's was *de rigueur*. It's comforting to be back.

I would exit Interstate 40 at Biscoe on those trips to Mississippi, leaving the heavy truck traffic behind and beginning a more relaxing trip through the heart of the Arkansas Delta. I would take U.S. 70 east for a time before heading south on Arkansas 17 and then east on Arkansas 241, connecting with U.S. 49 well south of Brinkley and eventually crossing the Mississippi River at Helena. There are

One rarely encounters another visitor on trips down the boardwalk at Louisiana Purchase Historic State Park.

meetings to attend in Marianna and Parkin on this day. But the key assignment is to reach Jones Bar-B-Q Diner in Marianna before James Jones runs out of pork and locks the door. Sometimes the closed sign goes up as early as 11 a.m.

Paul Austin, the Imboden native who heads the Arkansas Humanities Council, has never been to Jones, and I'm determined that he gets to savor the experience. At Martin's, he comments that one can purchase fresh Arkansas peaches and the latest edition of the *Grand Prairie Herald* out of Hazen along with that cup of coffee for the road. Just east of the store, where U.S. 70 crosses the Cache River at Brasfield, the sign at W. O. and Patsy Prince's Riverfront Restaurant & Fish Market advertises not only catfish and buffalo but also caviar and turtles. It's a clear signal that one is now deep into east Arkansas.

Because of the early start, there's time for a morning walk at the Louisiana Purchase Historic State Park. The park, just off U.S. 49 south of its intersection with U.S. 79, was declared a National Historic Landmark by the National Park Service in 1993. The park houses the monument that marks the initial point for the surveys of the land that had been acquired by the United States in the Louisiana Purchase. The state park covers just 37.5 acres, and I've rarely encountered another visitor on trips down the boardwalk through the headwater swamp. Yet this is without a doubt one of the most historic spots in Arkansas.

In 1815, President James Madison ordered a survey so a system could be established for distributing land to veterans of the War of 1812. The crossing of a north-south line (known as the fifth principal meridian) with an east-west baseline became the initial point from which later surveys of the Louisiana Purchase lands would originate. A November 1815 party led by Prospect K. Robbins marked two trees as witness trees.

The boundary between Lee and Phillips counties was being surveyed in this swamp in 1921 when surveyors Eldridge Douglas and Tom Jacks discovered those two witness trees. In October 1926, the L'Anguille Chapter of the Daughters of the American Revolution at Marianna placed a monument there. That monument was pretty much hidden for years.

The Arkansas Legislature authorized a state park at the site in 1961, but it wasn't until 1977 that the Arkansas Natural Heritage Commission supplied the funds needed to purchase the surrounding land. Facilities were built from 1977 to 1980, including a 950-foot boardwalk from the swamp's edge to the monument. Renovations were later made in anticipation of the 2003 bicentennial of the Louisiana Purchase.

Walking beneath the huge tupelo, bald cypress, oak and sweet gum trees, visitors can visualize the vast bottomland hardwood forest that once covered the Arkansas Delta. It's easy to see how the ivory-billed woodpecker once made a home here along with the black bears that gave the state the early nickname of the Bear State. Row crops rather than forests have characterized the Delta for decades now, with the hardwoods having been harvested and the swamps having been drained in the early decades of the 20th century.

An intricate network of levees and irrigation ditches allowed cotton to become king. With corn and soybeans bringing high prices, the Arkansas cotton crop is an estimated 320,000 acres this summer, down 46 percent from last year. From Little Rock to Hazen, the fields on either side of the interstate are filled with soybeans, rice and corn. The first cotton of the trip is spotted just off the Biscoe exit from Interstate 40. Cotton is a labor-intensive product, and many farmers say the prices the crop brings can no longer offset the production costs. The problems were compounded by a rainy spring that delayed planting. Pigweed, which is hard to control once it reaches maturity, is always a problem during an Arkansas summer. And though the boll weevil is pretty much history in Arkansas, various types of plant bugs still must be controlled.

On the drive from the Louisiana Purchase monument to Marianna, it's evident that the July rains have helped the crops. The summer of 2013 is shaping up to be far different from the drought-plagued summer the state suffered through last year. It's not even 10:30 a.m. when we arrive at Marianna, and there already are customers at Jones Bar-B-Q Diner. It was March of last year when the announcement came that Jones, which is among the oldest black-owned restaurants in the country, would receive the prestigious James Beard Foundation American Classics Award.

The smoked pork here is served on white bread rather than a bun, and the sandwiches feature a thin, vinegar-based sauce. They're smoking pork shoulders, ribs and even turkeys on this Friday morning, and the smell permeates the surrounding residential neighborhood. The oak and hickory is burned in a fireplace behind the restaurant, and the coals are transferred to the cinder-block pits where the smoking is done. On the wall of the tiny dining room, Mr. Jones has hung his James Beard Award right next to the poster listing the sandwich prices. There's no trophy case or lights for the award. The only nod to celebrity is the guest book that shows diners from as far away as California and Florida have visited the hard-to-find restaurant in recent weeks.

There's still a long day ahead in the Arkansas Delta. But as far as getting sandwiches before the day's supply of pork is gone at Jones: Mission accomplished.

September 25, 2013
Historic Harding

Something unusual occurred in Searcy on Friday. They inaugurated a new president at Harding University.

It was a rare event. Bruce McLarty, after all, is only the fifth president in Harding's 89-year history. The first president, John Nelson Armstrong, served from 1924 to 1936. He was replaced by George Benson, who was president from 1936 to 1965. Clifton Ganus Jr., who was on the stage of the Benson Auditorium for Friday's ceremony, was the president from 1965 to 1987. David Burks, who also was on the stage Friday, served as president from 1987 until earlier this year.

"There is something remarkable, perhaps unique in the world of higher education, on the stage here today," McLarty said in his inaugural address. "Seated behind me are two men who represent between them 48 years of presidency at Harding. I count them both as respected mentors and cherished friends. We are assembled here in an auditorium that is named in honor of Harding's second president, Dr. George S. Benson. If we were to add in the 29 years of his tenure, then we could say that 77 years of Harding University's presidency is physically represented here today."

With more than 6,000 students, Harding is by far the state's largest private institution of higher education. The visitors who filled the campus on a rainy Friday afternoon saw new construction at every turn. When Ganus took over as president in 1965, what then was known as Harding College had just 1,472 students.

Harding started in Morrilton in 1924 when a pair of struggling junior colleges—Arkansas Christian College of Morrilton and Harper College in Kansas—combined their assets and formed a four-year college. Both institutions were affiliated with the Churches of

70

Christ. Adlai Croom had started Arkansas Christian College in 1922. Harper College students and faculty members moved to Morrilton in time for the 1924 fall semester. Harding College was named in honor of preacher and educator James Harding. On a campus just north of Morrilton, classes began with 284 students from 17 states and 26 teachers. Just 75 of those students were in college. The rest were scattered from elementary school through high school.

By the fall of 1933, there were 430 Harding students from 25 states, and Mexico and Canada. The Great Depression had taken its toll on Harding and other higher-education institutions across Arkansas. One of those institutions was Galloway Women's College at Searcy. Galloway had been established in 1889 by the Methodist Episcopal Church, South. It was named in honor of Bishop Charles Betts Galloway. The school's largest enrollment was 269 students during the 1925–26 school year. With money scarce, Arkansas' Methodists decided to concentrate their efforts on Hendrix College at Conway. What's now Henderson State University at Arkadelphia had been a Methodist school that was founded in 1890. It was decided in 1929 to consolidate Henderson-Brown College with Hendrix. Henderson-Brown was taken over by the state that fall and renamed Henderson State Teachers College. Hendrix saw its name changed to Hendrix-Henderson College for a couple of years before reverting to just Hendrix College.

Back in Searcy, Galloway became a two-year college and enrollment fell to 75 students by the 1932–33 school year. The school closed following commencement in June 1933, and operations were merged with Hendrix. The Harding board voted in 1934 to buy the property that had housed Galloway. When Harding College opened in Searcy in the fall of 1934, there were 461 students from elementary school through college.

In April 1936, Armstrong told the board that a younger man was needed as president. The choice was Benson, an Oklahoma native who had been attending Harper College in Kansas when *it* merged with Arkansas Christian College in 1924. Benson was among those who moved to Morrilton that year. After graduating from Harding in 1925, he and his new wife moved to China so Benson could serve as a missionary. The communist uprising in China forced Benson to leave the country. He first went to Hong Kong and then to the Philippines.

Benson returned to China in 1928 after Chiang Kai-shek took control of the government. He founded the Canton Bible School. Benson came home to the United States in 1930 to obtain his master's degree from the University of Chicago before moving back to China. Then came the call from Harding. He took over a school in 1936 that was more than $80,000 in debt. Benson spent the next several years soliciting support from corporate leaders throughout the region. The debt was paid by November 1939. On Thanksgiving Day, students and faculty gathered in the rain with Searcy business leaders to watch the mortgage papers dropped onto a bonfire.

By the early 1940s, Benson was becoming well known nationally as a crusader against communism and an advocate for the free enterprise system. He established an organization based on the Harding campus that was known as the National Education Program. It promoted what were called Freedom Forums for high school students across the country. By the 1950s, Benson's syndicated column "Looking Ahead" was being published in more than 4,000 newspapers. His radio program *Land of the Free* ran on more than 300 stations. Benson announced his retirement as Harding president in April 1965 but continued to head the National Education Program, write his column and speak nationwide. He lived until December 1991, long enough to see the collapse of communism in the Soviet Union and Eastern Europe.

Harding's enrollment almost doubled during Genus' first 10 years as president. Burks continued that growth. Now add to the short list of Harding presidents a man who came to Searcy from Memphis as a freshman student in 1975. McLarty met his wife at Harding. After spending 15 months as a missionary abroad and then preaching in several states for a number of years, McLarty returned to Searcy as the pulpit minister for the College Church of Christ. He joined Harding's administrative team in 2005 after having spent 14 years at the nearby church. If the past is any indication, his tenure as Harding's president will be a long one.

February 5, 2014
At the Abbey

Looking at his hooded black robe—the daily dress of a Benedictine monk—I knew immediately that this was my tour guide.

"Father Hugh?" I asked early that Saturday afternoon as I entered the Coury House at Subiaco Abbey. "You must be Mr. Nelson," Father Hugh Assenmacher said quietly.

Since 1963, the Coury House has served as the abbey's retreat center. A modern conference center later was added. With 36 overnight rooms, the facility stays busy as people come to this rural setting in Logan County to pray, reflect and learn.

Father Hugh has seen a lot of people come and go at Subiaco since he entered school as a ninth-grade student in the fall of 1947. He was born Gerald Anthony Assenmacher in Billings, Missouri. He graduated from high school in 1951, took one year of college courses at Subiaco, entered the abbey as a novice in the fall of 1952 and said his vows in September 1953, receiving the name Hugh. Seminary courses were conducted at Subiaco at the time, and Father Hugh

The cornerstone for the current abbey church at Subiaco was laid in 1953.

was ordained to the priesthood in May 1958. He taught at Subiaco Academy until the fall of 1960, when he enrolled at St. Louis University to earn a master's degree in history. When he returned to Subiaco, he taught religion, history, sociology and music. He also served as the abbey's organist and was, from time to time, the band director and choral master for the academy.

In 1977, the Rose Publishing Co. of Little Rock published Father Hugh's book, *A Place Called Subiaco: A History of the Benedictine Monks in Arkansas*. Father Hugh, who will turn 81 on February 16, now serves in the role of abbey historian and archivist. No one knows more about the history of the Arkansas landmark, which began as St. Benedict's Colony in 1877. Subiaco Academy and Subiaco Abbey were founded in 1891 in this area of rolling Arkansas River Valley farmland near the base of Mount Magazine. The railroads were building lines through the area in those years. Little Rock & Fort Smith Railroad executives were anxious to see development along their line. A bit farther south, the Choctaw, Oklahoma & Memphis Railroad completed a line from Oklahoma City to Memphis in 1899. The railroads focused on attracting German Catholic immigrants due to their reputation for being industrious and thrifty. Farmland was offered at attractive prices, and the towns of Scranton, Subiaco and Ratcliff were established. The railroad through Subiaco ceased operation in 1949, two years after Father Hugh arrived, but the abbey and academy lived on.

It's quiet on this Saturday as we leave the retreat center and begin our walking tour of the grounds. Father Hugh explains that the resident students at the academy—which now serves boys from the seventh through the 12th grades—like to spend their Saturdays sleeping and reading in their rooms. There are almost 200 students at the academy, though several dozen of them are area students who don't live at Subiaco. There are more than 30 international students in residence. The academy even runs a bus to Fort Smith each day. Meanwhile, the abbey is the home to more than 40 monks from diverse backgrounds.

In 1877, Abbot Martin Marty of St. Meinrad's Abbey in southern Indiana heard about the large number of German Catholics settling in western Arkansas and contacted the Little Rock & Fort Smith Railroad to see if he could obtain land.

In December of that year, Father Isidor Hobi of St. Meinrad's found the site of what's now Subiaco. The first recorded mass was celebrated in March 1878. By 1879, 150 Catholic families were calling St. Benedict's Colony home. Additional funds and monks were supplied by the Abbey Maria-Einsiedeln in Switzerland. In the summer of 1891, Pope Leo XIII raised the status of St. Benedict's Priory to that of an abbey. The name Subiaco Abbey was born for what was now an independent monastery ruled by an abbot.

The first monastery was destroyed by a massive fire in December 1901. The new monastery was built at its present hilltop location. Seminarians have been trained at Subiaco since 1891. A high school for boys was added in 1902, meaning that Subiaco was no longer just a seminary. Another fire struck the abbey in 1927. With finances tight during the Great Depression, Subiaco did not fully recover until the 1950s. The building destroyed by fire in 1927 was where St. Benedict Church now stands. The site remained vacant until 1953, when the cornerstone was laid for the abbey church. The church wasn't completed until 1959.

We enter the church with Father Hugh. The Saturday mass won't begin until 6 p.m., so the church is empty. A soft light comes through the 182 stained-glass windows, which were designed by the Franz Mayer Co. of Germany. The columns of what's known as the high altar are 18 feet high. A canopy and cross of carved wood are covered with goldleaf. There are 52 tons of marble in the sanctuary. The white marble came from Italy, and the red marble came from Spain. Behind the altar are the pews where the monks gather several times each day.

A typical day for the monks includes morning prayer at 5:45 a.m., mass at 6:35 a.m., breakfast at 7:15 a.m., noon prayer, lunch immediately following, readings at 5:30 p.m., supper at 6 p.m. and vespers at 7:05 p.m. The Benedictines believe in a life of "prayer, community and work." In addition to his teaching duties, Father Hugh spent thousands of hours through the decades working on the immaculate grounds—cutting grass, trimming shrubs, raking leaves. He proudly notes that the monks wash their own dishes. He generally takes his turn at lunch. I go into the gift shop at Coury House and buy a bottle of Monk Sauce, the brand name for the pepper sauce the monks bottle and sell commercially. Father Hugh walks me to the parking lot and then turns and heads slowly back to the place he has called home since 1947, a special place known as Subiaco.

April 16, 2014
In the Ouachita Mountains

Wednesday of last week was the perfect day to drive through the Ouachita Mountains of west Arkansas. The temperature was in the upper 30s when I awoke in Mena, where I had spoken to a banquet the night before, but it rose quickly on the sunny spring day. There was little traffic as I made my way east on Arkansas Highway 88. The redbuds were in full bloom and the dogwoods were just starting to bloom as I drove through the communities of Ink and Cherry Hill.

Just after crossing from Polk County into Montgomery County, I found myself in tiny Pine Ridge. On my left was a classic Arkansas attraction, the Lum and Abner Museum. There were no other visitors, just the proprietor and her two dogs sitting on the front porch, enjoying the early April weather. I already was dressed for a speaking engagement later in the day at the Hot Springs Rotary Club.

"I bet you don't get many people in here wearing a coat and tie," I said. "It has been awhile," she replied.

This is perhaps the most remote museum in Arkansas, but it brings to life an amazing chapter in the state's cultural history that starred two bright Arkansans who were among the country's most popular performers during the Great Depression. The network radio comedy program *Lum and Abner* aired from 1931 to 1955. Chet Lauck, who was born in October 1902 at Alleene in Little River County, played Lum. His friend Norris "Tuffy" Goff, who was born

Arkansans Chet Lauck and Norris Goff, also known as Lum and Abner, were among the country's most popular performers during the Great Depression.

in May 1906 at Cove in Polk County, played Abner. Lauck and Goff's families had moved to Mena in 1911. Goff's father, Rome Goff, owned a wholesale general merchandise business that served several counties. Lauck's father was prominent in the banking and timber industries. Though Lauck was more than three years older than Goff, the two boys became close friends and often entertained Mena residents at various events. Both attended the University of Arkansas after graduating from Mena High School. Lauck was the co-editor of a university humor magazine known as *White Mule*.

They began their radio program when they were in their late 20s, playing two old men who ran the Jot-Em Down Store in the then-fictitious Arkansas community of Pine Ridge. The characters were created when Lauck and Goff were invited to appear on a flood relief broadcast on Hot Springs radio station KTHS in April 1931. They came up with the character names Lum Edwards and Abner Peabody just seconds before going on the air.

KTHS officials liked what they heard and began airing a regular program. Soon, Lauck and Goff were in Chicago auditioning for a nationally broadcast network show on NBC. The program was picked up, marking the start of an incredible run of almost 5,800 daily

15-minute programs that aired live through the years on four radio networks: NBC, ABC, CBS and Mutual. Sponsors included some of the nation's best-known companies and brand names: General Mills, Quaker Oats, Alka-Seltzer and Ford Motor Co.

In 1933, *Lum and Abner* became the first network program broadcast from Radio City in New York. Lauck and Goff were the first radio stars to host marathon charity broadcasts and the first to do a transatlantic simulcast, with Goff in Chicago and Lauck in London. During World War II, Armed Forces Radio aired their daily program to troops around the world. The radio show had moved to Hollywood in 1939 so Lauck and Goff could also pursue movie careers. They made six movies during the 1940s and one more in Europe in 1956 that was intended to be a television pilot. That seventh movie was never released to theaters.

Lauck and Goff based their Jot-Em Down Store on a real store at Waters in Montgomery County. Henry Waters had operated a sawmill and a cotton gin there in the late 1880s. When he established a post office at his store in 1886, the community was named for him. A. A. McKinzie built a general store at Waters in 1904. Five years later, Dick Huddleston built a store across the street, which housed the post office in the 1920s and again became the post office in 1983. The Jot-Em Down Store in the radio series was based on the McKinzie store.

In 1936, residents of Waters asked the federal government to designate the post office there as Pine Ridge. The current museum contains a 1936 letter from then-U.S. Rep. Ben Cravens noting that while Postal Service officials initially had balked since there were so many communities named Pine Ridge across the country, he had convinced the postmaster general to change the name. Cravens, a Fort Smith attorney, represented a large part of western Arkansas in Congress from 1907 to 1913 and again beginning in 1933. He died on January 13, 1939, in Washington, D.C., of bronchial pneumonia. He was just 10 days into his seventh term.

The name change from Waters to Pine Ridge was spotlighted during a ceremony at the State Capitol that was part of the 1936

Arkansas centennial celebration. The McKinzie store later was moved a few hundred yards and connected to the Huddleston store. The Huddleston store contains a gift shop and still serves as the Pine Ridge post office. The museum portion, which opened in 1971, is in the McKinzie store. Both buildings were placed on the National Register of Historic Places in October 1984.

Goff and Lauck retired from regular performances in 1955. Goff and his family remained in southern California. Goff died in June 1978 at Palm Desert, California, and is buried there. Lauck continued to portray Lum for Conoco Oil Co., where he was the vice president of public relations. He returned to his Arkansas roots in 1963, opening a public relations firm at Hot Springs and serving on the state Racing Commission. He died in February 1980 and is buried at Hot Springs.

May 14, 2014
That Bookstore

It was a sad day in the winter of 2012 when Mary Gay Shipley, the nationally known proprietress of That Bookstore in Blytheville, announced that one of the finest independent bookstores in the country was for sale. I figured the end was near.

She began her message on the store's website by quoting a famous verse from Ecclesiastes: "To everything there is a season, and a time to every purpose under the heaven."

I knew then what was coming. She wrote: "It is now time for change. It has been a privilege to serve you all these years. I am proud of the role That Bookstore in Blytheville has played in the life of our community. It is my sincere hope that someone or some group will come forward and continue TBIB in some fashion. I am not going anywhere and would be happy to help a new owner transform TBIB into their own vision. I believe the next few years will be exciting for independent booksellers who embrace the multiple reading formats and who are located in areas with a strong buy-local economy. It would be a fun challenge, if only I were a decade younger. And so

Mary Gay Shipley's dream was to bring a nationally recognized bookstore to economically depressed Blytheville.

I am ready to turn loose of That Bookstore in Blytheville and spend more time with my family. Thank you for the wonderful times."

Shipley was about to turn 68 at the time she wrote the message. I figured she was tired and said so on my blog. A few days earlier, I had written a blog post about the death of McCormick Book Inn in Greenville, Mississippi, which closed its doors in November 2011 after 46 years in business. It also was among the best bookstores in the South. I made many stops there during the years I worked for the Delta Regional Authority. I understood the decision owners Hugh and Mary Dayle McCormick had made. Running a small business in a struggling Delta town is no easy proposition. I passed the building that housed McCormick Book Inn on South Main Street in Greenville a few weeks ago. It still sits empty. Greenville and Blytheville, proud Delta towns, both have had their struggles.

"The economy in Blytheville has been marginal during most of our bookselling years," Shipley wrote for *Publishers Weekly* in 2009. "We have always operated in a community with both a low literacy rate and a low median income. When our local U.S. Air Force base closed in 1992, one-fourth of the population (and a greater percentage of our readers) left."

I wrote on my blog in February 2012: "Will a buyer be found in the next several months? I wish I were more optimistic. We may lose another Delta treasure." I quoted Jerry Seinfeld, who once said that a bookstore is "one of the only pieces of evidence we have that people are still thinking." I sulked about what I figured was the imminent loss of yet another favorite Delta haunt.

Shipley, who became a respected board member of the American Booksellers Association, had been a teacher before becoming a small-business owner. She opened a paperback exchange store affiliated with a Memphis group known as The Book Rack. She was looking to fill a void in Mississippi County. Shipley found space in a former jewelry store in downtown Blytheville in 1976, though the store didn't become known as That Bookstore in Blytheville until 1994. She said she would sell the store for just $35,000. "I really don't want someone to take it over with such a heavy debt load that they can't enjoy it," Shipley said in 2012. "It is my real hope to find someone who will make it theirs."

I was pleasantly surprised in November 2012 when it was announced that a 22-year-old writer named Grant Hill was moving to Blytheville from Mountain Home to buy the store. Hill took over That Bookstore in January 2013. I was in the store two months later and found that the inventory had diminished greatly since the Shipley days. On Good Friday, I was back in Blytheville, half expecting the store to have closed in the year since my previous visit. Instead, a man behind the counter offered a friendly greeting. It was Chris Crawley, who, along with attorney Yolanda Harrison, bought the store from Hill at the first of the year. "Come on in and make yourself at home," he called out. "We have some fresh coffee on, and there are cookies." It was almost as if Shipley were back in charge.

"I had been talking to my folks and doing the math—and checking my blood pressure—and came to the conclusion that I needed to look for a way to, in a sense, minimize any damage to the bookstore and my own health," Hill told the *Courier News* at Blytheville in December. "So I hadn't really even told anybody that I wanted to sell the business, and Chris came in and said, 'I'd like to talk to you about us possibly working out a deal to buy the bookstore.'"

Crawley, the son of sharecroppers, had eight siblings. The Mississippi County native worked as a talent and literary manager in the Los Angeles area before moving back to Blytheville. He bluntly told me that he thought he was coming home to die.

"I had suffered three strokes because of toxic black mold infestation in my lungs and digestive tract," Crawley said. "It's true when they say everything grows well in sunny California. For a time, I could not see, speak or walk. I thought I was done for. I came back to Blytheville to die, but God had other plans for me. He resurrected me, restored me and gave me new life. In return, I want to give new life to That Bookstore and in doing so give new life to Blytheville."

Crawley said he views the bookstore as "an opportunity to help rebuild the Blytheville community. I see the bookstore as a mechanism to uplift the town's spirit. I see it as a way to build literary awareness. I see it as a vehicle to increase literacy for our kids and adults. I see it as a way to make a difference. I see the bookstore as a way to fulfill my mission to make a difference in my hometown."

July 2, 2014
A Saturday in Jasper

Standing alongside Arkansas Highway 7 at the bottom of the steep hill that leads into downtown Jasper, one could smell the brakes of the big trucks headed north on a warm summer Saturday. The large sign next to the road advised drivers to slow down because there was a festival in progress. The 71st annual Buffalo River Elk Festival brings visitors from across the state to one of Arkansas' most remote, beautiful and least populated counties. Following a wet spring, the countryside is greener than usual at the end of June. The Little Buffalo River flows swiftly through Jasper. Just under the Highway 7 bridge, a fisherman stood in water up to his waist in the middle of the stream.

Newton County's population peaked at 12,538 in the 1900

census. It hit bottom at 5,963 in the 1960 census and had moved back up to 8,330 full-time residents by the 2010 census. Retirees had discovered the area in the years since 1960. If you were to count heads on a summer weekend, you would find even more folks in the county. Successful business leaders ranging from Oklahoma City oil and gas executives to northwest Arkansas automobile dealers to central Arkansas advertising magnates have bought homes in the county. One convert even built his own private airstrip to facilitate a quick trip from Oklahoma.

The venerable Ozark Cafe, which has been around in one form or another since 1909, was filled with breakfast patrons Saturday morning. The Ozark once was selected by *New York* magazine's Grub Street blog as Arkansas' entry on its list of the top 50 "foodie destinations." Across the street on the grounds of the Newton County Courthouse, which was completed in 1942 as a Works Progress Administration project, arts and crafts vendors peddled their wares. Just off the square, a Dutch oven cook-off was being held as part of the festival activities. A few yards down the highway from the cook-off, Eddie Watkins was selling his products from the Buffalo River Honey Co. Watkins has 100 hives scattered throughout the county. His bees harvest nectar from wildflowers that are untouched by chemical pesticides. Watkins sounded like a winemaker as he described the character of his honey. He talked excitedly about "floral scents" and "finishing notes."

At the nearby American Legion hut, 15 homemade pies had been entered in the pie contest. There were coconut, chocolate, apple, blackberry, raspberry, pumpkin, pecan, possum pie and more. A coconut pie captured this year's grand prize. Back at the courthouse square, a covered stage hosted the musicians who played on Friday and Saturday during the festival. This year's featured attraction was Jeannie Kendall, who along with her late father Royce made up the well-known country music duo the Kendalls. From the 1960s into the 1990s, the Kendalls released 16 albums with more than 30 singles finding their way onto *Billboard*'s country singles charts. Their most famous hit—"Heaven's Just a Sin Away"—made it to the top of the charts in 1978. It also won the Grammy award for best country vocal by a duo or group. That was, of course, the song Jeannie Kendall closed with Saturday just before the fireworks show that ended the Elk Festival.

Many of the out-of-town visitors had headed out following the 5 p.m. Saturday drawing by Trey Reid of the Arkansas Game & Fish Commission for three coveted fall elk-hunting permits. The people leaving after the drawing backed up area streets for blocks, creating the only annual traffic jam in Newton County. Some of those leaving Jasper made it a point to stop at the Low Gap Cafe, a fine-dining establishment in an old store on Arkansas Highway 74 between Mount Sherman and Ponca. It comes as a surprise to find fine dining in such a rural area of the Arkansas Ozarks, but that's exactly what chef/owner Nick Bottini provides. Bottini learned to cook from his Sicilian relatives. He studied at a culinary school in New York, worked in California and eventually wound up living in Arkansas after visiting relatives and liking what he saw. There's live music on Friday and Saturday nights on the wooden deck that's connected to the restaurant. The restaurant and deck were packed on this final Saturday evening in June.

"If you serve good food, people will find you," Bottini said.

The word about Bottini's restaurant certainly has gotten out to those who visit Horseshoe Canyon Ranch and the Boy Scout facility at Camp Orr. At Horseshoe Canyon, Barry and Amy Johnson prepare for one of their busiest weeks of the year. They were enrolled at Brigham Young University when they met while working at a dude ranch in Wyoming. The couple was determined to one day open a similar facility and found the perfect place in the Ozarks. They now offer everything from horseback riding to rock climbing to zip lines, and they've gained a national reputation in the process of building the ranch.

There were high hopes in Newton County back in 1966 when a Harrison real estate broker named Oscar Snow bought a trout farm between Jasper and Harrison and came up with the idea of a theme park. Snow recruited investors and then gained the confidence of Al Capp, who had created the *Li'l Abner* comic strip. The town of Marble Falls even changed its name to Dogpatch (the name was changed back to Marble Falls in 1997). Capp came down from Boston to speak at the groundbreaking ceremony for the 825-acre park in October 1967. Investors in Dogpatch USA claimed that 300,000 visitors entered the park in 1968. Developer Jess Odom bought controlling interest in the park that year. Four years later, he bought out most of the remaining partners and began construction on a winter sports complex known as Marble Falls. It would prove to be his undoing, as Odom lost hundreds of thousands of dollars on the winter resort. Dogpatch declared bankruptcy in November 1980, though a scaled-down version of the amusement park would continue to operate until 1993.

Dreams of an Ozarks version of Disney World, a facility that would create an economic boom in Newton County, were never realized. In its place is a more relaxed atmosphere where one can experience a float on the Buffalo River, a country breakfast at the Ozark Cafe, Eddie Watkins' honey, Nick Bottini's cooking, the beauty of grazing elk and the rock walls of Horseshoe Canyon.

January 28, 2015
Dear Little House

Margaret Moore Jacobs was a fascinating Arkansas character. Born in 1900 as the oldest daughter of John Burton Moore of Clarendon, she contracted tuberculosis as a teenager and was confined to bed in a sanatorium in Denver. After returning to Clarendon, she married John B. "Jake" Jacobs, a partner in the city's recently established Ford dealership. The couple was given the former house of Margaret's grandfather, John Wesley Moore. The house was built in 1870 and was later moved across the street by Margaret and Jake Jacobs.

Margaret, a prolific writer, was the first female contributing editor for *Furniture World* magazine and wrote for the *Presbyterian Observer.* Her subjects ranged from religion to antiques to gardening. She also was published in more than a dozen Christian periodicals and wrote books with titles such as *My Master Has a Garden* and *A Lifetime of Sundays.* She developed a large following during the 1940s and 1950s. Margaret Moore Jacobs Avenue was dedicated in Clarendon in 1948, and Margaret Moore Jacobs Day was held there on April 3, 1952.

Jake Jacobs died in 1965, and his wife died in 1976. Their estate was left in a trust with instructions that the property at Clarendon be turned into a park and museum. A 700-acre farm was also left to the trust to produce the income needed to operate the museum. Margaret Jacobs' brother, John B. Moore Jr., was appointed as the trustee. As Clarendon and the surrounding area lost population, nothing was done with the house for years. Things began to change when Margaret's nephew, John B. Moore III (who goes by Burton), became the curator and trustee. The house and surrounding gardens were cleaned up. Burton's son, John B. Moore IV, now oversees the museum with help from his younger brother, Jeremiah.

On the front page of the *Arkansas Democrat-Gazette* last week, a feature story on the Moore brothers by Noel Oman focused on their efforts to preserve the U.S. 79 bridge over the White River at Clarendon for cyclists, hikers and other outdoor enthusiasts to use once a new highway bridge opens. John Moore IV is a 26-year-old married father of two (including John Moore V) who returned to Clarendon two years ago at a time when far more people were moving out than moving in. In the 1920 census, Monroe County had 21,601 residents. By the 2010 census, the population was down to 8,149 people. Monroe County lost a higher percentage of its residents (20.5 percent) between the 2000 and 2010 census than any county in Arkansas. John IV and Jeremiah, who is 20, have a deep love for their home county and the Delta as a whole. The website for the Jacobs Park & Museum states: "Our vision at the Jacobs Trust is to create a small spark in a place where the power grid has largely been switched off, and for that spark to strike up a small flame."

Margaret Moore Jacobs always described her home as the Dear Little House. I became familiar with the brothers' efforts in Clarendon last summer when Jeremiah sent an email inviting me to pay a visit. He wrote: "Your forthright love for our state and its history bring a certain kindred feeling that leads me to invite you down to Monroe County for a visit, tour and a catfish lunch." Paul Austin, who heads the Arkansas Humanities Council, shares my fascination with the lower White River region. He also shares my love of a good catfish lunch. So it was that we found ourselves in the Dear Little House having lunch with the Moore brothers.

Clarendon has a rich history. The area was settled in the late 1700s by French hunters and trappers who built cabins where the Cache River empties into the White River. The Military Road from Little Rock to Memphis, which was constructed during the 1820s, crossed the White River at Clarendon. The settlement had a ferry crossing and a post office. Clarendon became the county seat when Monroe County was carved out of Arkansas and Phillips counties in 1829. Numerous skirmishes were fought in the Clarendon area during the Civil War. A railroad bridge for the Cotton Belt Line was constructed at Clarendon in 1883. Meanwhile, the ferry continued to operate until 1931 when the current highway bridge was constructed. The Monroe County Courthouse, designed by well-known Arkansas architect Charles Thompson, was built in 1911.

The flood of 1927, the onset of the Great Depression in 1929, the drought of 1930–31 and the flood of 1937 all helped spark a decades-long decline. The Dear Little House is an oasis on the residential part of Main Street. The gardens surrounding the home include cast-iron sculptures from the 1800s, a large bell that came from a church at Helena and landscaped gardens. The house itself is filled with antiques ranging from an 1880 music box to a fireplace mantel crafted in Naples, Italy. John Wesley Moore, who built the Greek Revival–style house, came to Clarendon from Sussex County in Virginia. Documents from the Arkansas Historic Preservation

Program note that "the strong architectural influences of his Virginia upbringing are evident in the home he constructed for himself. The house was built on a lot that ran down to the river's edge and gave a spectacular view of the heavy traffic on the White River until the construction of a levee following the 1927 flood, which devastated the town.

"Following his death, the house went to his son, who had established himself as an attorney as well as the owner of extensive landholdings in Monroe County. He married Bessie Branch of Holly Grove in the early 1900s. Bessie was the daughter of William F. Branch, who had established the Bank of Holly Grove, and Ella Walls Branch, whose family held large amounts of acreage in the county."

The Dear Little House was moved on log rollers by mules to its new location in 1931. The lot had been the site of an early schoolhouse. Margaret Moore Jacobs not only restored the house but also landscaped the grounds with plantings mentioned in the Bible. Now two great-nephews are working to preserve the Dear Little House and gardens along with her legacy.

September 9, 2015
Where Cotton Was King

For many years when I thought of Holly Grove in Monroe County, I thought of Sonny Gordon. He was the coach at the high school for four decades, a legendary mentor whose football teams won 21 consecutive games at one point in the early 1960s. The annual Thanksgiving game between Clarendon and Holly Grove once was a major event in east Arkansas.

Gordon was inducted into the Arkansas Sports Hall of Fame in 1984. He coached another Hall of Fame inductee, Ken Turner, who spent 17 years as an assistant football coach at the University of Arkansas and another decade as the head football coach and later the athletic director at his alma mater, Henderson State University. My father sold athletic supplies across the state, and Gordon was among his friends in the coaching profession. Following a night spent last month at the home of Raymond and Mackie Abramson, I began to think of Holly Grove in a different light. I contemplated the fate of similar towns across the Delta. These communities served the sharecroppers and tenant farmers who lived in surrounding rural areas. The streets were full on Saturdays when farmers would come to town to buy supplies during the day and find entertainment at night. With the increased mechanization of agriculture and the subsequent loss of Delta residents, dozens of such communities are struggling to find an economic reason to exist.

For most of the 20th century, cotton was king in the Delta. Turner says he went out for football "to keep from picking cotton after school. I told people a hoe handle and a cotton sack made a coach out of me." Holly Grove's population peaked at 977 residents in the 1920 census and was down to 602 by 2010. The town is named for the holly trees that are native to the area. When the Arkansas Central Railroad came in 1872, John Smith and James Kerry platted a new city.

Holly Grove was incorporated in 1876 and had seven general stores, a drugstore, a restaurant, a livery stable, a cotton gin, a gristmill, a grocery store, three churches, a funeral home and two doctors' offices by 1890.

Rue and Venda Abramson, who built the 1921 house where I spent the night, were Holly Grove natives. Their parents had been among the first people to settle in the area after the Civil War. Raymond Abramson, who now serves as a judge on the Arkansas State Court of Appeals, is the grandson of Rue Abramson and part of a rich tradition of Jewish farmers and merchants in the Delta that's rapidly disappearing. In addition to farming, Rue Abramson operated a bank and several businesses. He opened the town's first modern garage and service station in 1927. The official listing of the Abramson house on the National Register of Historic Places notes: "The Abramsons were active in the commercial life of Holly Grove as merchants, ginners and plantation owners. By 1922, they also founded the First National

Bank of Holly Grove. They were active in civic affairs. They were leaders in such organizations as the Crowley's Ridge Council of the Boy Scouts of America, the Monroe County Fair Association, the Sahara Temple of Pine Bluff, the American Red Cross, B'nai B'rith, Temple Beth El of Helena and various other Jewish organizations."

Rue Abramson selected a well-known Memphis architect, Estes Mann, to design his home. Mann had a remarkable career, designing more than 1,800 residences across the Mid-South, including some of the finest houses in Memphis.

Mann, a Marianna native, even designed the administration building at what's now Arkansas State University at Jonesboro. The elaborate Craftsman-style home was designed to make a statement. A few blocks away in the city's commercial district, Rue Abramson's R. Abramson Co. owned four buildings. Rue's son, Ralph, later took over the family's businesses. Ralph's wife, Rosemary, was a Memphis native who married Ralph in 1946 and spent the rest of her life in Holly Grove. Rosemary died in January 2013 at age 93. She had become a familiar figure through the years on the Mid-South horse show circuit, winning championships in Arkansas, Mississippi, Missouri, Kentucky and Tennessee on five-gaited horses with names such as Mr. Memphis, Denmark's Liberty Miss and Candyman. Her last horse was named Magic. Raymond Abramson keeps his mother's riding trophies on display in the family home along with photos of the horses and paintings by his wife, Mockie, an artist. Raymond Abramson received his undergraduate degree from the University of Virginia in 1973 and his law degree from the University of Arkansas at Fayetteville in 1976. He and Mockie, a Virginia native, split their time between Little Rock and Holly Grove but maintain deep ties to Monroe County. The Abramson family led the effort to turn the former depot at Holly Grove into a library.

"Even into the 1950s, Holly Grove flourished, with bands playing in downtown establishments that offered beer and dancing," Steven Teske writes for the Encyclopedia of Arkansas History & Culture. "Meanwhile, railroads diminished in importance as automobile traffic increased. Interstate 40 crosses northern Monroe County more than 20 miles north of Holly Grove. State highways 17 and 86 intersect in Holly Grove, but they do not host nearly as many travelers as the interstate. The railroad tracks have been removed. The school district was consolidated into the Clarendon School District. The Holly Grove elementary school continued to be used by the district until the building was destroyed by fire in December 2006."

A history of Holly Grove, written for the city's 1976 centennial celebration, sounded a hopeful note, noting that the town is "situated in one of the best cotton-growing areas in the country and ships a large quantity of that commodity. Rice and soybeans are grown extensively. Herds of fine cattle may be seen grazing in lush pastures. Holly Grove is noted for its lovely trees, old Southern atmosphere and hospitality. Although the town is small, it's an active little town, developing into a prosperous community." Almost four decades after those words were written, Holly Grove struggles to hold on. Between the 2000 and 2010 censuses, Monroe County lost a larger percentage of its population than any county in Arkansas. Like other farming communities in the Delta areas of Arkansas, Mississippi and Louisiana, Holly Grove celebrates its past while wondering if there's a future.

November 25, 2015
Thankful for Arkansas

As another Thanksgiving approaches, I'm thankful to live in a state like Arkansas. I'm thankful to live in a place where I can eat a turkey sandwich at the original Burge's in Lewisville, grab a plate lunch at the Pickens Store in Desha County, consume some buffalo ribs at the Lassis Inn in Little Rock, pig out at Jones Bar-B-Q Diner in Marianna and have a Friday night catfish dinner at The Whippet in Prattsville.

I'm thankful to live in a place where I can go to a winery near Altus before visiting the monastery at Subiaco, climb Pinnacle Mountain, visit one of the most beautiful state capitols in the country,

One thing to be thankful for is living in a state that supports classic restaurants.

fish for smallmouth bass on the Kings River and attend the seasonal craft fairs at War Eagle. I'm thankful to live in a place where I can stand along the rail at Oaklawn Park on Arkansas Derby day, hang out on Dickson Street in Fayetteville after a Razorback football game, listen to the music on a Saturday night in downtown Mountain View and take a hot bath on Bathhouse Row in Hot Springs. I'm thankful to live in a place where I can spend the night on a houseboat on Lake Ouachita, drive the Pig Trail through the Ozarks and watch the elk graze in the Boxley Valley. I'm thankful to live in a place where I can read the Civil War markers at DeValls Bluff before having some of the country's best barbecue at Craig's, tour the Johnny Cash boyhood home at Dyess, see the English Tudor architecture at Wilson and eat an entire hubcap cheeseburger at the original Cotham's in Scott.

I'm thankful to live in a place where I can float a canoe down the Buffalo River when the dogwoods are blooming, search for the Gurdon Light late at night, fish for trout early in the morning on the upper White River and run jugs for giant catfish at night on the lower White River. I'm thankful to live in a place where I can attend a Battle of the Ravine college football game between Ouachita Baptist University and Henderson State University each November in Arkadelphia, watch the sun rise on a winter morning from a duck blind on the Grand Prairie and sample dozens of versions of duck gumbo in Stuttgart on the weekend after Thanksgiving. I'm thankful to live in a place where I can spend the night in both the Arlington Hotel at Hot Springs and the Crescent Hotel at Eureka Springs, drive along the Talimena Scenic Drive when the leaves are changing, spend the day walking around Historic Washington State Park when the jonquils are blooming and wrangle an invitation to one of the Sunday night wild-game dinners at Gene's in Brinkley. I'm thankful to live in a place where I can eat the famous gear salad and a filet mignon at Herman's in Fayetteville, hang out with some bikers at Roy's in Paragould, have a steak on a Friday night at Jerry's in Trumann, combine fried chicken with spaghetti at the Venesian Inn in Tontitown and drink the water at the Mountain Valley headquarters in downtown Hot Springs.

I'm thankful to live in a place where I can watch the toad races during Toad Suck Daze in Conway, have breakfast at The Pancake Shop in Hot Springs, attend the annual Gillett Coon Supper each January and then show up a few weeks later for the annual Slovak Oyster Supper. I'm thankful to live in a place where I can be a part of the all-tomato luncheon during the Bradley County Pink Tomato Festival at Warren, see people in kilts at the Scottish Festival at Lyon College in Batesville, attend a meeting in the room behind the kitchen at Doe's Eat Place in Little Rock and buy an ice cream cone at the Ernie Dunlap Store in Kirby. I'm thankful to live in a place where I can watch the rice harvest near Weiner on a fall day, go to Garvan Woodland Gardens on Lake Hamilton when the tulips are blooming, attend the St. Patrick's Day Parade in Hot Springs and have my photo taken while straddling the Arkansas-Texas line at the federal courthouse in downtown Texarkana. I'm thankful to live in a place where I can get a room at the Mather Lodge atop Petit Jean, tour the Lakeport Plantation near Lake Village, walk the boardwalk through the swamp between Brinkley and Marvell to see the Louisiana Purchase monument and eat a slice of melon at the Hope Watermelon Festival.

I'm thankful to live in a place where I can try to finish a tamale spread at McClard's in Hot Springs, attend the King Biscuit Blues Festival at Helena, eat a turkey leg at the Arkansas State Fair and sit on the east side of Mount Nebo while watching the sun rise over the Arkansas River Valley. I'm thankful to live in a place where I can spend a summer Saturday morning at the farmer's market on the square in Fayetteville as the locals walk their dogs, take a slow walk through history at Mount Holly Cemetery in Little Rock, visit a sand blow in northeast Arkansas while contemplating the New Madrid Earthquakes of 1811–12 and get a sunburn while attending Riverfest along the banks of the Arkansas River in Little Rock. I'm thankful to live in a place where I can dig for diamonds at the Crater of Diamonds State Park near Murfreesboro, buy strawberry shortcake in the spring at The Bulldog in Bald Knob, sample the fried chicken at the Mount Nebo Chicken Fry at Dardanelle, gather wild blackberries in the summer and eat some peaches picked that day at the Johnson County Peach Festival.

I'm thankful to live in a place where I can go kayaking on the Mulberry River, cross the U.S. Highway 62 bridge over Norfork Lake on a clear day, visit Judge Parker's courtroom at the Fort Smith National Historic Site and attend the Fourth of July community picnics at Corning and Piggott. I'm thankful to live in a place where I can take a boat onto Grassy Lake in southwest Arkansas to look for alligators and sit outside in Basin Spring Park at Eureka Springs on a fall Saturday evening while enjoying live music. I'm thankful to live in a place where I can walk around the courthouse square in El Dorado, have a catfish dinner at Dondie's on the banks of the White River at Des Arc and buy a stack of books at That Bookstore in Blytheville. I'm thankful to live in a place where I can watch Sonny Payne do his *King Biscuit Time* radio show at the Delta Cultural Center in Helena, fish for bream on a south Arkansas oxbow during the day, gig frogs on the same lake at night and watch the cardboard-boat races at Greers Ferry Lake before having dinner at the iconic Red Apple Inn.

Arkansas People

July 27, 2011
Lunch with the Solomons

It might have been the most pleasant lunch I had all year. It was a year ago when I made the trip to Helena—Friday, July 23, 2010, to be exact.

Noted Arkansas historian Trey Berry and I walked into the home of David and Miriam Solomon for lunch just before noon that day. They greeted us warmly, and Miriam made sure everyone was comfortable. I immediately noticed that the home was filled with art and books, signs of a cultured life well lived.

David had just turned 94 at the time of our visit. Miriam, his wife of 68 years, was three years younger. Both were Helena natives and stalwarts in what once was a strong Jewish community along the lower Mississippi River. The Delta Jews, who had thrived in towns on both sides of the river from St. Louis to New Orleans, were rapidly disappearing. I was there to do a magazine story for *Arkansas Life* on the decline in population of those Delta Jews. During the course of that delightful afternoon, I made new friends.

Miriam Solomon died earlier this month at age 92 from injuries suffered in a fall. She was described in her obituary as someone who "worked to advance the quality of life for the Helena community and for all its citizens."

That's an understatement. Longtime friend Cathy Cunningham, who shared lunch with us at the Solomon home a year ago, said Miriam "felt everybody was equal and deserved the same treatment. That wasn't the popular thing to do....It takes a special person to be that blunt and loved by so many."

Her obituary also touched on the rich life she lived. It described her as an "avid reader" who in her later years "was the center of an informal reading group of friends in Helena and around the country. She and David loved to travel and journey over most of the world. She was a gourmet cook with a particular passion for Southern specialties, a collector of art and antiques and an enthusiastic golf and bridge player."

The most enjoyable part of my afternoon in the Solomon home was watching the couple spar verbally in a good-natured way. I'm not sure which one had the sharper wit. By the end of the day, I felt like their lifelong friend.

David has long been one of the state's most respected attorneys, putting on a suit and bow tie each morning into his 90s and reporting to his law office on Cherry Street. Once the busiest commercial street in east Arkansas, Cherry Street is now a place where a number of the buildings are empty and crumbling. After the closing of Temple Beth El five years ago, some of the area's remaining Jews would gather in the Solomon home for Friday night services. "There are only about six or seven of us," David told me. "One lady drives over from Marvell. Another comes from Holly Grove. There was just no way to maintain the temple. There were too few of us left, and we certainly weren't going to give it to another religion."

He smiled as he said that. His wit is as much a part of his persona as his bow tie.

There are three highly successful Solomon sons. David P. Solomon of New York retired as executive director of the American Jewish Historical Society. Rayman L. Solomon became dean of the Rutgers School of Law in Camden, New Jersey. Lafe E. Solomon of Washington, D.C., was named last summer by President Obama as the acting general counsel for the National Labor Relations Board and has been much in the news lately.

David Solomon's grandfather arrived from Germany shortly before the Civil War and had eight children: six boys and two girls. That second generation eventually would own a department store, a shoe store, a wholesale dry goods operation and cotton farms. Miriam Solomon's father, Charles Rayman, operated Helena Wholesale Co. Her older brother, David Rayman, was among those who would attend the Friday night services at the Solomon home.

"I basically run an upscale nursing home," Miriam told me. "We live a long time in this family."

David and Miriam were married in September 1942. David

traveled back to Helena from Camp Carson in Colorado Springs, Colorado, where he was stationed in the Army. Miriam had been working as an occupational therapist in a Chicago hospital. The wedding was in Miriam's family home.

"If she were a woman of today, she probably would still have her career," her oldest son said following his mother's death. "She may have lived somewhere else. But being a homemaker was the tradition for women back then."

She carved out a full life for herself. When the temple was closed in 2006, she saw to it that many of its artifacts were given to the Etz Chaim congregation in Bentonville. She also ensured that the Department of Arkansas Heritage would take over the building that had housed Temple Beth El and that there would be an endowment to maintain the Jewish cemetery at Helena.

As our seafood lunch came to an end, Miriam looked over at Katie Harrington, the director of the Delta Cultural Center at Helena.

"I had made up my mind that we weren't going to have the temple standing there with weeds growing out of the gutter," Miriam said. "That wasn't going to happen on my watch. In my mind, I gave it three years. If we hadn't found a use for it by then, we were going to have it torn down. Then Katie came into our lives with a plan to use the temple for the good of the community."

David Solomon interjected, "We can go peacefully now that Katie has the temple."

August 10, 2011
Stanley Reed: Cotton Farmer

A lot was written last month about Stanley Reed, the Marianna farmer who died the morning of July 15 in a one-vehicle accident on U.S. Highway 64 east of Augusta.

It was duly noted that Reed had been among the four finalists for the job of president of the University of Arkansas System. The day before the accident, the UA Board of Trustees selected Donald Bobbitt, a former dean of the Fulbright College of Arts and Sciences at the University of Arkansas at Fayetteville, to serve in that position.

It also was noted that in December 2003, Reed won an election to become president of the influential Arkansas Farm Bureau Federation.

During the almost 10 years I spent on Governor Mike Huckabee's staff, we had few better friends than Stanley Reed. When I was Huckabee's campaign manager in 1998, Reed consistently went to bat for us at a time when it was still rare to find Delta business leaders who would openly support a Republican for governor, especially in a race in which the Democratic nominee was from east Arkansas. Reed never wavered in his support.

The governor appointed Reed to the UA Board of Trustees in 1998, and he would go on to serve as chairman from 2006 to 2008. Despite his many civic accomplishments through the years, here's what I believe to have been Reed's greatest contribution to our state: He never tired of reminding folks of the importance of agriculture to the Arkansas economy.

The population loss in the Delta is not a secret. According to an Associated Press story published last month, "Rural America now accounts for just 16 percent of the nation's population, the lowest ever. The latest 2010 census numbers hint at an emerging America where, by mid-century, city boundaries become indistinct and rural areas grow ever less relevant. Many communities could shrink to virtual ghost towns as they shutter businesses and close down schools, demographers say. More metro areas are booming into sprawling megalopolises. Barring fresh investment that could bring jobs, however, large swaths of the Great Plains and Appalachia, along with parts of Arkansas, Mississippi and north Texas, could face significant population declines."

You'll notice that Arkansas is among the states singled out in this story. During the four years I served as a presidential appointee to the Delta Regional Authority (which covers 252 counties and parishes in parts of eight states), I dealt on a daily basis with population loss issues. But when writers feel obligated to include the adjective "struggling" each time they write the word "Delta," they leave out an important fact: While agricultural mechanization means that far fewer people are needed to produce a crop than was once the case, the land remains valuable. With crop prices generally high, it's perhaps even a more vital cog of the Arkansas economy than before.

Stanley Reed never tired of reminding us of that.

Reed graduated as the salutatorian of T. A. Futrall High School in Marianna and went on to receive his bachelor's degree in agricultural engineering from the University of Arkansas at Fayetteville. He also attended law school at Fayetteville. Each time, he graduated with the highest of honors. As an undergraduate, he was Mr. Everything—president of the Sigma Alpha Epsilon fraternity, president of the Interfraternity Council, etc.

In 1976, Reed made the highest score on the state bar exam. There's no doubt in my mind that with his drive and intellect, he could have gone on to become one of the South's top attorneys. Farming, though, was in his blood. He quickly determined that he had much rather be sweating in the Lee County cotton fields than sitting behind a desk in an air-conditioned law office.

In July of last year, Reed invited me to join him for lunch at Jones Grocery in Haynes, a community on Arkansas Highway 1 in Lee County between Marianna and Forrest City. Haynes had a population of just 150 people in the 2010 census (down from 214 in the 2000 census), but it's surrounded by some of the most fertile land in the state.

The tables were almost full when I walked in just past 11 a.m. Reed had saved me a seat. The farmers in the store ranged in age from their 20s to their 70s. They talked about the lack of rain, soybeans that were becoming stressed by dry conditions and pigweed that was beginning to show up in their fields. Reed wanted me to hear all of that. He loved the world of agriculture, and he delighted in sharing his world with others.

Reed, who usually showed up for meetings in Little Rock dressed in a suit, was in jeans and dusty boots that day. He was at home among these men who had just come from the fields and would return to the fields once lunch was over. Reed was anxious to introduce me to his son, Nathan. He was proud his son had followed him into farming. They farmed almost 6,000 acres together.

Following lunch, I climbed into Reed's vehicle to tour his farm. We left Haynes and drove east on Arkansas Highway 131 toward the St. Francis River. Thousands of acres of soybeans, cotton and rice could be viewed on either side of the road. Crowley's Ridge provided a brief interval of trees. On the other side of the ridge, the land flattened again and the crops were planted as far as the eye could see.

On the way back to Haynes, we stopped at a shady spot atop Crowley's Ridge to visit. Reed was happy that day, having had the opportunity to show off his farm and talk about the importance of Delta agriculture. We need more like him.

February 8, 2012
The Newspaper Publisher

Hundreds of Arkansans will gather in downtown Little Rock on Friday night as the Arkansas Business Hall of Fame inducts its newest members. This will be the 14th class of the Hall of Fame, a project of the College of Business at the University of Arkansas. The inaugural class in 1999 consisted of business legends Sam Walton, Jack Stephens, Charles Murphy and Bill Dillard Sr.

Subsequent inductees have included such familiar names in Arkansas history as Don Tyson, J. B. Hunt, Col. T. H. Barton, Harvey Couch and Albert Yarnell. Inductees this year include advertising giant Wayne Cranford, timber industry innovator John Ed Anthony and longtime Walmart executive Jack Shewmaker.

The fourth member of the Class of 2012 is the publisher of the newspaper that publishes this column, Walter E. Hussman Jr., a man for whom I worked for 10 years in several stints at the *Arkansas Democrat* and later the *Arkansas Democrat-Gazette*. I haven't worked full time at a newspaper since 1996 but still think of myself as a newspaperman. Hussman is a lifer. He was born into a newspaper family and still oversees a family-owned media conglomerate at a time when family-owned newspapers have become somewhat of a rarity.

I recently did something that I had never done in all the years I worked for him: I sat in Hussman's office for several hours and discussed his family's history in the business. It's a fascinating story, one that would make a good subject for a book. Following graduation from the University of North Carolina, Hussman applied to the journalism school at Columbia University in New York. He was turned down and instead became a student at Columbia's business school, where he earned his master's degree in 16 months.

Enjoying life in the big city, Hussman decided he wanted to be a business writer at *Forbes*, *Business Week* or *Fortune*. He landed at *Forbes* and was carving a niche for himself when his father in Camden called. Hussman's two older sisters weren't involved in the day-to-day operations of a family media business that had grown to include newspapers, radio stations, a television station and cable television franchises. Hussman's father was 63 and wanted to know if his son would consider returning to Arkansas. If he declined, the elder Hussman would consider selling the business.

Hussman became his father's administrative assistant in 1970. When the general manager of the *Camden News* was dismissed, Hussman was told by his father: "You're going to run the paper until you find somebody else to run it."

Hussman had wanted to be on the writing side of journalism because he thought that's where the creativity was. He soon learned a valuable lesson: One can be just as creative on the business side. In 1973, Hussman moved from Camden to Hot Springs to become the vice president and general manager of the Palmer Newspapers, which included dailies at Camden, Hot Springs, Texarkana, El Dorado and Magnolia. Just a year later, the company purchased the *Arkansas Democrat*, the struggling afternoon daily in Little Rock. The *Democrat* had a daily circulation of 62,405. The *Arkansas*

Gazette, the morning newspaper that was in my family's driveway each morning when I was growing up, had a circulation of 118,702.

Hussman's father was wary but decided to give it three years to see if there was progress. The Hussman family paid $500,000 down, along with a note of $3 million to be paid over 20 years at 7 percent interest. Walter Hussman Jr. was just 27 when he became a newspaper publisher in the state's largest city.

"I thought I really knew a lot about the newspaper business," he told me. "I didn't realize how little I really knew." Hussman was able to bring down costs during his first three years as employees voted to decertify four unions.

Revenues were flat, however, leading Hussman to approach *Gazette* publisher Hugh Patterson Jr. with the idea of a joint operating agreement (JOA). Hussman had studied the 22 agreements already in place across the country. He proposed giving the *Gazette* 100 percent of the JOA profits until the morning newspaper had made as much money as the year before. In a decision that has become famous in journalism annals, Patterson turned him down.

Soon afterward, Hussman decided to go head-to-head against the *Gazette*. His father consented reluctantly, and the *Democrat* began publishing a morning edition in 1979 in an effort to reverse years of declining market share. Front-page color was added, free want ads were offered to non-commercial advertisers, the size of the "newshole" was increased by 58 percent and the news staff was doubled. Revenues increased, but expenses also soared.

I went to work at the *Democrat* in late 1981, my first job after college. I was young, and the idea of working for the underdog in what was becoming one of the country's great newspaper wars was exciting. Little did I realize the anxiety downstairs among those who were trying to make the numbers work from a business standpoint.

"We caught a tiger that was bounding through the jungle by the tail, but he was going so fast we couldn't get off," Hussman said.

Finally, there was a small monthly profit in May 1984. Huge losses would follow, but psychologically that was a turning point. As

Hussman puts it, "I think the owners of the *Gazette* realized that once we made money, we weren't going away."

I was working in Washington for the *Democrat* in 1986 when the Patterson family sold the *Gazette* to Gannett Corp., the nation's largest newspaper chain. My assignment that day was to cross the Potomac River, go to the Gannett headquarters in Arlington, Virginia, and write about the company. Those of us who worked at the *Democrat* were scared to have a giant enter the fray. Hussman admitted in our interview that he also was scared.

The rest, as they say, is history. Walter Hussman Jr. took on the nation's largest newspaper chain and won. The final editions of the *Arkansas Gazette* and the *Arkansas Democrat* were published October 18, 1991. The first edition of the *Arkansas Democrat-Gazette* was published the next day.

February 15, 2012
The Timber Baron

It's chilly on this winter morning as John Ed Anthony throws another piece of wood on the fire. I'm at Anthony's Shortleaf Farm, a scenic piece of property on Arkansas Highway 290 near Hot Springs.

Last Friday night, the University of Arkansas' Sam Walton College of Business inducted Anthony into the Arkansas Business Hall of Fame.

Anthony long has been among my favorite Arkansans, dating back to my days as a young sportswriter when his Loblolly Stable was among the top thoroughbred racing and breeding operations in America. On this morning, we talk about the timber industry and his family's long history in south Arkansas.

"Most people only ask me about racing, and that's just a small part of who I am," Anthony says.

To his core, he's a lumberman. After all, he spent the first years of his life in a timber camp started by his father, Ted Anthony.

"It was called Smead," John Ed says. "It was about 25 miles from Camden in the middle of nowhere. The place was named for

Lamar Smead, a former Ouachita County sheriff....My dad would tell stories of how men would walk up and down the railroad line looking for work."

His parents later moved to a tiny community between Fordyce and Bearden named Hopeville. John Ed began the first grade at Bearden in 1945. At Christmas that year, the family moved to Woodville, Texas, a town deep in the piney woods between Lufkin and Beaumont. He stayed in Woodville until his high school graduation.

By the 1930s, the Anthony family had one of the largest private lumber operations in the country. With multiple partnerships, the family ran between 20 and 30 mills in south Arkansas, north Louisiana and east Texas. John Ed's grandfather, Garland Anthony, and Ted Anthony had come to the realization that cut-over pine land left behind by large companies would renew itself in 20 to 30 years if properly managed. The Anthony family was a pioneer in selective harvesting techniques.

Any discussion of what's now Anthony Timberlands Inc. must start at Bearden, which had a population of 966 people in the 2010 census, down from a high of 1,300 in 1950. Bearden was founded as a railroad stop along what would become the Cotton Belt Railway. The city limits were set in 1882 by the Southwest Improvement Association, an agency of the Railway Land Office. Bearden was named for Judge John T. Bearden, a lawyer for the association. Surrounded by virgin forests, the community prospered. In 1885, the Cotton Belt Lumber Co. picked Bearden as the site of a mill.

The online Encyclopedia of Arkansas History & Culture notes that lumber was "the driving force of Bearden's economy. Four large lumber mills—the Cotton Belt mill, the Freeman-Smith Lumber Co., the Eagle Lumber Co. and the Stout Lumber Co.—operated within six miles of the town from 1885 to 1930. At one point, the mills employed and supported more than 2,000 area men and their families. Most of the mill workers were farmers or sons of farmers. They would work the mills by day and the fields before and after work. While the success was long lasting, Bearden, like many communities in the early 1900s, experienced the results of unsound lumber practices. Many acres were cut and not replanted correctly or at all, resulting in a shift in milling. The first mill to leave was in 1923."

Garland Anthony's grandfather, Addison Anthony, came to south Arkansas in the 1840s from Virginia. Garland Anthony was born in 1884 and grew up near Bearden, where his family farmed and raised livestock. The man known across south Arkansas simply as Mr. Garland teamed up with an uncle to build a sawmill in 1907. By 1910, the uncle had turned the operation over to Mr. Garland, declaring that he was headed back to the farm to raise cotton. Ted Anthony, Mr. Garland's oldest son, took things to the next level.

John Ed had never set foot in Fayetteville until his first day at the University of Arkansas, where he majored in business. A month before graduation in 1961, he received word that his father had died of a heart attack at age 48. John Ed, just 22, leased a house in Bearden and took his wife and one-month-old son Steven there so he could work with his 77-year-old grandfather. Mr. Garland would live to age 97, dying in 1981 soon after an automobile accident at Bearden.

John Ed drove to Union County each day to manage a mill at Mount Holly. One day in 1962, his grandfather informed John Ed that he would manage the flagship Bearden mill. John Ed began pulling together the partnerships his family had entered into through the years. It wasn't an easy task. He found deeds in cigar boxes and agreements scribbled on the backs of envelopes.

When John Ed approached his partners in the early 1970s with expansion plans, they declined. He moved forward by himself, forming Anthony Timberlands Inc. Steven Anthony has been the ATI president since 2004. With significant declines in the housing market, the timber industry has suffered in recent years.

"I wish I could be optimistic about the future," John Ed says. "It has been a bloodbath the past five years or so. We now have a huge inventory of uncut timber. Trees that were planted in the 1980s and 1990s are cutting size, but there's no demand for them."

The Anthony family won't be leaving the timber business anytime soon, though. John Ed's grandson Addison makes the seventh generation of Anthony family members working in those south Arkansas forests.

March 7, 2012
Tommy May's Journey

On July 4, 1939, Lou Gehrig, the New York Yankee star known as the Iron Horse, stepped to the microphone at Yankee Stadium for what would become one of the most memorable moments in baseball history.

"Fans, for the past two weeks you have been reading about the bad break I got," said Gehrig, 36. "Yet today I consider myself the luckiest man on the face of the earth."

During the noon hour last Wednesday, several hundred Arkansans gathered at the Clinton School of Public Service in Little Rock to hear Arkansas' own Iron Horse, Tommy May. The Simmons Bank chairman from Pine Bluff had made the short trip to the capital city for a talk titled "A Journey with Many Crossroads."

It was standing room only in the old depot that now houses the Clinton School. Bankers wearing expensive suits sat by those dressed in casual clothes. The thing they all had in common was respect for May. They gave him a standing ovation when his wheelchair was rolled to the podium at the start of the address, and they gave him another standing ovation 45 minutes later as he concluded his remarks.

May, an avid runner, noticed in September 2005 that his running had slowed and his feet felt heavy. Following months of tests, he was diagnosed with what's commonly known as ALS or Lou Gehrig's disease. The official name is amyotrophic lateral sclerosis. The degenerative disease is progressive and fatal. There's no known cure, and many patients die within two to three years.

May, his voice hoarse from recent surgery, noted that about 20,000 Americans have ALS. He said almost 5,000 people are added to the rolls annually while another 5,000 "finish their journey" each year. Gehrig talked about being "lucky." May echoed those sentiments, making it clear he's thankful for the things that have occurred during his 65 years of life. He quoted from the Bible, talked about the strength of his faith and referred simply to "my medical challenge."

The room was silent as he talked, the silence broken by occasional laughter as May displayed his trademark sense of humor. He noted the large number of bankers in attendance and said, "If I knew they were going to be here, I would be out calling on their customers."

May said people had given up their lunch hour just to hear "an Arkansas banker, nearing retirement, just out of surgery who can hardly talk."

In November 2008, the J. Thomas May Center for ALS Research was dedicated at the University of Arkansas for Medical Sciences. Frank Broyles, the legendary former University of Arkansas football coach and athletic director, told the crowd that day: "I'll never forget when I called him after hearing about the diagnosis. What he said was 'we're going to stay positive. We're going to keep working.' He will always be an inspiration to me."

May indeed has remained positive. He also has continued to work at the bank as he has gone from using a cane to a walker to a wheelchair.

May, who was born at Prescott in 1946, grew up at El Dorado. After two years of college at the University of Arkansas, his father pulled him out of school because he was unhappy with his son's grades. May went to work for a time in the pine woods of south Arkansas where he said "the mosquitoes were as big as sparrows." He joined the U.S. Marine Corps in 1967 and was sent to Vietnam, where he was assigned to psychological operations. After his discharge, he returned to college in Fayetteville, determined to do better this time around.

May received his bachelor's degree in 1971 and a master's degree in 1972. The chief executive officer of First National Bank of

Commerce in New Orleans was an Arkansas native and came to the Fayetteville campus for interviews. He was impressed with May and offered him a job, which May accepted.

May returned to El Dorado in 1976 to work for Exchange Bank. In 1987, Arkansas business legend Louis Ramsay convinced May to come to Simmons. Under May's leadership, Simmons has become not just a statewide but a regional banking powerhouse.

May urged those in attendance last week to "eliminate the personal pronoun 'I' and focus on 'we.' The real fun begins when we find ways to help others help themselves....Things don't just happen. People make them happen."

He admitted that the days following his ALS diagnosis were filled with "fear, anxiety and disbelief" but added that his faith eventually led to a "sense of peace that remains with me today....Sometimes we forget the power of our faith until we have a crisis. Life is uncertain and has many twists and turns. At best, life is fragile."

May spoke of the joy of being a grandfather and added, "I believe the Lord has many things left for me to do." He said two of his inspirations in life were the late construction contractor Bill Clark of Little Rock, with whom he served on the UA Board of Trustees, and the late KATV, Channel 7, sports director Paul Eells.

"God fully expects us to help others," May said. "Those two men helped others, and they did it for all the right reasons. We all have our challenges. Mine is just a bit more definitive. I choose to get up each morning with a positive attitude....Every day is a good day, and every day we get to think about what we can do to help others."

He closed by urging the crowd to "lead by example in bad times as well as good." Tommy May has set the example for us all.

August 6, 2014
South Arkansas' Renaissance Man

On the front of the *Arkansas Democrat-Gazette*'s Perspective section on July 20, there was a guest column by an El Dorado–based geologist named Richard Mason. The column explained the

110

fracking technology that has revolutionized the oil and gas industry and set the United States on the road to energy independence. For the uninitiated, it should have been pointed out that Mason is much more than just a geologist. He is, in some ways, south Arkansas' renaissance man.

Along with his wife, Vertis, Richard Mason led the way in taking a dying downtown at El Dorado and transforming it into one of the best downtowns for any city its size in the South. He's an ardent environmentalist, having angered untold numbers of business lobbyists after then-governor Bill Clinton appointed him in the 1980s to the state Pollution Control and Ecology Commission. He's a former president of the Arkansas Wildlife Federation. He's also an incredibly prolific author, having recently finished the ninth and 10th books in a series of novels that he calls the Richard the Norphlet Paperboy series. The novels are set in south Arkansas in 1944.

"My first book in the series was titled *The Red Scarf* and was published by August House," Mason says. "It sold out the 7,500 copies in the first edition. It was picked up by a Hollywood executive and is under a movie option. Since that time, I've worked with a self-publisher to publish another 18 books. They're all on Amazon. I've found that I love to write but hate to promote my books."

In the final book of the Paperboy series, *Runaways*, the two principal characters are caught up in a flood and become reluctant runaways, winding up in New Orleans. Mason's nonfiction books have titles ranging from *Surviving Marriage* to *Haunted*. It has been quite a ride for someone who grew up at Norphlet, a small town deep in the pine woods of Union County that rose to prominence along with El Dorado and Smackover during the south Arkansas oil boom of the 1920s. Norphlet had a population of 1,063 people in 1930. By the 2010 census, the population had dropped to 844 residents.

Like a character in his novels, Mason was a paperboy, delivering the *Arkansas Gazette*, the *Shreveport Times* and the *El Dorado Daily News*. He spent much of his time hunting, fishing and trapping. He would watch as salt water ran from area oil wells into streams, killing fish and vegetation. Mason once told a reporter that he thought the crusted salt, glinting in the south Arkansas sun and crunching beneath his feet during dry periods, was "the natural order" in south Arkansas.

The St. Louis, Iron Mountain & Southern Railway built a line from Gurdon to El Dorado in 1891, and Norphlet was among the stops along the route. The railroad opened up opportunities for those in the timber industry. Writing for the Encyclopedia of Arkansas History & Culture, Steve Teske describes when the business focus of Norphlet turned from timber to oil and gas: "Seeking to tap into the Smackover Oil Field, workers for Oil Operators Trust were drilling a well in Norphlet designated Murphy No. 1. On May 14, 1922, their drilling struck a large pocket of natural gas, which began to escape at a rate estimated at 65 to 75 million cubic feet of gas per day. Efforts to cap the hole were ineffective. On the morning of May 16, the gas ignited, shooting flames more than 300 feet into the air and creating a crater at least 450 feet across and 75 feet deep. The explosion and fire, which demolished the oil derrick, sent fragments of shale up to 10 miles away from Norphlet. A second well, drilled a few weeks later in an effort to reduce the fuel supply of the fire, also caught fire and created a second crater."

Still, the industry thrived. Workers moved to Norphlet by the hundreds, and gamblers and prostitutes followed. Mason, who's in his 70s, graduated from Norphlet High School steeped in the culture of the oil and gas industry. He then worked his way through the University of Arkansas, earning bachelor's and master's degrees in geology. His father, who had worked for more than two decades at an asphalt plant, was killed in an automobile accident when Mason was a college sophomore. His mother later ran a women's clothing store at El Dorado. Mason and his wife, a Smackover native, headed to Houston following graduation in search of a job. He was hired by what's now Exxon Mobil as an exploration geologist. Mason worked on the famed King Ranch in south Texas for two years and then worked another two years in Libya before being transferred to

Corpus Christi, Texas. It was in Corpus Christi that he decided he didn't want to spend the remainder of his career working for a large corporation. He left the company in 1968 and eventually teamed up with a Corpus Christi wildcatter named Joe Baria to form Gibraltar Energy Co.

The company drilled 28 wells and made small finds. Mason then met a geologist in Mississippi named Hilton Ladner, who wanted to explore an area known as the Black Warrior Basin near Columbus, Mississippi. Their first two test wells showed promise. A third well confirmed that they were onto something big. They had discovered a gas field eight miles long and two miles wide. Mason and his wife were thinking about moving to Columbus in 1975 when he saw a sign on a 20-acre tract at El Dorado that had been home to what he described as a "barbecue-and-beer joint." The couple bought the property, built their home and have been in El Dorado ever since. After his business partner retired in 1977, Mason became the sole owner of Gibraltar.

Mason was simply looking for office space in El Dorado when he was bitten by the historic preservation bug. He also realized that his home county was in the midst of a long economic decline and decided to do something about it. Since then, Mason and his wife have purchased and renovated 17 buildings. He also has planted more than 1,000 trees in the downtown area while adding park benches, planters and even English-style phone booths. Through it all, he never lost his love of writing. Mason began writing while in Libya since there was nothing else to do with his free time in the Sahara Desert. His first book was written in longhand.

April 8, 2015
John Paul

In January 1967, two Republicans entered the U.S. House of Representatives and became friends. They couldn't have been more different.

George Herbert Walker Bush, born in June 1924, was a native of

Massachusetts and the son of a former U.S. senator, Prescott Bush. He graduated from Yale University, where he was the president of the Delta Kappa Epsilon fraternity and the captain of the baseball team. He also was on the cheerleading squad and in the Skull & Bones secret society. Bush moved his family to west Texas after graduation and entered the oil business, becoming a millionaire by age 40. He moved from Midland to Houston in 1958 and lost a U.S. Senate race in 1964 to the Democratic incumbent, Ralph Yarborough. Two years later, Bush was elected to Congress, becoming the first Republican to represent Houston in the House. He was a blueblood in the truest sense of the word.

John Paul Hammerschmidt, born in May 1922, was raised in a family of German descent in a modest home on the outskirts of Harrison. He headed to South Carolina following graduation from Harrison High School in 1938 to attend The Citadel. After a year there, Hammerschmidt received an appointment to the U.S. Naval Academy but requested a change to allow him to attend the U.S. Military Academy with a friend from Harrison. During the interim, he enrolled at the University of Arkansas. After the Japanese attacked Pearl Harbor, Hammerschmidt joined the Army Air Corps and began pilot training rather than starting school at West Point.

One thing Bush and Hammerschmidt had in common was their admirable service record during World War II. Bush joined the Navy after graduating from Phillips Academy in Andover, Massachusetts, and became an aviator at age 18. He was commissioned as an ensign in June 1943 after 10 months of training. It was three days before his 19th birthday, making him the youngest naval aviator to date. Bush was forced to bail out of his TBM Avenger on September 2, 1944, when it was hit by flak. He waited for four hours in an inflated raft in the Pacific Ocean before being rescued by a submarine crew. Bush flew 58 combat missions and received the Distinguished Flying Cross.

After being commissioned as a second lieutenant in the Army Air Corps, Hammerschmidt volunteered for overseas missions. He flew an amazing 217 combat missions, many of which took place over the area of the eastern Himalayan Mountains known as the Hump. Hammerschmidt received four Distinguished Flying Cross medals, the Air Medal with four oak-leaf clusters and three battle stars. He served in the U.S. Air Force Reserves from 1945 to 1960. Hammerschmidt enrolled at what's now Oklahoma State University after World War II before being called back home to help run the Hammerschmidt Lumber Co. due to an illness in the family. He married Ginny Sharp of Bellefonte in October 1948 and served on the city council in Harrison from 1948 to 1954 and 1961 to 1962.

Hammerschmidt, who died last week at age 92, was active in the Republican Party and eventually was elected state chairman. Winthrop Rockefeller, who had lost his race for governor in 1964 to Orval Faubus, was going to give it another try in 1966 and wanted a strong field of GOP candidates for other offices. He urged Hammerschmidt to take on Congressman Jim Trimble, a Carroll County native who had served the district as a Democrat in Congress since 1945.

There had long been Republicans in the Ozarks, dating back to mountain residents who were upset that planters from the Arkansas Delta led the drive for secession at the outset of the Civil War. *The Almanac of American Politics* once described it this way: "The hills of northwestern Arkansas have always harbored more Republicans than any other part of the state, and for most of the 20th century this was the only part of Arkansas with two-party politics. The Republicanism here was the ornery type, often encountered in Southern hill country, a vestige of opposition to slavery and the Civil War."

Hammerschmidt forged a coalition of the mountain Republicans and Democrats who were looking for a change, defeating Trimble with 53 percent of the vote. In Washington, he befriended Bush, who loved to race up and down the Potomac River in his speedboat with Hammerschmidt as a passenger. Years later, Hammerschmidt would delight in telling how Bush would drive up next to the presidential yacht *Sequoia* while President Lyndon Johnson was entertaining dignitaries. The two freshmen established a tradition of getting together occasionally in the House members' dining room of the U.S. Capitol for a lunch of salty country ham from Virginia, grits and turnip greens. Bush served in Congress until 1970, when President Richard Nixon convinced him to run for the Senate again. A moderate Democrat, Lloyd Bentsen, defeated Yarborough in the Democratic primary and then defeated Bush. Even after leaving Congress, Bush kept up the tradition of country ham lunches with Hammerschmidt at the Capitol. He did so as ambassador to the United Nations, as chairman of the Republican National Committee, as director of the Central Intelligence Agency and even as President Ronald Reagan's vice president from 1981 to 1989.

I was the Washington correspondent for the *Arkansas Democrat* when Bush was elected president in 1988. About a week after the election, I called Hammerschmidt to ask if he thought the new president might continue the lunch tradition. In that familiar Ozarks drawl, the congressman said: "No. It would be too hard as president. They would have to do a security sweep of the Capitol and shut down Pennsylvania Avenue for the motorcade. The president only comes here for the State of the Union address." Within weeks of Bush's January 1989 inauguration, the phone rang in the Capitol Hill basement where I worked. It was Hammerschmidt. He got right to the point: "Well, what I told you back in the fall was wrong. The White House just called. The president will be here at noon for ham, grits and greens." Obviously, we ran the story on the front page the next day.

July 22, 2015
W. R.

Most mornings on my way to work, I drive by the hotel on Capitol Avenue in downtown Little Rock now known as the Legacy. In its day, when it was the Hotel Sam Peck, it was among the top hotels in the South. On summer days like this one, I often think of Governor Winthrop Rockefeller as I pass the old building.

In some respects, Petit Jean was the state capital during the four years Winthrop Rockefeller served as governor, from 1967 to 1971.

The Sam Peck was the place Winthrop Rockefeller first called home when he fled to Arkansas from New York at the invitation of an Army friend named Frank Newell. Rockefeller's arrival date was June 9, 1953. Within a year, he had purchased a large tract atop Petit Jean Mountain and set out to create a model ranch. Ultimately, he would change an entire state. I was at the hotel on a June day in 2003 when then-lieutenant governor Winthrop Paul Rockefeller re-enacted his father checking into the hotel to mark the 50th anniversary of that important date in Arkansas history. The lieutenant governor even used the suitcase his father had carried in 1953. In 1955, Winthrop Rockefeller accepted Gov. Orval Faubus' invitation to become the first chairman of the Arkansas Industrial Development Corp. and went to work reversing a long trend of population loss in the state.

The 2010, 2012 and 2014 election cycles changed the face of Arkansas politics. The Republican Party became the state's majority party for the first time since Reconstruction. The modern breed of Arkansas Republicans would do well on this 60th anniversary of Rockefeller taking over the state's economic development efforts to study this Republican who came to our state to escape the constant scrutiny of the Manhattan media. Rockefeller, a far different man from his brothers, had withdrawn from Yale University after three years and gone to the oil fields of Texas as an apprentice roughneck. He later would tell friends that it was one of the happiest periods of his life. Just as he had fallen in love with west Texas, he would fall in love with Arkansas and its people. In a letter to his son, Rockefeller wrote: "While we lived comfortably with that which we inherited and earned, we had the responsibility to see that these resources were also used wisely in the service to our fellow man."

In some respects, Petit Jean was the state capital during the four years Rockefeller served as governor, from 1967 to 1971. He preferred his ranch to the Capitol and would spend days at a time on the mountain, entertaining visitors from around the world. A landing strip made access easy for those who were flying in. Rockefeller's own jet could fly him wherever he needed to be. Where he needed to be and wanted to be often were different things. He wanted to be at the ranch with his prized Santa Gertrudis cattle and the majestic views of the Arkansas River Valley below. Former Arkansas Supreme Court justice Bob Brown said at an event I attended on Petit Jean several years ago: "He wanted to make this a showcase so the world could see what could happen in Arkansas. He was economic royalty and this was his citadel." Brown, whose father was the Episcopal bishop of Arkansas, remembered a 1967 visit by the archbishop of Canterbury. He said the archbishop was anxious to meet this scion of one of the world's wealthiest families.

Rockefeller was in his first year as governor in 1967. It wasn't until the end of his four years in office that the list of his contributions could be appreciated. Only now, decades later, is the full impact of what he did to change this state being properly examined. William "Sonny" Walker, the man Rockefeller hired in 1967 to head the state's economic opportunity office, was believed to be the only black man in the cabinet of a Southern governor at that time. Walker once told me: "They just didn't do that back then, and they certainly didn't do it in the South. I had some of the same ideas that Rockefeller had.

I just didn't have the money he had." Walker advocated the hiring of black state troopers. He felt that having black troopers would send a positive message to other black Arkansans. Rockefeller made it happen. The governor also set out to reform the Arkansas prison system, which Brown described as "a cesspool," adding, "Let's face it. Most of the prisoners were African-Americans."

Dorothy Stuck, a former Marked Tree newspaper publisher who became one of Rockefeller's friends and advisers, said after his death: "It just amazed me how quickly he came to understand what we needed in this state. He opened the Capitol's front door and let a fresh wind blow through."

Rockefeller helped fund voter registration drives designed to enfranchise black Arkansans. He also underwrote an organization known as the Election Research Council, which trained lawyers to root out election fraud. On the Sunday after the Reverend Martin Luther King Jr. was assassinated just across the Mississippi River from Arkansas in Memphis, Rockefeller joined black ministers on the front steps of the State Capitol. He held hands with the ministers as a crowd of almost 3,000 people sang "We Shall Overcome." Remember, it was 1968, it was in the South and Rockefeller was on the ballot that fall. No other Southern governor would make such a gesture.

"I don't think he knew the words to the song, but he was there," Walker said. "That's what mattered." Brown called it "his defining moment. He never gave up. That was the thing about him. Eventually the things he stood for prevailed."

Legislative defeats were common during the 1967 and 1969 legislative sessions. Stuck said those defeats hurt Rockefeller more than he would let on. "Although he didn't live to see it, the seeds he planted have come to fruition," she said. "What happened here radiated out across the country."

In April 1971, after Dale Bumpers had moved into the Governor's Mansion, Rockefeller was presented a silver plaque that was described as being from "the black people of Arkansas." It read: "Governor Winthrop Rockefeller, an inspiration to the young, a symbol of security for the old, full of love, warmth and compassion; a champion of human rights, brotherhood and dignity, who brought the Rockefeller family tradition to Arkansas and sacrificed time, resources, energy and public office for the causes of unity, justice and equality. Thank you for all you have done, for all you are doing to make our state the Land of Opportunity for all Arkansans. God bless you."

August 5, 2015
The College President

On a Thursday morning earlier this summer on the campus of Ouachita Baptist University at Arkadelphia, a group gathered to dedicate the new home of the Ben Elrod Center for Family and Community. For almost two decades, the center has helped instill an ethos of community service into the school's students while celebrating the legacy of Ben Elrod, a former Ouachita president who's now retired in North Little Rock.

Elrod hails from a prominent south Arkansas family with roots deep in the pine woods of Cleveland County. His memories provide insight into the development of that part of our state. Elrod once described his hometown of Rison as a place "with a population of about 1,206 or 1,207, depending on how everybody was getting along." He had the benefit of an extended family that he described as including "my mom and dad, all of my grandparents and an abundance of aunts and uncles."

Elrod's parents had married when they were 20. They borrowed $1,000 from Ben Elrod's grandfather and built a white frame house. The bank where Elrod's father worked failed in the early years of the Great Depression, and his father wound up as the local postmaster for a time before taking a job with the Federal Land Bank as an appraiser. Elrod says: "My mother was pretty well the disciplinarian. She was the one who answered the day-to-day questions from me. My father was away all week. He would come in on Friday, stay the weekend and then leave on Sunday night or Monday morning. He decided that he was tired of that traveling, and he bought a little sawmill that we called the groundhog sawmill. These were mills that could be moved to the timber supply. He started his own business that way, and it ultimately employed 400 to 500 people in Rison. He had quite a going business there."

The Texas & St. Louis Railway, commonly known as the Cotton Belt, had given rise to Rison. A railroad official named Samuel Wesley Fordyce planned the route in 1882 and named the community that formed along the tracks after William Richard Rison, a former business partner in Alabama. Fordyce, an Ohio native who moved to Alabama after the Civil War, began visiting Hot Springs in 1873 in hopes that the waters there would heal his war injuries. He moved to Hot Springs in 1876 and was active in the decades that followed as a financier for thousands of miles of railroad lines.

Former state historian Wendy Richter described the Cotton Belt route as one that "spurred development of the modern timber industry of southern and southwestern Arkansas by creating access to the region's vast pine forests. Completion of the line in 1883 changed Arkansas, making major cities out of towns such as Pine Bluff and Texarkana. New communities sprang up along the rail line as well, including the town of Fordyce."

The Southwest Improvement Association, a subsidiary of the railroad, set aside a parcel of land for homes in Cleveland County in 1883. Rison was incorporated in 1890. The Cleveland County seat was moved to Rison from the community of Toledo in 1891. Elrod and Rufus Buie wrote for the Encyclopedia of Arkansas History & Culture: "The railroad remained Rison's point of reference for decades. 'Rison on the Cotton Belt' was the affectionate way residents referred to their community. The commercial value of the railroad was felt from the beginning. The economy depended on the production of cotton, lumber, and, ultimately, a wide variety of wood products, including pulpwood, piling, pallets, broom handle squares, ammunition boxes, and U.S. Army pup tent poles."

Several cotton gins operated in and around Rison when Elrod was a boy. The largest and most efficient gin was owned by Ira E. Moore. It was built in 1933. But with the soil becoming depleted after having the same crop grown on it year after year, landowners in the region began turning more to harvesting pine trees than raising cotton. The Clio Lumber Co. mill was built in 1887 five miles north of Rison. According to a 1909 issue of *Lumberman's Magazine*, the Clio mill owned several thousand acres of timberland and had 432 employees in the sawmill, 130 on the woods crew and 80 working the tramlines used to transport logs. Other mills in the area were operated by the J. L. Sadler Lumber Co., the C. L. Garner & Sons Lumber Co. and the Elrod Lumber Co. By the 1950s, the company owned by the Elrod family employed almost a third of Rison's population.

"I can remember that my family did a lot of bartering," Elrod says. "We had a lady who would bring us milk and eggs. In return, we bartered something to her. Such bartering went on all the time because everybody was poor."

For parts of two years, Elrod served as a page for the U.S. House of Representatives. He vividly remembers the day the House pages had lunch at the White House with President Harry Truman and First Lady Bess Truman. The 15-year-old boy from Rison could not have predicted that Truman would be the first of six U.S. presidents with whom he would shake hands in his lifetime. The other five were Dwight Eisenhower, Gerald Ford, Jimmy Carter, George H. W. Bush and Bill Clinton. During his senior year in high school at Rison, Elrod considered attending the University of Arkansas, the school from which his brother had graduated. He was concerned, though, about the lack of religion courses since he had decided he wanted to be a Baptist minister.

"We had an interim pastor who was enrolled at Ouachita along with his wife," Elrod says. "They talked with me about Ouachita, and I got interested through them. My first contact with the school was to call Dr. J. R. Grant, who was the president, and tell him I was interested and wanted to look into the possibility of attending.

He gave me an appointment to come to Arkadelphia. I drove over, visited with him and decided to attend. That was about it. It was a pretty simple transaction." So it was that Elrod found himself in the fall of 1948 at the Southern Baptist institution that had been founded in 1886 with 235 students. The Arkansas Baptist State Convention had voted in November 1885 to authorize an institution of higher education, and the school's board voted in April 1886 to locate the college in Arkadelphia. In June 1886, the board selected J. W. "Dr. Jack" Conger to be Ouachita's first president at age 29. Classes began on September 6, 1886, and Ouachita has continued to operate at the same location along the banks of the Ouachita River ever since.

Little could the freshman from Rison have known that he would end up spending much of his career at Ouachita, in two stints as vice president of development and then as president from 1988 until 1997, when he stepped down to take on the title of university chancellor. Elrod had accepted the job at age 57 when some of his friends were already taking early retirement. He explained at the time: "I have always had my greater joy in my work. Work has never seemed to be drudgery to me. It has always been a pleasure."

January 12, 2016
The Bumpers Magic

[*Dale Bumpers died on January 1, 2016, at age 90.*]

Senator Dale Bumpers had no reason to like the *Arkansas Democrat*, which often was critical of him on its editorial page. But he was always open and fair to me during my time as the *Democrat*'s Washington correspondent in the late 1980s.

In that era before cell phones and the Internet, we did what I call shoe-leather reporting. I was in all six offices of the Arkansas congressional delegation on a daily basis, checking to see if there were news stories I needed to write. My favorite days were those in which one of our state's U.S. senators—Dale Bumpers or David Pryor—would invite me into their offices and tell off-the-record stories. I love Arkansas history and politics, and I could listen to

Bumpers and Pryor spin yarns for hours. It might sound strange coming from someone who would go on to work for a Republican governor and a Republican president, but I likely became too close to the two Democratic senators from Arkansas. When I left Washington after four years on the beat, it was time for a new reporter who could be more objective when it came to Bumpers and Pryor. I still could ask the tough questions when I needed to do so, but my fondness for both men had grown through the years.

Bumpers, a former Marine, knew he could tell me a salty joke or an inside story. Off the record meant off the record. What I never could get him to explain fully was why he never pulled the trigger and ran for president. Bumpers came close several times to seeking the Democratic presidential nomination. The first time was in 1976. Bumpers was in his second year in the Senate. Who knows? Bumpers rather than Jimmy Carter might have been the young president from the South had the Arkansan chosen to run. The last time he came close to running was during the 1988 election cycle. It was early 1987, and Bumpers was giving every indication that he would enter the race.

I vividly remember taking the train from Union Station in Washington, D.C., to Penn Station in New York City with Bumpers' press secretary, Matt James, to cover what was billed as a major foreign policy address at Columbia University. Earlier that day, Bumpers met with potential donors in New York and received millions of dollars in commitments. Before Matt and I took a late-night train back to Washington, I filed two stories—one about the meeting with donors and one about the foreign policy speech. The announcement that Bumpers would run for president seemed like a mere formality at that point. John Robert Starr, the *Democrat*'s managing editor, told me that I would cover the Bumpers presidential campaign on a daily basis. These days, I can't think of anything much worse than spending the winter in Iowa and New Hampshire. At age 27, however, I couldn't wait to be one of the boys on the bus.

Everything changed on a Friday night that spring. James had a leading role in a community theater presentation on Capitol Hill. He was about to leave the office for opening night when Bumpers walked by his desk, handed him a sheet of paper and said, "Get this out to the media." It was a short statement, making clear that he would not be running for president. In a telephone interview the next day, Betty Bumpers told me that while she would have supported her husband's decision regardless, she had finally put her foot down and told him to make a decision in order to calm his restlessness and end the sleepless nights.

By the fall of 1992, I had returned to Little Rock and was the political editor of the *Arkansas Democrat-Gazette*. With Bill Clinton's presidential race dominating our political coverage, I decided it was time to give the Senate race between Bumpers and a young Baptist minister named Mike Huckabee some attention. I spent two days on the road with each of the two candidates and wrote long stories on each campaign for the Sunday edition of the newspaper. My two-day trip with Bumpers ended with an evening event in Camden. We were flying back to Little Rock from Ouachita County on a small plane late that night when I asked my final question: "Senator, something you used against J. William Fulbright when you beat him in 1974 was the accusation that he was out of touch with Arkansas; that he had become a part of the East Coast establishment. Let me ask you: Had you rather be at a fish fry in Camden or at a dinner party at Pamela Harriman's townhouse in Georgetown?"

Harriman, who died in 1997, was an English-born socialite whose first husband was the son of Winston Churchill. Her third husband, beginning in 1971, was the well-known American diplomat, politician and businessman Averell Harriman. She became an American citizen the year she married Harriman and also became a key fundraiser for the Democratic Party. The dinner parties she threw at her Georgetown townhouse were the stuff of legend. Bill Clinton appointed her as the U.S. ambassador to France in 1993.

Bumpers looked at me when I asked the question and smiled that famous smile: "Oh hell, Rex, you know how I have to answer that."

125

The thing is, he was at home at the toniest events in Washington and also at the most down-home events in Arkansas. I can't count the number of times I saw him speak to a civic club in Arkansas when the members would start the meeting mad about his vote on some issue. After about 20 minutes, those club members would be laughing and smiling. He had them eating out of the palm of his hand. The Bumpers charisma isn't easy to put into words. You had to experience it.

It was my great fortune to cover him as a newspaper reporter, experiencing that magic on a daily basis. We'll never see another one quite like him.

January 20, 2016
A Coach Called Red

There must be something in the soil of the south Arkansas pine woods that produces football coaches. Paul "Bear" Bryant, who became the most famous college coach of them all at the University of Alabama, came out of the Moro Creek bottoms and played high school football at Fordyce. Sam Bailey, who was Bryant's right-hand man for years, hailed from rural Union County and played college football for two years at what's now Southern Arkansas University (SAU) at Magnolia and for two years at what's now Ouachita Baptist University at Arkadelphia.

Barry Switzer, who won national championships at the University of Oklahoma and coached the Dallas Cowboys to a Super Bowl victory, was from Crossett. Larry Lacewell, who was Switzer's defensive coordinator at Oklahoma and then was a successful head coach at Arkansas State University, likes to say that he was a "bug all my life"—a Chigger and Redbug at Fordyce and then a Boll Weevil at what's now the University of Arkansas at Monticello. Tommy Tuberville, the current University of Cincinnati head coach, played high school football at Camden Harmony Grove and college football at SAU. I used to spend a week each year working in media relations at the Cotton Bowl. I found myself walking out of an event with Tuberville at the Hilton Anatole Hotel in Dallas one night when

Tuberville was the head coach at Auburn University. I said: "I'm also from south Arkansas and remember when you played for Coach Rip Powell at Southern Arkansas." Tuberville looked at me, smiled and then said: "You know, the last name I expected to hear mentioned in Dallas tonight was Rip Powell."

Charles McClendon, who had success as the head coach at Louisiana State University from 1962 to 1979, was a native of Lewisville. The man affectionately known as Cholly Mac had played college football under Bryant at the University of Kentucky. I could go on and on with the list of coaches from south Arkansas who achieved success at the high school and college levels. Some had more championships, but none worked at it longer than Jimmy "Red" Parker, who died earlier this month at age 84. Parker coached his last game on the evening of Friday, November 13, as his Benton Harmony Grove team lost to Fordyce, 22-8, in the first round of the Class 3A playoffs at Paul "Bear" Bryant Stadium in Fordyce. It was fitting that Parker's career ended in the town where he first achieved success as a head coach in the 1950s. Like Bryant, Parker was dead within weeks of his final game.

Parker was born in 1931—in the midst of the Great Depression—to Madelyn Parker and Floyd Raymond Parker of Hampton. He graduated from Rison High School in 1949 and headed to Arkansas A&M (now UAM), where he was a halfback for the Boll Weevils from 1949 to 1952. Parker's wife, Betty Ann, also hailed from south Arkansas—from Herbine in Cleveland County, to be exact. She died last April after 64 years of marriage.

"As a young boy in Hampton, there were only two things that Parker ever dreamed of becoming," Doug Crise wrote for the *Pine Bluff Commercial* in 2003. "And neither of them had anything to do with football. 'One of them was to be a big league baseball player,' Parker said. 'The other one was to be a cowboy.' Parker spent his youth throwing himself into his twin passions—playing baseball and riding horses and bulls. When he moved with his mother to Rison, the cowboy interests faded when he was introduced to football.

While his dreams were still pointed toward the diamond, Parker at least now had a more viable fallback option." The coach told the newspaper: "The only thing I ever had in my mind was playing big league baseball or being a big league football coach. I don't know if it was a calling, and I don't know if it was elimination. But those were the two things that motivated me, and I knew I could be happy doing them."

Parker was offered a $10,000 signing bonus by the Detroit Tigers organization, but he decided he didn't want to play for a minor league team in Wisconsin with a wife and young child back in Arkansas. So Parker accepted a coaching job at Fordyce. He was eager to learn. Parker used his own money to travel to Florida for a coaching clinic. While there, he met one of the nation's best-known coaches, Bud Wilkinson from the University of Oklahoma. Parker said: "For some reason, Bud Wilkinson just took a liking to me. I just kind of got into his head and listened. I was running plays and calling defenses and had no idea of what it was all supposed to mean together. He made me understand."

Parker coached at Fordyce from 1953 to 1960, compiling a 76-15-4 record. The Redbugs had a 37-game winning streak from 1957 to 1960. His college alma mater called, and Parker moved down the road from Fordyce to Monticello, where he was the head coach of the Boll Weevils from 1961 to 1965. His teams won two Arkansas Intercollegiate Conference championships during that time. Parker's climb up the coaching ladder continued when The Citadel, a well-known military school in South Carolina, hired him. He coached there from 1966 to 1972 and then was hired at Clemson University, where he was the head coach for four seasons. The rest of Parker's career—serving as the head coach at three smaller colleges, as the offensive coordinator at the University of Mississippi and as the head coach at five Arkansas high schools at an age when most men would be retired—was well-documented following his death.

Parker said back in 2003: "No matter how bad we are, I always feel like there's going to be something happens to give us a chance to win. What I don't do now is I don't get nervous before a game because I know we've prepared well. I can honestly say that once the game begins, I don't know the difference between Neyland Stadium (at the University of Tennessee) and Redbug Field."

Like other men from south Arkansas such as Bryant, Switzer, Tuberville, Lacewell and McClendon, "Red" Parker was born to be a football coach.

February 24, 2016
Fitz

This month marks a decade since Fitz Hill was selected as the president of Arkansas Baptist College in Little Rock. He inherited an institution that was on the verge of closing. Hill, who many Arkansans still remember from his days as the assistant head football coach and recruiting coordinator at the University of Arkansas, will announce this week that he's stepping down after a decade at the helm. Every day has been a struggle at the small institution, but progress at Arkansas Baptist and in the surrounding neighborhood is undeniable.

"Our mission has always been unique because we never erected barriers but rather sought to include anyone who desired an opportunity to be empowered by education," Hill says. "Most colleges invest significant resources reaching out to the gifted students while excluding those who for one reason or another have not ranked in the top tier. Arkansas Baptist has a rich tradition of extending its hand to students who simply need a chance to achieve their fullest potential. I always desired to be known as a premier institution for serving the underserved. Our goal was to be exclusively inclusive to those left out."

Arkansas Baptist was founded in 1884 by the Colored Baptists of the State of Arkansas. The first classes were held at Mt. Zion Baptist Church in Little Rock as the children of former slaves were trained to be ministers. The name of the school was changed from the Ministers' Institute to Arkansas Baptist College in August 1885 when the school moved to its present location at 16th and High Street (now Dr. Martin Luther King Jr. Drive).

I've known Hill since he was a child. We both grew up at Arkadelphia, where his mother was the beloved high school secretary. The public schools there were integrated when I entered the fourth grade, and Hill's older brother and I were friends from then through high school. When Hill was a star receiver on the football team at Arkadelphia High School, I broadcast his games on the local radio station and wrote game stories for the Arkadelphia newspaper. When he starred as a wide receiver at Ouachita Baptist University, I again called his games on the radio.

After graduating from Ouachita, Hill became a graduate assistant football coach at Northwestern State University in Louisiana, where he received his master's degree. He later became a graduate assistant for the Razorbacks but was summoned to military duty in 1990, serving in Operations Desert Shield and Desert Storm. During that time, he often would send me letters, outlining dreams that went beyond football. Hill served on the Razorback staff for almost a dozen years. In December 2000, he was hired as the head football coach at San Jose State University in California. Hill was one of the few black head coaches in NCAA Division I and later would team up with *San Jose Mercury News* columnist Mark Purdy to write a book on the dearth of black head coaches in college football.

When Hill left coaching at the end of the 2004 season, he returned home to Arkansas and took a job at Ouachita, raising money for scholarships at his alma mater. I always thought that Hill could be the first black governor of Arkansas if he set his mind to the task. But his mission was different. When he called a decade ago to tell me that he had taken the job at Arkansas Baptist, I thought he had made a huge mistake, riding a sinking ship that would derail his own career. I should have known better than to underestimate Hill. He launched a $50 million capital campaign and began buying up old houses and even a car wash in the surrounding neighborhood. Enrollment soared from fewer than 200 students to more than 1,000.

One move that Hill made was to convince Charles Ripley, the former Little Rock Parkview High School head basketball coach who's a legend in sports circles, to serve as athletic director and men's basketball coach. Ripley knew what he was facing. "Look, we serve what may be the poorest student body in America," Ripley says. "We don't have an endowment. We don't get money from the United Negro College Fund. Probably 98 percent of our students depend on Pell Grants. A lot of them are kids that no other school would take a chance on. We handed out 141 degrees last spring. When I came over there, there were 150 students total."

Hill opened the African American Leadership Institute to help students develop leadership skills and then practice those skills in central Arkansas. Last year, Arkansas Baptist dedicated the Scott Ford Center for Entrepreneurship and Community Development with the goal of teaching students how to start businesses in underserved neighborhoods.

When Hill became president, Old Main, the centerpiece of the small campus, was boarded up. Old Main, which had been constructed in 1893, reopened in 2012 after a $6 million renovation. Crime has been reduced in the surrounding neighborhood, which was featured in the infamous 1994 HBO documentary *Gang War: Bangin' in the Rock*.

"With the opening this spring of the Derek Olivier Research Institute for the Prevention of Black-on-Black Violence, Arkansas Baptist will take the lead in finding and promoting solutions to the problem of homicides among black males ages 15 to 35," Hill says. "Derek was murdered across the street from our campus in September 2012 when another black male walked into the area and began firing. This institute will promote a movement to make our most dangerous communities safe again. I call it putting the neighbor back in the hood. The college and the community are linked. Both need each other. Black-on-black violence is an unfortunate reality that begs for a solution."

As Hill considers his next move, he looks back on an often

stressful decade at Arkansas Baptist: "Serving the population of students that we attempt to serve is a high-risk, high-reward task. There's a constant battle regarding graduation rates and student loan default rates when you serve those who need education the most but have the fewest opportunities. If we don't invest in this population on the front end, we do so on the back end through prison costs. Arkansas Baptist has made a special effort during the past decade to invest in this population and work through the challenges that come with serving these students."

March 9, 2016
The Washington Insiders

It was an eclectic collection of people who gathered on the final Friday of February at the old house on South Izard Street in Little Rock. The house has been remodeled to serve as the Little Rock office for two former U.S. senators—David and Mark Pryor—and many of those in attendance have connections dating back decades with the Pryor family. They had come together on this day, though, to remember a Blytheville native named Ann Pride, who died February 21 at age 68.

We all shared a love for Pride and shared stories about her. We talked about how she mentored us in Washington, D.C., where she had lived since David Pryor entered the Senate in 1979. My story was a bit different from the others. Pride, who worked for the elder Pryor from 1975 to 1991 in the governor's office and later on Capitol Hill, was the senator's press secretary when I arrived in Washington in 1986. I was new to the city as the *Arkansas Democrat*'s Washington correspondent, while the *Arkansas Gazette* had a veteran correspondent there and the Little Rock newspaper war was reaching a fever pitch. In other words, I was scared to death.

I had been the *Democrat*'s assistant sports editor and enjoyed my work. Weekends are the busy period in the sports world, so my days off were Monday and Tuesday. I vividly remember the phone ringing in my Little Rock apartment on a Monday morning in 1986. It was the newspaper's managing editor, John Robert Starr, and I assumed we had made a huge mistake in the sports section for Starr to be waking me up at home. Instead, he asked: "Why haven't you applied for the Washington job?" I answered, "Because I love sports. I have no interest in moving." Starr wasn't one to beat around the bush. He said: "Well, I've already decided you're the one going. Get used to the idea."

So it was that I went from covering that year's Super Bowl (the Bears over the Patriots in New Orleans) to working out of the House Press Gallery in the U.S. Capitol. The *Democrat* editorial page hadn't been kind to Pryor, so Pride had no political reason to take me under her wing. But here's the way she looked at it: I was a fellow Arkansan, I was young, I needed help. She was going to see to it that I succeeded. Along the way, we became friends. Like a lot of males in their twenties in those days, I was a devoted Jimmy Buffett fan and thus was impressed that Pride knew Michael Utley, the keyboardist for Buffett's Coral Reefer Band. Utley also grew up at Blytheville, where he was influenced by the so-called Memphis sound, and moved to Memphis to work full time as a musician after obtaining his bachelor's degree in zoology from the University of Arkansas. Pride and I attended two Buffett concerts together to watch the musician whose name is mentioned by Buffett during the song "Volcano." Right before the first keyboard solo, Buffett says, "Mr. Utley."

Pride joined Entergy Corp. as a lobbyist in 1991 but never stopped helping Arkansans who found themselves in the nation's capital. I'm not as familiar as I once was with the Arkansas expatriates who live in Washington, but I hope they're still as close-knit as we were in the 1980s. Those who were reporters, lobbyists and congressional aides from Arkansas tended to socialize on a regular basis. The fact that Arkansas is such a small state made us even closer. While cleaning out a drawer recently, I came across a copy of the Arkansas State Society of Washington's membership list for 1986. The members of the Arkansas congressional delegation took turns serving as chairmen of the society, and that year's chairman was Rep. John

Paul Hammerschmidt. I was struck by the 1986 address of former congressman Wilbur Mills and his wife Polly—1600 S. Eads St., in Arlington, Virginia. That was the Crystal Towers apartment complex, where Melissa Garcia lived when we started dating in 1988. We've now been married for more than 26 years. I would sometimes run into Mills, the former House Ways and Means Committee chairman, when visiting the complex. Also living there at the time was Margie Nicholson, who long had been the personal assistant to Sen. John L. McClellan.

Also on that 1986 list was the McLean, Virginia, address of Marcus Hollabaugh. Like Pride, Hollabaugh was an Arkansas native who wound up living decades in Washington but never stopped loving Arkansas and those who hailed from there. Soon after I moved to Washington, my phone rang one day. "*Democrat* Washington bureau," I answered. The first words I heard were, "You don't know me, but my name is Marcus Hollabaugh. I'm from Searcy County, I like to talk about my native state and I want to take you to lunch." He invited me to the National Lawyers' Club, which at the time occupied the second and third floors of the 12-story Federal Bar Building on H Street in downtown Washington. The building had been constructed in 1962 to house law firms and was torn down in 2003. The place practically screamed "old boys' club," and it was obvious from the moment we walked in that Hollabaugh was a regular. He wound up being one of the most interesting men I've ever met.

Hollabaugh was born at Marshall in 1913, graduated from Arkansas Tech with a degree in history and political science in 1935 and moved to Washington during the Great Depression. He became an FBI agent and obtained his law degree. Hollabaugh eventually became the chief of the special litigation section of the Antitrust Division of the U.S. Department of Justice before entering private practice. As an attorney in private practice, he was among the nation's experts on antitrust issues. There was nothing he would rather talk about, however, than Arkansas history and the colorful characters the state has produced through the decades. We met one Friday a month for lunch at the National Lawyers' Club (he would never let me buy) until I moved back to Arkansas. Following my return to Little Rock, we continued to exchange Christmas cards, even after Hollabaugh moved to California to be near his son, daughter-in-law and grandchildren. Hollabaugh died in 2006 at age 92.

I'm not sure if Ann Pride knew Marcus Hollabaugh. I bet she did since she made it a point to know everyone in Washington with Arkansas ties. While they weren't close in age, Hollabaugh and Pride shared this: They were native Arkansans who spent most of their lives in the nation's capital, never forgetting their roots and working overtime to make fellow Arkansans feel welcome in the big city.

April 13, 2016
The Preservationist

It was my first meeting as a member of the Historic Arkansas Museum Commission. I sat in the Loughborough Room, looking up at the portrait of Louise Loughborough. Arkansans have Loughborough to thank for what long was known as the Arkansas Territorial Restoration in downtown Little Rock. She's a fascinating figure in Arkansas history, though it's a safe bet that the vast majority of Arkansans can neither spell nor properly pronounce her name.

She was born in Little Rock in 1881, the daughter of Louisa and William Fulton Wright. Her father was a Confederate veteran. The state's last territorial governor, William Savin Fulton, was an ancestor. She married a Rose Law Firm attorney named J. Fairfax Loughborough in October 1902 and then threw herself into the Arkansas capital city's civic scene.

"She was a charter member of the Little Rock Garden Club and a member of the National Society of Colonial Dames of America," says Bill Worthen, who has headed what's now the Historic Arkansas Museum since 1972. "She served as vice regent of the Mount Vernon Ladies Association of the Union, the organization that restored and maintains the home of George Washington. Her involvement in historic structures in Little Rock began when the Little Rock

Garden Club sought to improve the appearance of the War Memorial Building and its grounds in 1928. The grounds were littered with signs and monuments, and the roof of the Greek Revival building sported figurative statues of Law, Justice and Mercy, which had been installed above the pediment after being salvaged from the Arkansas exhibit at the Philadelphia Centennial of 1876. To take the façade of the edifice back to its original 1830s appearance, Loughborough had the statues removed without the permission of the War Memorial Commission, which had legal authority over the building."

The War Memorial Building, now known as the Old State House, is an Arkansas treasure, recognized nationally as the place where Bill Clinton spoke on the night he was elected president in November 1992. Without Loughborough's efforts, who knows what would have happened to that building? Loughborough was appointed to the Little Rock Planning Commission in 1935 and again made her mark when she heard of a plan to condemn houses near the intersection of Cumberland and Third streets. One of those was the Hinderliter House, the oldest building in the city. No one denied that the area was a slum, with several of the houses used for prostitution. Loughborough had heard that the Hinderliter House had been the last territorial capitol. She recruited well-known architect Max Mayer, and they came up with the term "town of three capitols" in an effort to gain support, giving what they thought was the old territorial capitol the status of the state Capitol and the Old State House.

The Hinderliter House had been built in 1827 by Jesse Hinderliter as a tavern. Loughborough was persuasive and was able to convince Floyd Sharp of the federal Works Progress Administration to help fund the project. During the 1939 legislative session, the Arkansas Territorial Capitol Restoration Commission was created. The WPA provided labor and materials, and Loughborough raised private capital to complete the restoration project.

The Arkansas Territorial Restoration opened July 19, 1941. Worthen calls it "the first Arkansas agency committed to both the restoration of structures and the interpretation of their history, and it served as a model and inspiration for historic preservation in the state." Loughborough was the founding chairman of the commission. The restored Hinderliter House was joined on the grounds by three other antebellum structures that used the names of Arkansas pioneers William E. Woodruff, Elias N. Conway and Charles Fenton Mercer Noland. In 1960, the National Trust for Historic Preservation included the Arkansas Territorial Restoration on its list of the 12 outstanding museum communities in the country.

Loughborough stepped down as board chairman in 1961 due to declining health, and architect Ed Cromwell took over. Next to Loughborough's portrait in the conference room where the commission now meets is a portrait of Cromwell. That's fitting because he took the museum to the next level, serving as commission chairman until 1977. Cromwell, a 1931 Princeton University graduate, came to Arkansas during the Great Depression as an architect for the federal Resettlement Administration, a New Deal program in 1935–36 that relocated struggling families to planned communities. When prominent architect Theo Sanders left the firm then known as Thompson, Sanders & Ginocchio, Cromwell was hired to replace him. Frank Ginocchio and Cromwell designed the Governor's Mansion. Under Cromwell's leadership, what's now Cromwell Architects Engineers grew into one of the top firms in the region. Cromwell practiced architecture in Little Rock until 1984.

Worthen, a Little Rock native, graduated from Little Rock Hall High School and Washington University in St. Louis. He taught high school in Pine Bluff for three years and then became director of the Territorial Restoration in 1972. In 1981, it became the first history museum in the state to be accredited by the American Association of Museums. Earlier this year, during the annual Governor's Conference on Tourism, Worthen was inducted into the Arkansas Tourism Hall of Fame. Prior to Worthen's arrival, Cromwell used funds from the federal and state governments to acquire additional land downtown. A former Fraternal Order of Eagles building was turned into a reception center, and the Hinderliter House was listed in March

1970 on the National Register of Historic Places. Beginning in 1972, Cromwell teamed with Worthen to secure a more professional staff, more educational outreach programs and more historic research. It was determined that there was only circumstantial evidence that the last territorial assembly had met at the Hinderliter House. Additional research led to the names of the Noland and Conway houses being changed. In 1976, the antebellum Plum Bayou log house was moved from its original location near Scott. And in 2001, the name of the complex was changed to the Historic Arkansas Museum as the size of the former reception center was doubled. Loughborough died in 1962, and Cromwell died in 2001. Their legacies, however, live on at the Historic Arkansas Museum.

Arkansas Food

BAR-B-QUE PER POUND   6.00
1 POUND   12.00
2   18.00
3   24.00
4   30.00
5   36.00
6   42.00
7

ICE COLD
Coca-Cola
SOLD HERE

October 30, 2010
Arkansas Barbecue

I recently had the honor of being asked by my friends at the Southern Foodways Alliance on the University of Mississippi campus to write the introduction for the Arkansas section of what's called the Southern BBQ Trail. You already can find oral histories posted from Alabama, Mississippi, North Carolina, Tennessee and Texas at www.southernbbgtrail.com. Oral histories are now being collected from Arkansas.

I've never felt that the Arkansas barbecue culture gets the credit it deserves. Unlike our boastful Texas neighbors, Arkansans quietly prepare great barbecue, enjoy eating it and then move on with our lives. Because we don't brag, Arkansas barbecue has never received proper national recognition.

Some of the best barbecue anywhere can be found in Arkansas, though national television shows and magazine articles tend to focus on North Carolina and Texas barbecue. In addition to the modesty of Arkansans, a reason for the lack of recognition might be the fact that people from outside the state have a hard time figuring Arkansas out. We're a fringe state, not solely a part of any one region. We're a state that's mostly Southern but also a bit Midwestern and a tad Southwestern. Northwest Arkansas is far different from southeast Arkansas. Northeast Arkansas isn't the same kind of place as southwest Arkansas.

The thing all parts of Arkansas have in common is that our people, while never boastful, are proud. So what if outsiders can't figure us out? Those of us in Arkansas already know we have a good thing going when it comes to food.

I've long believed that the strongest barbecue area of the state is east Arkansas. The barbecue is pork here (beef has crept from Texas into parts of southwest Arkansas), though the sauces vary from place to place. At Craig's on U.S. 70 in DeValls Bluff, you can walk into the ramshackle building and immediately be asked if you want your barbecue mild, medium or hot. The hot sauce is just that, which is why most folks go the medium route. The crowd is a mixture of locals, hunters from Little Rock and Memphis when it's duck season and those who are wise enough to get off Interstate 40 and find their way to DeValls Bluff.

In Marianna, meanwhile, Jones Bar-B-Q Diner is in an old house in a residential area. Jones has been around since at least the early 1900s. While it's hard to determine the exact year it opened, there are certain food experts who believe it's one of the oldest continually operated black-owned restaurants in the South.

Up in the far northeast corner of the state, you can find the Dixie Pig at Blytheville, whose fan page on Facebook has almost 1,500 members. For more than 70 years, the "pig sandwiches" there have drawn people from as far away as Memphis and the Missouri Bootheel.

It's common, of course, for restaurants to use the name "pig" in a state where the beloved athletic teams at the University of Arkansas are called the Razorbacks and people "call the Hogs" at football games. Among the oldest barbecue joints in central Arkansas is the venerable White Pig in a working-class neighborhood of North Little Rock. The Pig Pit at Caddo Valley changed its name to Fat Boys a few years back, though barbecue is still on the menu.

While East Arkansas is regarded as barbecue country, the most famous barbecue restaurant in the state is likely McClard's in Hot Springs. Given the fact that Bill Clinton grew up in Hot Springs, McClard's has received plenty of national media attention through the years. The attention is deserved, even in a barbecue-rich city that has other quality establishments with names like Stubby's. Alex and Gladys McClard owned the Westside Tourist Court in the 1920s. When a traveler couldn't come up with $10 he owed them, he asked the couple to accept a recipe for barbecue sauce instead. By 1928, the Westside Tourist Court was Westside BarB-Q with barbecued goat as the featured item on the menu. McClard's moved to its present location in 1942 and hasn't changed much since, though the goat has disappeared from the menu.

I explained in the Southern BBQ Trail introduction that while Clinton was born in Hope, he moved to Hot Springs as a young child, finishing elementary school, junior high school and high school there. Most of us from Arkansas considered Clinton a Hot Springs product. During the 1992 presidential campaign, he became the man from Hope once his consultants determined that "I still believe in a place called Hot Springs" just didn't have the same ring to it.

It's another example of how this state of contradictions known as Arkansas confounds outsiders. The same goes for our barbecue, which varies from region to region and even restaurant to restaurant. Define Arkansas barbecue, you say? Impossible. Just shut up and eat, Arkansans will tell you.

April 16, 2011
Fried Chicken

The question comes often: Which restaurant serves the best fried chicken in Arkansas?

Whenever I think of barbecue, I tend to think of the Delta. But when it comes to fried chicken, northwest Arkansas is the part of the state that first comes to mind. Maybe that's because my parents would take me to the AQ Chicken House in Springdale as a child if we were in that neck of the woods. There was even an AQ in Russellville for a short time, and it was the place we would visit after making the curvy drive up Arkansas Highway 7 from Arkadelphia to watch Ouachita take on Arkansas Tech in football and basketball.

I often would spend two consecutive nights in northwest Arkansas during my decade of working in the governor's office, and my two restaurants of choice for dinner were the Venesian Inn at Tontitown and the Monte Ne Inn near Rogers. At Monte Ne, it's chicken or nothing. You sit down in the small but spotless restaurant near the place Coin Harvey tried to make famous, and they start bringing food—lots of food.

It's all you can eat at Monte Ne. Maybe that's why I like it so much, since I find it hard to stop when eating fried chicken. You'll start with the bean soup. That will be followed by fried chicken, mashed potatoes, gravy, corn, coleslaw, rolls and apple butter. It's best to call ahead for reservations at a restaurant that serves from 5 p.m. until 8 p.m. each Tuesday through Saturday and from noon until 7 p.m. each Sunday.

As far as the Venesian Inn is concerned, thousands of people who've attended Razorback football and basketball games through the years have stories of long waits outside just to get what might be the best rolls at any Arkansas restaurant. There's far more than fried chicken on the menu, though I usually find myself going for the No. 1: three pieces of fried chicken served with spaghetti and meat sauce.

Ordering the No. 1 is a good way to combine the Italian heritage of Tontitown with the poultry heritage of the Arkansas Ozarks. Italian immigrant Germano Gasparotto opened the restaurant in 1947. The wooden tables are the same ones Gasparotto installed in 1947, and the brick walls and hardwood room dividers are original.

Gasparotto sold the Venesian Inn to two other native Italians, John and Mary Granada. They, in turn, passed it on to their daughter, Alice Leatherman, who became a beloved proprietor for customers from across the state. Her nephew, Johnny Mhoon, joined his wife, Linda Mhoon, in taking over the restaurant in 1992.

"Mhoon says some of her regular customers recall the days when a Venesian Inn No. 9 steak cost only $1.50," the restaurant's website states. "As one of the restaurant's original waitresses, Elsie Mae Pianalto, explains, the Venesian Inn charm is what keeps customers coming back again and again: 'People who came here as children bring their children here....They say it's neat to see everything the same.'"

The No. 9, by the way, is a 16-ounce sirloin that will set you back $18.95 these days. I consider it a bargain at that price. In fact, I happily pay the additional $2 to replace the fries with spaghetti.

The AQ Chicken House in Springdale opened the same year as the Venesian Inn. In case you're wondering, AQ stands for "Arkansas quality." The founder, Roy C. Ritter, was among the poultry industry pioneers in the Ozarks. He had large chicken houses and his own processing plant. Thousands of customers still come weekly.

AQ has quite a history. In 1966, for instance, it shipped 400 dinners to Miss Universe contestants. By 1972, franchises were available. An outlet opened for football games in the expanded Donald W. Reynolds Razorback Stadium in 2001.

What about fried chicken in Little Rock? I would cast my vote for the Kitchen Express on Asher Avenue. If you want more of an upscale dining experience, the day fried chicken is served for lunch in the Capital Bar & Grill at the Capital Hotel is worth marking on your calendar. I've also found the two Franke's locations to have consistently good fried chicken.

There are a number of places that are no longer with us whose fried chicken I miss. I miss Paul's in the Park Hill area of North Little Rock, where the fried chicken was worth the wait. I especially miss Mrs. Miller's near Lake Hamilton in Hot Springs, which was probably my father's favorite restaurant in the state. Fisher's in North Little Rock also had great fried chicken, as did Browning's in the Heights area of Little Rock.

March 21, 2012
An American Classic

The James Beard Awards are to the food industry what the Pulitzer Prizes are to journalism, the Academy Awards are to the movies, the Emmy Awards are to television, the Tony Awards are to the theater and the Grammy Awards are to music.

It's big news in the Arkansas Delta when a Beard Award finds its way to Lee County. One of the highest honors a restaurant can earn is about to be bestowed on a business in a nondescript building in a residential area of Marianna—219 W. Louisiana St. to be exact. Jones Bar-B-Q Diner, owned by James and Betty Jones, was selected by the James Beard Foundation of New York as one of five America's Classics Award honorees for 2012.

Most Arkansans have never heard of Jones Bar-B-Q, but that's

Jones Bar-B-Q at Marianna is an American classic in more ways than one.

about to change. According to the foundation, the America's Classics Award goes to restaurants with "timeless appeal that are beloved for quality food that reflects the character of their community." The Jones family will be honored in May when the foundation's annual awards dinner is held at Lincoln Center in New York.

"The presentations of our five America's Classics Awards are favorite moments at our ceremony," says Susan Ungaro, the foundation president. "Attendees at our awards love meeting these folks and hearing their stories because they represent the diverse heritage, heart and community of our country's national cuisine. James Beard would have loved visiting them all."

Beard, who died in 1985, was a cookbook author and teacher who educated several generations of chefs and other foodies. The Oregon native published the first of his 20 books in 1940. He established the James Beard Cooking School in 1955 and for the next three decades taught men and women how to cook.

"Through the years, he gradually became not only the leading culinary figure in the country but the dean of American cuisine," Julia Child once said.

The foundation's website describes him as a "tireless traveler, bringing his message of good food, honestly prepared with fresh, wholesome, American ingredients, to a country just becoming aware of its own culinary heritage." I have no doubt Beard would have enjoyed Jones Bar-B-Q, which has existed in some form for almost 100 years and is among the oldest black-owned restaurants in the country.

Several years ago, when I became active in the Southern Foodways Alliance, I became acquainted with John T. Edge, the alliance director and a nationally known food writer who's based on the Ole Miss campus. I urged him to spend more time on the west side of the Mississippi River, since I've long considered the barbecue culture of the Arkansas Delta to be superior to that of the Mississippi Delta. Jones Bar-B-Q was among the places Arkansans urged Edge to try.

Edge drove over from Oxford to visit the restaurant and discovered that James Jones is a man of few words. Edge came back again and again, finally wearing down Jones enough for an *Oxford American* article titled "In Through the Back Door." The article was nominated for a Beard Award.

In a later article for *Saveur*, Edge wrote: "Jones' story is similar to many I've heard from pitmasters around the South. For their ancestors, barbecue was an opportunity—a way to leverage equity and muscle to build successful businesses. By the late 1930s, as new roads stretched across the South and community barbecue traditions begat city commerce, young entrepreneurs began selling sandwiches from roadside shebangs. And in a leap that would give a lexicographer whiplash, a vocation that had been built largely on the labor of enslaved African-Americans began referring to its best practitioners as pitmasters."

Walter Jones began the operation by selling barbecue from his back porch on Fridays and Saturdays. His son Hubert Jones said the meat was smoked in "a hole in the ground, some iron pipes and a piece of fence wire, and two pieces of tin." James Jones is the son of Hubert Jones.

"My father would sell the meat in town at this place they had," James Jones told Edge. "They called it the Hole In the Wall. That's what it was. Just a window in a wall where they sold meat from a washtub."

Here's a tip if you're planning a pilgrimage to Marianna for a sandwich: Arrive early.

"Mr. Jones is there early in the mornings and leaves early in the afternoon," says Kim Williams, a travel writer for the Arkansas Department of Parks & Tourism. "If you want barbecue, you get it in the morning."

Jones usually arrives by 7:30 a.m. each Monday through Saturday. Williams lists the closing time as 2 p.m., but if Jones runs out of meat, he's gone. I've arrived during the noon hour and found the place locked tight. There are no buns. The sandwiches are served on white bread, with or without slaw. There are no sides with the exception of some small bags of chips for sale. A lot of people buy the barbecue by the pound.

"I grew up on Jones," Williams says. "I can only eat barbecue on white bread. The slaw, which is basically the only slaw I will eat, is mustard based, I guess, because it's yellow. The sauce is vinegar based and relatively thin. I'm craving it now. It's only four blocks from my house."

Several years ago, Kane Webb wrote a feature article for the *Arkansas Democrat-Gazette* on my so-called Arkansas Delta Barbecue Trail. I took Webb and our driver for the day, Bubba Lloyd, to Jones Bar-B-Q for the first time.

"I've never had smoked meat that was so good," Lloyd remembers. "It's also the restaurant where I was offered the opportunity to buy a pit bull dog from a clothes basket in the back seat of a Buick in the parking lot."

It's indeed an American classic.

April 4, 2012
The Barbecue Capital

In a state that loves its barbecue, the question often comes up: Which town has the best and the most barbecue restaurants? When it comes to quality smoked pork per capita, I would have to proclaim Blytheville as this state's barbecue capital.

Blytheville has suffered economically in recent decades with the outmigration of thousands of sharecroppers and the closure of Eaker Air Force Base, but barbecue restaurants continue to thrive. It's a long tradition there.

Food historian Robert Moss of Charleston, South Carolina, writes, "In Blytheville, Ernest Halsell opened the Rustic Inn in a log cabin in 1923, later moving the restaurant to a rock building, and finally to Sixth Street in the 1950s....It operated as a drive-in with curb service during the 1950s and 1960s but later scaled back to just a regular family-style restaurant."

Any visit to Blytheville requires a stop at the Dixie Pig, a direct descendant of that log cabin where the Halsell family began serving food in 1923. The Dixie Pig has hundreds of loyal patrons who drive from all over northeast Arkansas, the Missouri Bootheel and Memphis to buy what's known locally as a "pig sandwich." It's also a regular stop for those traveling on Interstate 55.

In 2009, a book with the intriguing title *America's Best BBQ: 100 Recipes from America's Best Smokehouses, Pits, Shacks, Rib Joints, Roadhouses, and Restaurants* was published. A co-author of that book, Paul Kirk from Kansas City, declared that the Dixie Pig has the best barbecue in the country. Jennifer Biggs, who writes about food for the *Commercial Appeal* in Memphis, headed to the Dixie Pig soon after the book was released.

"In Memphis, we can passionately discuss the merits of first, whether to put slaw on your sandwich and second, the merits of mayo-based slaw vs. one of mustard or vinegar," Biggs wrote. "At the Dixie Pig, that's no issue. It was just cabbage, dressed with a smidge of vinegar. And I do mean a smidge; it wasn't even wet.

149

Adding the hot vinegar sauce greatly improved it."

The thing about Blytheville is that there are choices other than the Dixie Pig. There are a lot of choices, in fact.

There are two locations of Penn's Barbeque, operated independently by members of the same family. Unfortunately, it appears the original location is about to be replaced by a Dollar General store. One of my Blytheville barbecue correspondents thinks the best barbecue in town can be found at Benny Bob's on East Main Street.

Others swear by the pork sandwich at the Kream Kastle on North Division Street, a Blytheville institution that serves a variety of other dishes. There's Yank's Famous Barbeque on East Main Street and Johnny's BBQ on South Lake Street.

I'm also told of a man who split from Yank's and now serves barbecue off a grill behind a barber shop. That sounds like a true Delta experience.

"Yes, it's confusing," my correspondent admits when asked about the various barbecue joints. "We have a whole bunch of barbecue for a town this size."

I especially want to try a spot a Blytheville resident describes like this: "There's a place here that has some of the best barbecued pork I've ever tasted. It's in a travel trailer parked in front of Hays Supermarket. I don't think the stand has an official name. He has been there for a decade or so, and the locals just refer to it as Old Hays Barbecue."

Though Blytheville's population dropped from 20,798 in the 1960 census to 5,620 in the 2010 census, the town is still filled with fascinating places thanks to its rich history. Rigel Keffer writes in the online Encyclopedia of Arkansas History & Culture that Mississippi County has "long held its place as the number one cotton-producing county in Arkansas, and Blytheville sits near ten cotton gins. One of the largest cotton gins in North America lies on Blytheville's western edge....Blytheville lies along Highway 61 of blues music fame. Generations of blues musicians passed through Blytheville as they traveled from Memphis north toward St. Louis, Missouri, and Chicago, Illinois. The 1932 Greyhound bus station at 109 North 5th St. is one of the few surviving Art Deco Greyhound bus stations in the United States."

After writing on my Southern Fried blog about barbecue in Blytheville, I discovered that the folks there are passionate about pork.

"I've been eating barbecue from Penn's, Dixie Pig and Kream Kastle for more than 43 years," one wrote. "Not only have I eaten at these establishments almost all my life, but they are the standard by which I measure all of my barbecue eating....Blytheville has had a hard way to go over the past couple of decades, but if you've never tried one of these chopped barbecue sandwiches, you owe it to yourself to make the drive to Blytheville and check them out. I make this 150-mile trip about once a month just for a Penn's barbecue." Another person wrote, "Finally somebody gets it besides the natives."

And in the words of one enthusiastic native, "The pig sandwich from Blytheville is the best in the world. I grew up on it and have not been able to replicate it anywhere I've lived. I'm hoping to visit Blytheville in a few months and will want to eat pig sandwiches for breakfast, dinner and supper."

July 18, 2012
Pass the Crappie

A website owned by the giant Hearst Corp. recently had a feature titled "All-American Eats: Must-Try Foods from the 50 States." The editors at the Delish website (www.delish.com) chose one ingredient or dish to represent each state.

What did they choose for Arkansas? Chocolate gravy. That's right, chocolate gravy.

I had two grandmothers who were great Southern cooks and lived into their 90s. Neither ever prepared chocolate gravy. I conducted an informal poll on my Facebook page and my Southern Fried blog. While there were some Arkansans who grew up eating chocolate

Pan-fried crappie makes for an iconic Arkansas meal.

gravy on a regular basis, it was nowhere near a majority.

But here's what the folks at Delish wrote about Arkansas: "Chocolate gravy (a thickened chocolate sauce) is a common accompaniment for biscuits in the South. It's a breakfast staple in Arkansas. It is thought that recipes for the decadent Southern treat were developed using chocolate pudding as a base in the 19th century. While there is no documentation about the addition of biscuits to the mix, it makes sense that a common baked good was grabbed at some point to dip in the chocolate gravy—and thus a breakfast tradition was born."

Chocolate gravy as a breakfast staple in Arkansas? Hardly. Had they said cream gravy or redeye gravy, I would have given them a pass. Too often writers and editors in places far from Arkansas come up with what they think those of us who live here should be eating and drinking as opposed to what we actually eat and drink. Sweet tea and fried green tomatoes have become trendy in Arkansas restaurants and represent the height of Southern cuisine for many Americans. In my house and the homes of my grandparents, if you wanted your tea sweet, you took a spoon and put sugar in it. It wasn't automatically brewed that way.

My grandmothers fried everything from okra to squash. But we were much more likely to have fried green apples than fried green tomatoes. If the green tomatoes fell off the vine early, they were put in the window to ripen. Be careful when using too broad a brush to define Arkansas cuisine. Don't get me wrong. I like chocolate gravy, sweet tea and fried green tomatoes. But they're far from traditional Arkansas staples.

The editors at *Arkansas Life* magazine were nice enough to ask me to come up with my perfect Arkansas summer meal for the July issue, which focuses on summer food. I chose fried crappie and bream as the main course. Neither fish would have made the Delish list since the Yankee editors likely couldn't pronounce "crappie" or "bream" correctly.

I told the *Arkansas Life* editors that I had never been asked one of those High Profile–style questions about what I would have for my last meal. After giving the subject some serious thought, I came to the conclusion that my perfect summer meal would consist of freshly caught pan fish (bream, crappie or a combination of both), fried potatoes with a bit of onion, slices of cornbread slathered in butter, and sliced tomatoes, bell peppers, cucumbers and green onions straight from an Arkansas garden.

I specified that the fish be pan fried, not deep fried, and caught that day if possible. It also would be best to gather the vegetables from the garden on the same day. Dessert could be a wild berry cobbler using either blackberries or dewberries. The gatherer of those berries should have the chigger bites to prove they came from the wild. This was often what I had for lunch during childhood summers spent at the small cabin my paternal grandparents owned on Lake Norrell, a Benton city water supply lake that covers about 280 acres in northern Saline County.

I learned to swim, water ski, fish and frog gig on that lake. My grandmother and I spent our mornings fishing for bream on the dock in front of the house with poles made from cane my grandfather had cut. My grandparents sank their Christmas tree at the end of that dock each year to attract bream and regularly threw in large sacks of dog food with holes punched in the side.

Our bait consisted of either the red wigglers my grandfather raised in his worm bed (I got to pour in kitchen scraps and coffee grounds on a daily basis to "feed" the worms) or the catalpa worms gathered off the giant tree out back. My grandmother cleaned whatever we caught—"If it's big enough to bite, it's big enough to eat," she would say—and pan fried the fish for lunch. I've never had better meals.

If you pick up a copy of the magazine, you'll see a photo of a couple of cleaned crappie adjacent to my short article. I had warned the editors at *Arkansas Life* that they shouldn't try to pass off a piece of fried catfish in a photo as crappie or bream, since Arkansans are savvy. For the sake of authenticity, I had to give up a bag of my precious crappie for the photo shoot.

In thinking about what I would rate second on my list of Arkansas summer meals, I came up with this: A bacon and tomato sandwich (no lettuce for me) using Arkansas tomatoes and high-quality bacon. Wash it down with a cold glass of milk and then have half an Arkansas cantaloupe for dessert. And, yes, I put salt on my cantaloupe just as I do my watermelon and grapefruit.

You'll recognize the common denominator in both of my meals: Arkansas tomatoes. You can have your chocolate gravy, I'll take one of those tomatoes.

August 8, 2012
Arkansas Caviar

One of the things I enjoy most about writing this column is sharing stories about Arkansas that readers might not otherwise know. It's a safe bet that most people don't realize Arkansas is a caviar producer.

That's right. Caviar.

I was delighted earlier this year when the editors at *Arkansas Life* magazine asked me to learn what I could about Arkansas caviar. I made the trip to Marvell to interview 62-year-old Jessie George—his friends call him John—about the caviar he ships from George's Fish

Market each winter and early spring. He gave me a container of the caviar to try at home. I like anything salty, and this was something I found hard to stop eating.

"It's comparable to the taste of Russian caviar," George says.

This is a man who knows what he's talking about when it comes to the rivers of the Arkansas Delta and the things those rivers produce. He grew up on a houseboat at St. Charles on the lower White River during the river rat era when hundreds of Arkansans lived on houseboats on the Arkansas, White, Cache and St. Francis rivers. These families scratched out a living by catching fish, trapping for the fur market and gathering mussel shells for the button industry.

George has picked cotton, worked in grain elevators, fished commercially for catfish and buffalo and overcome alcoholism in his life. One brother was killed in a boating accident while fishing on the White River at Indian Bay. Another brother was killed when the truck he was driving, which was carrying 750 pounds of catfish, was hit by a train at Almyra. It hasn't been an easy life.

"People were out there picking the fish up before they could even get his body removed from the vehicle," George says of the truck-train collision.

Back when Arkansas restaurants sold river-caught catfish rather than farm-raised catfish, the George brothers supplied the owners of the best-known catfish restaurants in the state—men such as Virgil Young of North Little Rock and Olden Murry of DeValls Bluff. George says he threw "tons" of paddlefish back in the water through the years, never realizing there might be a demand for the eggs. Paddlefish can reach more than five feet in length and weigh more than 60 pounds.

George began moving into the caviar business in 1998. At one point, he drove from east Arkansas to Portland, Maine, just so a wholesaler could sample his product. Within a few years, George was no longer selling buffalo or catfish. He explains it this way: "I would be selling someone $4 worth of buffalo and let $100 worth of caviar spoil in the process."

About 15 commercial fishermen supply George from late November until early April with eggs from paddlefish (often known in Arkansas as spoonbill), shovelnose sturgeon and bowfin. There was a time when George shipped almost 10,000 pounds of eggs annually. He says it's too hard these days for him to find seasonal labor. He also has a bad back. Pulling in fishing nets day after day can take its toll.

"If you meet a commercial fisherman who is as old as I am, you'll meet someone with a bad back," he says.

Output at the Marvell facility is now about 5,000 pounds a season. George's biggest buyer is the Great Atlantic Trading Co. of Ocean Isle Beach, North Carolina, which describes paddlefish roe on its website as ranging from "light to dark steel gray, and comparable in taste to Caspian Sea Sevruga." The eggs from shovelnose sturgeon, which are known in the business as hackleback caviar since the term "shovelnose" apparently turns consumers off, are described as "dark, firm with a very mild, subtle flavor." George also supplies Great Atlantic with bowfin eggs that are marketed by the company as "black caviar roe with an earthy and distinctive flavor."

Armenian brothers Melkoum and Mouchegh Petrossian, who were born on the Iranian side of the Caspian Sea and raised on the Russian side, are credited with popularizing caviar in Paris during the 1920s and spurring a worldwide interest in the product. The brothers went to France to continue their studies of medicine and law, which had been interrupted in Russia by the Bolshevik Revolution.

The Petrossian website tells the story this way: "Paris welcomed exiled Russian princes, intellectuals and aristocrats with open arms, and Parisians embraced all things Russian, especially the arts, ballet, the choreography of Diaghilev and the music of Igor Stravinsky. Nonetheless, there was one thing missing from the Russian expatriates' lives: caviar. The French had yet to be introduced to this rare delicacy, a situation that the Petrossian brothers immediately set out to remedy.

"Their first attempts to create an awareness of caviar in Paris were assisted by Cesar Ritz, the great impresario of the European hotel trade. His initial reluctance to offer caviar in his prestigious establishment at the Place Vendome was quickly overcome as caviar caught on and assumed its own very special niche in the world of gastronomy."

Jessie George and the town of Marvell don't seem to fit alongside Cesar Ritz and Paris. But there's no doubt that Arkansas has found its niche in the world caviar trade.

January 16, 2013
Tamale Time

Winter has descended on Arkansas, and my thoughts have turned to tamales. I enjoy tamales any time of the year, but they seem better when it's cold outside. Three years ago, the Arkansas Educational Television Network had the debut of a program titled "On the Tamale Trail." AETN crews followed journalist Kane Webb, political consultant Bill Vickery and me through the Delta regions of Arkansas and Mississippi in search of the best tamales we could find.

In Arkansas, we ate Pasquale's Tamales at Helena and tamales from Rhoda's Famous Hot Tamales at Lake Village. In Mississippi, we visited Hicks' and Abe's in Clarksdale, John's in Cleveland, the White Front in Rosedale, Doe's in Greenville and Maria's (in the backyard of a man named Shine Thornton, who also played the fiddle for us) in Greenville.

Kane paced himself. Bill and I didn't. I'm not sure how we ate so many tamales in a two-day period. That's not to mention that we "chased" the tamales with a steak at Doe's in Greenville on the first day of our two-day excursion. AETN reruns the program from time to time during pledge drives. I know when it airs because the emails start pouring in, asking me where to find the best tamales in Arkansas.

Delta tamales are different from Mexican tamales. I like both. My Mexican-American mother-in-law won't eat Delta tamales, but I consider them to be in a separate category from those you find in Mexican restaurants. Those with an interest in the subject should go to the Southern Foodways Alliance's Delta Tamale Trail website at www.tamaletrail.com. In Little Rock, Doe's, the Arkansas Burger Co., Izzy's and Terri-Lynn's all offer decent Delta-style tamales.

"So what is this food, so often associated with Mexico, doing in the Mississippi Delta, you might ask," writes Southern food expert John T. Edge. "Isn't this just an aberration? Like finding curried conch in Collierville, Tenn., or foie gras in Fort Smith? It's not that simple. Tamales have been a menu mainstay in the Mississippi Delta for much of the 20th century. Indeed, along with catfish, they may just be the archetypal Delta food. Mississippi bluesman Robert Johnson sang about them in the song 'They're Red Hot,' recorded in 1936."

Those from outside Arkansas seem perplexed when I tell them that our state has a long tamale tradition. Old-timers in my hometown of Arkadelphia still talk fondly about Joe Villa, who died in September 1963 just five days after I turned four. The *Southern Standard*, a weekly newspaper at Arkadelphia that no longer exists, published a lengthy article on Villa following his death.

Written in a simpler and less politically correct time, the article stated: "Joe Villa was an institution of a bygone day in Arkadelphia. He and his large family came here many years ago from Old Mexico. He denied any kinship with the famous bandit Pancho Villa, and his life in this city certainly showed he had none of the undesirable traits of that other one. Joe was a hot tamale specialist, and he made the best there was to be had. Joe's tamales were tasty, and you bet his utensils were clean and the ingredients pure. Joe reared and educated a large number of children on his tamale sales to his fellow townsmen and townswomen and certainly to the boys and girls.

"One of the local churches got Joe enlisted and all his children into Sunday school. None of the dozen children, more or less, of Mr. and Mrs. Villa ever became a juvenile delinquent or gave any trouble. This Mexican family was law-abiding and decent in every way. Several of the boys played on the athletic teams at Arkadelphia High and acquitted themselves creditably. Anybody who follows the right kind of road in this life like Joe Villa ought not to have much trouble finding the pearly gates open when he arrived up yonder, nor have too much trouble orienting himself in that new community."

Villa was born in Mexico in 1877, married a native of Laredo, Texas, and moved to Arkadelphia in 1910, where the couple raised a family of three sons and seven daughters. Joe and Millie Villa are buried in the city's Rose Hill Cemetery. An ad in the 1921 yearbook at what's now Henderson State University read: "Hot Tamale Joe. You know me, girls. Ice cream sandwiches and hot tamales. Delivered a la carte. Joe Villa."

Late last year, my phone started ringing with the news that George Eldridge, who owns Doe's in Little Rock (which became as famous as the Greenville original when staffers for Bill Clinton's 1992 presidential campaign began hanging out there), had opened a restaurant in rural Woodruff County called The Tamale Factory. It's in his horse barn at Gregory, which is 10 miles south of Augusta, and is open each Friday and Saturday from 5 p.m. until 10 p.m. In addition to tamales, there are steaks and shrimp. It has become a popular place in that part of the Arkansas Delta.

Arkansas' tamale heritage isn't confined to those of Mexican descent such as Joe Villa. Joe St. Columbia of Pasquale's in Helena is Sicilian American. Rhoda Adams of Lake Village is African American. Pasquale St. Columbia, Joe's father, came to Helena from Sicily in the late 1800s.

"Pasquale never met a stranger and made friends fast," Joe says. "He was jolly, friendly and talkative. Because they could understand each other's languages, the cultural exchange between Pasquale and the Mexican immigrants he met and befriended was easy. Pasquale learned to prepare and eat tamales from the Mexican farm workers. He shared his recipe for Italian spaghetti and, in turn, they taught him to make the traditional Mexican hot tamales."

Farther south in Lake Village, Rhoda Adams has become so famous that Little Rock executives occasionally come down in private jets for lunch. Now in her 70s, Adams began making tamales four decades ago when her husband's aunt suggested that it would be a good way to make money. Her husband bought her a machine to craft the tamales, and the mother of 15 children went to work. She's another in a long line of well-known Arkansas tamale makers dating back to Pasquale St. Columbia and Joe Villa.

March 6, 2013
The Tamale Factory

The invitation proved irresistible. Don Tilton, one of Arkansas' most famous lobbyists, called to say that he would be picking up Paul and Mary Berry of Little Rock for a Friday afternoon trip to Gregory in Woodruff County. Would I like to tag along? Paul is among this state's most colorful lobbyists and gifted storytellers. Mary also can tell stories with the best of them. Among the three of them, I knew there would be plenty of tales told about Arkansas politicians, musicians and other characters past and present.

I wasn't disappointed. Mary hails from the Eldridge clan, long a prominent Woodruff County family. Last year, her cousin George remodeled a barn on the family farm and opened a restaurant called The Tamale Factory. The place has been packed every Friday and Saturday night since it opened in November. People drive from as far away as Little Rock, Memphis and Jonesboro for tamales, steaks and fried shrimp.

George Eldridge, the owner of the Little Rock branch of Doe's Eat Place, long has had the golden touch when it comes to restaurants. For years, Eldridge had taken friends to the original Doe's on Nelson Street in Greenville, Mississippi, for tamales and steaks. The Greenville Doe's was opened in the 1940s by Dominick "Doe" Signa and his wife, Mamie. The family had operated a grocery store in the building since 1903. When business declined following the Great Flood of 1927, Doe Signa began bootlegging to supplement his income. In 1941, Mamie was given a tamale recipe, and she started selling them in the store.

Soon, the place had been transformed into a honky-tonk serving a black clientele. In addition to beer, Doe and Mamie sold chili, tamales and buffalo fish. In the back of the building, Doe cooked steaks for his white friends. Eventually, the honky-tonk was phased out and Doe's Eat Place was born. Doe retired in 1974 and turned the business over to his sons, Charles and "Little Doe." In the 1980s, Eldridge convinced the sons to let him use the Doe's name and menu in Little Rock. Eldridge bought an old building on the skid-row corner of Ringo and West Markham streets and opened the Little Rock Doe's in 1988.

Thanks to Bill Clinton, the Little Rock Doe's soon would be more famous than the original location. During Clinton's 1992 presidential campaign, staff members made Doe's their nightly hangout. The national political media followed and began writing about the place. When *Rolling Stone* brought P. J. O'Rourke, Hunter S. Thompson and William Greider to town in September 1992 to write a cover story on Clinton, the back room at Doe's was chosen as the location of the interview.

In November 1992, *People* magazine published a story on George and his chief cook, Lucille Robinson. The headline read: "Little Rock's Mecca for Gumbo and Gab." Eldridge escorted Robinson to an inaugural ball in Washington. An Annie Leibovitz portrait of the pair is among the many photos that hang on the restaurant's walls.

The Tamale Factory has a menu like that at Doe's. Delta residents don't mind driving long distances for great meals, and The Tamale Factory has ample ambience. On the other side of the barn that houses the restaurant, Eldridge keeps his quarter horses. Cats are a tradition in horse barns, and Eldridge has three. One pen is filled with goats. There's also an indoor show ring for the horses. Occasionally, the dirt is rolled, a wooden dance floor is put down and bands are brought over from Memphis.

Adjacent to the barn is the beautifully restored Eldridge family home, which was built in 1910. On the other side of the barn, which faces Arkansas Highway 33 south of Augusta, is the Eldridge family cemetery. Rolfe Eldridge bought the land on which The Tamale Factory sits in 1852 from Robert Adams, who had acquired a government deed three years earlier. Rolfe Eldridge died in 1859 at age 51 and was buried in the cemetery.

A son named Rolfe, who was born in 1842, served in the Confederate army in the battles at Prairie Grove and Helena. After the war, he returned to Woodruff County to grow cotton and corn. He later would own four cotton gins and become president of the Augusta & South Eastern Railway Co., which had its office at Gregory. J. D. Eldridge acquired the family farm in 1891. In 1923, J. D. Eldridge moved to Little Rock, where he managed the Arkansas Cotton Growers Association. The family later moved back to Gregory. J. D. Eldridge practiced law and was president of the Southern Cattlemen's Association.

Roots run deep in this part of Arkansas, and that was evident as Mary Eldridge Berry gave me a cemetery tour. Toward the west, a brilliant winter sunset could be seen across the flat landscape. The trip to Gregory was, in many ways, a trip back in time for me. We exited Interstate 40 at Hazen and made the drive north along Arkansas Highway 11 to Des Arc.

It was a trip I had made countless times as a child to visit my grandparents in Des Arc. I asked Tilton to drive down Main Street so I could point out the building my grandfather, W. J. Caskey, had built almost a century ago to house the Caskey Hardware Co. It's still home to a hardware store. Just across the street is the Prairie County Courthouse, where my grandfather served as assessor, county clerk and finally as county judge from 1939 to 1941.

We crossed the White River. I have a framed photo of the massive suspension bridge that was at Des Arc from 1928 to 1970. Locals knew it as the Swinging Bridge. The sun began setting and the ducks could be seen coming to roost as we drove east on Arkansas Highway 38. At Little Dixie, we took a left onto Highway 33, passing through Dixie and reaching Gregory just before dark.

Like other east Arkansas counties, Prairie and Woodruff counties have lost population. Prairie County only has half the population it had in 1920, falling from 17,447 that year to 8,715 in the 2010 census. Woodruff County has a third of the population it had in 1920, dropping from 21,527 that year to 7,260 in 2010. Those who remain, though, retain an intense sense of history and place. They also know how to have a good time, as evidenced by the line waiting for a seat at The Tamale Factory.

June 12, 2013
The Pig Sandwich

If Paul Austin, the director of the Arkansas Humanities Council, and I were going to travel all the way from Little Rock to Blytheville, we most certainly were going to take full advantage of that northeast Arkansas city's plethora of fine barbecue joints. We started by pulling into a stall at the Kream Kastle drive-in restaurant and ordering what's known in Blytheville simply as a "pig sandwich." The next stop was the venerable Dixie Pig, where we went inside for our sandwich. The third stop was the drive-thru window at Penn's for yet another "pig sandwich."

Yes, we had three sandwiches for lunch. Yes, they were all jumbos. What can I say? I was serious in that column last year when I declared Blytheville to be the barbecue capital of Arkansas. For quality smoked pork per capita, nothing comes close. What was once Arkansas' cotton capital has suffered economically for decades with the outmigration of sharecroppers from Mississippi County and the closure of Eaker Air Force Base. But properly smoking a hog still borders on a religion in these parts, and good barbecue restaurants continue to proliferate.

To show you just how serious the folks in northeast Arkansas are, I recently received a copy of a 34-page paper by Revis Edmonds, an adjunct history professor at Arkansas State University–Newport who is pursuing his doctorate in heritage studies on ASU's Jonesboro campus. The title of the paper is "The Kream Kastle and Its Place in Blytheville's Barbecue Mecca."

The Kream Kastle has been at the same location on North Division Street for more than 60 years. Edmonds writes: "Outwardly, the business appears to be one of those rundown relics of another era. However, it is one of Blytheville's most enduring community hot spots. It has gained a statewide reputation for its camaraderie as well as its positive contributions to the Blytheville community. It is truly one of those places where its loyalists meet, not just to swear by the pork sandwich but to hold onto their ideal of community."

Co-owner Suzanne Johns Wallace, the daughter of the Kream Kastle founder, says customers come by on a regular basis to talk about how they met their spouse at the Kream Castle, stopped there every day in high school or, in a few instances, actually were married at the restaurant.

"This has long been the place for the community's movers and shakers, those who travel in search of the perfect pig sandwich and the community's young people who were simply looking for a place to get a good meal and hang out with their friends," Edmonds writes.

In July 1952, the Kream Kastle was established as a window-service-only operation by Steven Johns. His son Hugh Johns says his father "kept it simple at first. When he opened, he just sold hot dogs, ice cream and bottled drinks. He would use his profits to add things."

Before long, the Kream Kastle was a drive-in restaurant with carhops in white uniforms. Customers would drive up and honk their horns or flash their lights for service. For several years, the Kream Kastle was best known for its hot dogs. Steven Johns decided to add barbecue in 1955. Edmonds notes that it was a gamble "in a market where barbecue saturation was quite obvious. There were other establishments in town that promoted barbecue, including the Old Hickory Inn, Ronald Penn's Barbecue, Rustic Inn, Brackin's Cafe, Roy Bunch's Barbecue and the iconic Dixie Pig."

Steven Johns, the hard-working son of Arab immigrants, often would be at the Kream Kastle from 7 a.m. until past midnight. Having added the barbecue pit, he decided to run a special on barbecue sandwiches for 69 cents along with another special of six sandwiches for $1 on Sunday nights after church. Soon, the Kream Kastle was selling more than 300 barbecue sandwiches a day. Hugh

Johns remembers that he "literally rubbed stone bruises from the pit on my fingers."

"Steven Johns got some assistance from an unexpected quarter— his local competitor," Edmonds writes. "On the last day of the special, Buddy Halsell of the Dixie Pig brought Steven and Hugh Johns two fully smoked pork shoulders so they were able to make it. This would appear to be a very unusual arrangement, but under the circumstances it really was not. In small communities dealing with some of the first incursions of national restaurant chains into what had been exclusively local markets, it was not that unusual."

Hugh Johns began working full time following his graduation from the University of Arkansas in 1968. Two of Steven Johns' other sons were involved in the business from time to time. Steven Johns died in January 1979. Steven Johns Jr. took over the business along with a friend in 1981. An Air Force veteran who had retired in Blytheville ran the business for a time. There were other owners and partners as the Kream Kastle experienced financial difficulties. In March 1986, Suzanne Johns Wallace and her husband, Jeff Wallace, took over the business.

Edmonds says Jeff Wallace has a reputation as "a man with a gruff exterior" who is "a good and thrifty businessman who puts out a quality product and cares about the people he serves. In some ways, he is perceived as being a better businessman than the founder, if thriftiness is the trademark. Wallace became known around town for driving a Cadillac that he would fill with firewood to use in the barbeque pit."

His wife says, "It was a big conversation maker around town. When he stopped driving it in September, people said that the Kream Kastle didn't look the same without that car sitting there every day." Cadillac or no Cadillac, the "pig sandwich" at the Kream Kastle is still something special. Paul Austin and I can attest to that following our culinary pilgrimage to Arkansas' barbecue mecca.

May 28, 2014

Good Friday

We gathered at 8 a.m. on Good Friday in the parking lot of the Clinton Presidential Center at Little Rock. The goal: To sample as much Arkansas Delta barbecue as possible in a single day, with catfish and tamales thrown in for good measure. I was joined by Denver Peacock, Gabe Holmstrom, Jordan Johnson and Jason Parker for an excursion that would take us more than 400 miles and allow us to eat at 10 places before dusk. The towns of the Arkansas Delta feature some quality dining opportunities, and we wanted to pack as many in as possible.

We began with fried catfish at the Wilson Café in the unique community of Wilson in southern Mississippi County. We warmed up for the barbecue portion of the day at the Hog Pen along the Great River Road—U.S. Highway 61—a couple of miles south of Osceola. We then headed to Blytheville, the barbecue capital of Arkansas, to sample pig sandwiches (that's what they call them in northeast Arkansas) from five places—the Dixie Pig, the Kream Kastle, Penn's, a trailer in the parking lot of the Hays grocery store and a trailer that's known as Razorback Carryout.

The next barbecue sandwich was from Woody's at Waldenburg, another east Arkansas dining hot spot. We made our way from there to The Tamale Factory at Gregory in Woodruff County to visit with George Eldridge, best known as the owner of Doe's Eat Place in downtown Little Rock. We sampled tamales, fried shrimp and boiled shrimp but had no room left for Eldridge's steaks. Our final stop was the legendary Bulldog at Bald Knob for strawberry shortcake, a spring specialty in a town that once proclaimed itself as the nation's strawberry capital. Cars were backed up onto the highway that Friday night as people waited to purchase shortcakes.

Between the food stops, we walked around the former company town of Wilson, visited the museum on the courthouse square at Osceola, went to Dyess to see the restoration work being done on the Johnny Cash boyhood home and checked out the Poinsett

County Courthouse at Harrisburg. At Wilson, chef Joe Cartwright is attracting people from miles around. His Wilson Café on the square of the historic town serves lunch Tuesday through Sunday from 11 a.m. until 2 p.m. and serves dinner on Friday and Saturday nights. Cartwright grew up at West Memphis and attended college at Arkansas State University in Jonesboro. He later moved to Memphis, where he was the chef at well-known restaurants such as Spindini and The Elegant Farmer. The Wilson Café reopened December 20, 2013, after having been closed for a number of years.

We headed north on U.S. 61 after leaving Wilson. The plan was to begin the barbecue portion of the tour at Blytheville, but we saw the Hog Pen on the east side of the road and decided to sample its pork. The piles of fresh-cut hickory out back let us know that this place takes barbecue seriously. We ate outside on a picnic table. The walls inside are covered with memorabilia from Cortez Kennedy, who played high school football at nearby Rivercrest High School and was inducted into the Pro Football Hall of Fame two years ago. Kennedy played college football for the University of Miami and spent his entire professional career with the Seattle Seahawks, participating in the Pro Bowl eight times. In the cotton country of south Mississippi County, which has a rich sports tradition, playing football was the thing to do. "Where I grew up, there was nothing else to do," Kennedy once told an interviewer. "We used to throw rocks at each other for fun."

The first Blytheville stop was the venerable Dixie Pig, the only barbecue joint where we actually ate inside. We picked up sandwiches from the other four establishments and took them to the bank of the Mississippi River behind the Nucor Yamato steel plant at Armorel. We laid the sandwiches out on the hood of the vehicle, sampled them and watched barges move down the river. Armorel was founded in 1899 by R. E. L. Wilson, perhaps the most famous cotton planter in Arkansas history. The town's name represents Arkansas, Missouri and the first three initials of Wilson's name. The community is the home of the Armorel Planting Co., headed by John Ed Regenold, the chairman of the Arkansas Highway Commission.

We drove through Dyess and Harrisburg with the next eating stop being Waldenburg, which has one of the best food intersections in the state where Arkansas Highway 14 and U.S. Highway 49 meet. There's the D-Shack, a dairy bar known for its hamburgers. There's the Crossroads Country Cafe, where I had an outstanding plate lunch last fall. There's also the original Josie's, known for its steaks. There has been a bigger, better-known Josie's on the banks of the White River at Batesville since 2004. But the restaurant started at Waldenburg, serving weekend dinners to area farmers and those who visit the region's many duck camps each winter.

The fourth dining spot at the intersection is the trailer from which William "Woody" Wood sells barbecue. Wood and his wife began preparing barbecue in 1985 in the months when things were slow for the family's crop-dusting service. There was such a demand that the couple began selling barbecue on a full-time basis in 1992. Their sauces and rubs are now sold across the state. The stand in Waldenburg—there are a couple of picnic tables to eat on—is open most Wednesdays, Thursdays and Fridays.

From Waldenburg, we drove south on U.S. 49 to Woodruff County. Eldridge's Tamale Factory is in a converted barn between his family home and family cemetery. The tamales for Doe's are made there, but steaks, shrimp and other items are served for dinner on Friday and Saturday nights. We saved room for a final stop, the Bulldog at Bald Knob in neighboring White County, the place where Denver Peacock's parents had first met decades earlier. The first strawberry association at Bald Knob was organized in 1910. In 1921, three businessmen built the longest strawberry shed in the world, a three-quarter-mile structure parallel to the railroad tracks. In the peak year of 1951, Bald Knob growers sold $3.5 million worth of strawberries. Berries ceased to be a major crop in the 1960s due to changing market and labor conditions, but the tradition of spring strawberry shortcakes at the Bulldog continues.

February 18, 2015
Sno-White Grill

The texts and emails began rolling in within minutes of each other that sad Friday earlier this month. People wanted to make sure I had heard that the Pine Bluff institution known as the Sno-White Grill would be closing. I had no way of knowing when the news would come, but I knew it was inevitable. Sno-White owner Bobby Garner is well past retirement age, and no one was waiting in the wings to replace him. Garner purchased the restaurant in February 1970 from Roy Marshall, who had owned it the previous 27 years. He never dreamed he would have a 45-year run.

There was a newspaper clipping from the *Pine Bluff Commercial* framed on the wall of the restaurant. The story was dated November 29, 1991, and told of a fire that broke out at Sno-White at 12:26 a.m. on a Thursday. It was Thanksgiving morning. The fire destroyed the business at 310 E. Fifth Ave. The writer of the story said Sno-White had the reputation of serving the best hamburgers in the state. Garner told the newspaper: "I don't think I've gotten over the shock yet. I'm down, but I'm not out."

Within months, Garner was back behind the counter, serving as the short-order cook and dishing out those famous hamburgers. Across Arkansas, there are restaurants where locals gather to drink coffee, discuss the previous day's sports events, talk politics and catch up on the town's gossip. Few of those gathering spots have a history like that of Sno-White, which was founded in 1936, one year before Walt Disney produced his first full-length animated movie, *Snow White and the Seven Dwarfs*.

Garner was a hands-on operator who was quick to tell you that he was the only one with a key to the building. He would arrive six mornings a week at 5:30 a.m. and then come back on Sunday mornings to clean up. The restaurant served breakfast and lunch from Monday through Saturday and added dinner on Thursday, Friday and Saturday nights. When I interviewed Garner several years ago for a magazine story I was writing, I asked him why he had yet to slow

169

down. He smiled and said: "I checked with my board, and they said Sno-White doesn't have a retirement plan."

Of course, Bobby Garner *was* the board. From opening time until the last customer left, he ran the show. None of the coffee mugs matched, which was part of the charm of Sno-White. I drank coffee one morning from a mug that said "Sparkman Sparklers," the name of a girls' basketball team from Dallas County that was nationally known in the 1930s. It was as if the restaurant had become the repository of south Arkansas history. There once were a number of locally owned, full-service restaurants in Pine Bluff. As the city lost population and economic vitality through the years, those establishments closed. There was John Noah's Restaurant over by the Norton Lumber Mill. There was Wonderland and others that Garner named.

"Most of my friends have either died or moved," he told me. "There's a void there."

Business was good right up until the end. The prime rib special three evenings a week was popular. So were the plate lunches. Garner could list the lunch specials off the top of his head. Monday featured pork chops or chicken and dressing. On Tuesday, it was chicken and dumplings or grilled beef liver. The choices on Wednesday were fried chicken, baked ham or spaghetti and meat sauce. On Thursday, it was chicken-fried steak, chicken spaghetti or barbecued pork. Fridays featured salmon croquettes, fried catfish or hamburger steaks.

"We had a lot of people come in on Tuesdays just for the liver," Garner told me. "That's hard to find in restaurants these days, and folks won't fix that for themselves at home." He also was quick to tout the cornbread salad: "You make it like you would make tuna salad. But instead of using tuna, you use cornbread."

The mornings belonged to the coffee-drinking regulars. There were shifts that came in each hour. If you looked immediately to your left and to the back of the room when you walked in, you would see them in the famed Back Booth. It was the one with political posters covering the walls behind it: "I'm for Arkansas and Faubus,"

"John McClellan for Senate," "Dale Bumpers for Senate" and even "Monroe A. Schwarzlose, Democratic Candidate for Governor, the Law and Order Candidate." Schwarzlose hailed from nearby Kingsland and ran for governor in the Democratic primaries of 1978, 1980, 1982, and 1984. There was also a poster for Pine Bluff's Joe Holmes, who ran for governor in the Democratic primaries of 1990 and 2002. He was among the regular coffee drinkers. Bill Clinton even came in as president to have one of Garner's hamburgers.

"When I left the night before, there was a car across the street with two guys in it," Garner said. "They were watching the restaurant. I came back early the next morning, and these two guys were still in the car. The police later began blocking the streets several blocks away in every direction. If you were already in here, you could stay. But nobody else could come in."

Garner doesn't remember which hamburger the president had in those pre-vegan days. It might have been the Hutt Special, named after the owners of the Hutt Building Materials Co. over on Alabama Street. Or it could have been the Perdue Special, named after what was once Pine Bluff's largest office products and commercial printing company.

Garner, who grew up 18 miles west of Pine Bluff at Grapevine in Grant County, joked: "When I was coming up in Grapevine, I thought I might be president. I never thought I would cook a hamburger for one."

July 1, 2015
Gene's in Brinkley

Today marks 21 years since Gene's Barbecue in Brinkley opened. In fact, it has never been closed a day since Gene DePriest unlocked the doors on July 1, 1994. That includes every holiday and even the day after a fire.

"Thanksgiving and Christmas are two of my busiest days," says DePriest, a man with whom I've hunted ducks on many a cold morning. He's 78 now and, to put it mildly, is a colorful character. As an old newspaperman, I'm attracted to both colorful characters and independently owned restaurants where people gather at all hours of the day and night. So naturally I'm attracted to Gene DePriest and his namesake restaurant.

DePriest was born near the farming community of Monroe and attended school at Moro in Lee County. During the 1960s, he ran a restaurant in Brinkley called the S&K Grill. The aging "river rats" who live along the Lower White and Cache rivers know him best as the man who operated the 17/79 Club at Clarendon from 1971 to 1994. The club was named for the intersection of U.S. Highway 79 and Arkansas Highway 17.

It's said that the 17/79 Club hosted its fair share of high-stakes card games through the years. "We would have several hundred people in there on a Saturday night," DePriest says. "There would be live music and lots of fights." Things settled down when DePriest went from running one of the most famous nightclubs in east Arkansas to operating a restaurant that attracts families. That doesn't mean there haven't been exciting times. The ivory-billed woodpecker search stands out. Gene's menu reads: "More than 60 years after the last confirmed sighting of an ivory-billed woodpecker in the United States, researchers have evidence that the majestic bird still lives. On Feb. 11, 2004, a kayaker caught a glimpse of a huge and unusual woodpecker in the Cache River National Wildlife Refuge. The encounter spurred an extensive scientific search for a species that many feared had vanished forever, driven to extinction by the destruction of Southern old-growth forests."

There was never another sighting, and some experts consider the original sighting a hoax. DePriest still bills the two-patty cheeseburger on his menu as the "ivory-bill burger" and has a large poster in the main dining room that honors the woodpecker. The late Ed Bradley and his crew from CBS News ate their meals at Gene's while doing a story about the search for *60 Minutes*. An article in a Nature Conservancy publication in 2005 noted: "Gene's was a major hangout of the search team, a place where members sometimes met to dine after a day of working transects or checking cameras. We sit down and start to open our menus, but before we can order our waitress directs our attention to a board at the back with a new special, the ivory-bill cheeseburger."

Another memorable moment was the fire. A man driving down U.S. Highway 49 noticed the flames coming out of the restaurant on September 16, 2001. He called the fire department and then called DePriest at home. DePriest says: "I beat the firemen down here. The fire started in a fan in the women's restroom. They got it out before it affected the kitchen. It took us eight weeks to get things rebuilt up front. But we never missed a day of business." DePriest worked all night to clean up after the fire. He moved the main dining area from the front room to what's usually the private back room. As soon as the state inspectors left at 10 a.m. the next day, he was open for business.

When DePriest purchased the restaurant from his brother Louis, who died in 1996, it was known as Sweet Peas'. The business had been in Brinkley since 1971. The formal name became Gene's Barbecue, but the restaurant serves much more than barbecue. There are Southern favorites that have become hard to find in other restaurants. For breakfast, a customer can order pork chops, country ham or even a chicken-fried steak with eggs. At lunch and dinner there are fried bologna sandwiches and even buffalo fish, ribs, fried quail, frog legs and homemade stew.

Several years ago, the Southern Foodways Alliance at the University of Mississippi filmed a short documentary about the Sunday night wild-game dinners at Gene's. For years, the gravel parking lot on the side of the building would fill up with pickups late on Sunday afternoons. Men wearing jeans and camouflage would gather to eat and tell stories. They might have squirrel one week, crappie the next and rabbit the week after that. Duck, goose, dove, venison and baked coon would find their way onto the menu along with sides such as baked sweet potatoes, fried Irish potatoes, turnip greens and sliced tomatoes and onions from DePriest's home garden. An acquaintance of DePriest once described the menu as consisting of "whatever Gene shot, caught or ran over the previous week." As the Sunday night regulars aged and died, the wild-game dinners became more infrequent.

"I was killing a lot of squirrels," DePriest explains. "My wife wouldn't cook them at home, so I started to cook them here at the restaurant and invite my friends over to help me eat them. It just kind of mushroomed. But about everybody I hunted and fished with is now dead."

Like other men his age who live in the Delta, DePriest has spent a lifetime hunting and fishing. He also has been known to plant up to 125 tomato plants in the spring along with lettuce, radishes, onions, bell peppers and various kinds of peas and beans. He knows there's no greater expression of Arkansas culture than through our food, which can best be described as traditional country cooking using the freshest ingredients possible. John T. Edge, who heads the Southern Foodways Alliance, says men like DePriest are among those "for whom food is a caloric fuel sure, but also a means of cultural expression, on par with music and literature."

Arkansas Sporting Life

March 6, 2010
The Bird Hunters

It's cold on this final Friday of February as I cross the Ouachita River bridge at Arkadelphia. There's a bit of snow mixed in with the rain. I'm headed toward the southeast on Arkansas Highways 7 and 8, anxious to drive past some of the places where I hunted quail with my father.

After passing through open fields where row crops are grown, I cross Tupelo Creek and L'eau Frais Creek. The familiar pine forest almost envelops the highway. On the left is a home that the Clark County Historical Association lists as the Strong House. I've known it as the McCaskill place. Built in 1842 by a pioneer family, it was near a spring and became the center of a prosperous plantation. It has been beautifully maintained through the years. A family cemetery is adjacent to the home. In the front yard, the jonquils are blooming. They're the first jonquils I've seen this year.

I turn right onto a county road, and the memories begin to flow. The Pennington farm is down this road, and it was our favorite spot to hunt. As I near the entrance, I notice that the small fields that once were used to grow soybeans and cotton are no longer being farmed. There are now thick stands of pine.

In his column in last Sunday's *Democrat-Gazette*, Bryan Hendricks wrote about a quail seminar sponsored by the Arkansas Game and Fish Commission. He noted the huge drop in quail numbers in Arkansas since 1967, which was about the time I began hunting with my father. In an annual breeding survey, the commission recorded almost 30 birds per route in 1967. That number is now less than 10 birds per route. Quail hunting is almost a thing of the past in Arkansas.

On winter days such as this one, I miss it terribly.

"Habitat has greatly changed—and not for the better where quail are concerned," Joseph Greenfield wrote in his 2004 book *A Quail Hunter's Odyssey*. "Clean farming has all but eliminated the small fields and edges."

It was the form of hunting with which I was most familiar as a child. We considered it a regal sport. We always had at least two bird dogs at our house. There were pointers, English setters and Brittany spaniels. They had names like Susie, Mitzi, Bo, Boy, Little Boy and Ready. Rip, a hard-headed setter, was named after a college football coach in Magnolia. When the dogs were good, they were a joy to watch. Having one dog point a covey of quail with the partner backing on a crisp day afield became almost a religious experience. When the dogs weren't so good, they taught a man patience and humility.

In a 1998 essay titled "Why We Hunt," Arkansas writer Jim Spencer said, "Maybe, like me, you hunt the old-fashioned way, with a gun and a raggedy set of camo. I don't need Freudian substitutions; I'm just a hunter, in the old, original, outdated, politically incorrect way."

Dad and I were hunters in that old-fashioned way. Our hunting pants often were torn from crossing too many barbwire fences. But quail hunting made us feel like rich Southern gentlemen. For me, the Pennington farm along the Ouachita River was the most special place we hunted. There were fields of cotton. There were cattle and there was a trap to catch wild hogs.

There was a creek to cross and tall stands of bottomland hardwoods. Early each winter, we would pick black walnuts and even pull a few turnip greens from a riverside patch. It was a magical place for a boy to spend time with his dad.

There was a slough near the river filled with majestic tupelo gum trees. Often, we would put the dogs in the truck at the end of a long day of quail hunting and spend the final hour hunting ducks there. It was also a place to catch crappie and the occasional chain pickerel in the spring and gig frogs in the summer. Alligators were imported from Louisiana in the 1970s. Though it's not encouraged, we later would take my now 17-year-old son there when he was four and five to feed marshmallows to the gators. He likely was the only boy in his kindergarten class who fed alligators in the wild.

I pass the entrance to the farm but don't pull in. I don't want to bother anyone without advance notice. I continue south, passing the beautiful McDowell thoroughbred horse farm and going through what we called "the palmetto woods." Here, saw palmetto plants blanket the forest floor, making one feel more like he's in Florida than Arkansas. The palmettos made this area seem even more exotic to me as a boy. Continuing toward the Dallas County line, I drive through lovely, mature pine forests.

The rain comes down harder. Our bird dogs are gone. Dad is in a nursing home. Many of the fields where we hunted are pine thickets. The memories endure.

December 4, 2010
Sugar from the Sky

Sugar fell from the sky in Little Rock shortly after 6 p.m. last Saturday.

You couldn't see it, but you can bet it was there.

I glanced over at my 13-year-old son, who had yelled himself to the point of exhaustion during the previous four hours, and hoped he would remember this moment.

I could feel my eyes misting up as the memories came flooding back—memories of the drive from Arkadelphia to Little Rock in my father's big Oldsmobile when I was a boy to attend games at War Memorial Stadium, the anticipation building with each passing mile; memories of watching the crowd simply refuse to leave following Arkansas' victory over Texas in 1979; memories of looking over at my older son (who was 9 at the time) following the original Miracle on Markham in 2002 and hoping that he would cherish this moment.

Isn't that one of the reasons for attending such events? We're there not only to enjoy the moment but hopefully to create memories along the way, perhaps even picking up a new story to tell around the dinner table 10 or 20 years from now.

The University of Arkansas' 31-23 win over Louisiana State University last Saturday afternoon was one of those memory-making games. I've been attending games at War Memorial Stadium for more than 40 years and can never remember one when the fans stood for every play. We only sat during television timeouts, and goodness knows CBS requires plenty of those.

There can be magic in late-November games—the ones that start in the sunlight and end under the lights. As was the case after the wins over Texas in 1979 and LSU in 2002, no one wanted to leave. The stadium remained packed 10 minutes after the game had ended. I hope my son remembers that. In the north end zone, motorcycle officers in their helmets from the Little Rock Police Department protected the goal post from being torn down. In the south end zone, the goal post was protected by troopers from the Arkansas State Police. I hope he remembers that. Coach Bobby Petrino was surrounded by troopers (the more troopers around a Southern football coach, the bigger the game) and television cameramen as he exited the field, smiling more than I've ever seen him smile. I hope Evan remembers that, too.

The weather had cooperated fully on this Saturday after Thanksgiving. It was a gorgeous November day for college football. We parked in Hillcrest and made the trek down Harrison, Lee and Van Buren streets. I knew immediately this wasn't an average contest when I saw people who had charged $10 to park for the Louisiana-Monroe game now charging $30. There were fans wanting tickets—lots of them—at the intersection of Van Buren and Markham. No one was selling. The policeman signaled for us to cross Markham Street. We walked into War Memorial Park for what would turn out to be an afternoon never to be forgotten.

I've never made a secret of my fondness for Little Rock games. I cherish those traditions that make our state unique, and having the state's largest university play its home football games in two places sets us apart in an era when Alabama no longer plays at Birmingham and Ole Miss no longer plays at Jackson. When those who favored moving all home games to Fayetteville made the argument that this was no longer done in Alabama and Mississippi, it only strengthened my resolve.

"Good," I would say. "That's all the more reason *not* to change.

This makes us even more special. And since when did we start using Mississippi and Alabama as examples of how to do things anyway?"

After entering the park, we made our way to stadium commissioner Brenda Scisson's tailgate party in the lot directly behind the new press box. I can think of few things better than this: a beautiful November afternoon, good friends, what promises to be a great college football game, fried chicken and pimento cheese sandwiches. An integral part of a Little Rock game day for me is the time spent watching the fans walk by. I greeted friends from all sections of our state. It is, in a sense, a large family reunion.

When it was over after almost four hours of pressure-packed action, I looked at Evan as he joined thousands of his fellow Arkansans in chanting "BCS, BCS." No, I've never been in this stadium when it was louder. We returned to Brenda's party after the game and listened to the Hog calls, yells and whoops that were coming from the now dark golf course. It was a happy night in Arkansas.

Remember this sweet November day, Evan. Remember that you sat between your mother and father. Remember how you screamed at the top of your lungs each time LSU came to the line, feeling as if your effort were playing a role in the game. Remember that touchdown as time expired in the first half. Remember that fourth-down play that resulted in a touchdown right in front of you in the fourth quarter. Remember the smile on the coach's face and the fans who didn't want to leave, staying in their seats to savor it all for a few more minutes.

Remember the day sugar fell from the sky.

April 30, 2011
The Man

On the day I attended funeral services for Coach Buddy Benson in Arkadelphia, the sports section of this newspaper featured a story about how Ohio State head football coach Jim Tressel allegedly lied to hide violations by players who traded memorabilia for cash and tattoos.

I couldn't help but contemplate the contrast.

Benson, who died on Good Friday of congestive heart failure at age 77, was the head football coach at Ouachita Baptist University for 31 seasons. Growing up in Arkadelphia, I was in awe of him. From almost the time I could walk, fall afternoons after school were spent watching his Tigers practice (at least until I was old enough to have my own football practices to attend).

Benson, who ranked up there with the likes of Grambling's Eddie Robinson and Florida State's Bobby Bowden when it came to tenure at one school, had chances to move to bigger colleges. He chose, however, to remain at a small private institution with high academic standards, which limited recruiting. When he was offered the head coaching job there in 1965, it was a risky proposition at best. Few people across the state believed Ouachita could win in football. In fact, some of Benson's closest friends thought he had doomed his career by taking on an impossible task.

After all, the school had experienced just two winning seasons the previous 16 years. That's what makes this fact so remarkable in retrospect: Benson didn't have a losing season in his first 12 years. He worked his magic quickly, winning a share of the Arkansas Intercollegiate Conference championship by his second season as head coach.

The things people look for in a college football team at the start of any season are things such as size, speed and depth. Usually, Benson's teams weren't very big and weren't very fast. There rarely was much depth. But some way, somehow, those squads consistently won more games than they lost. Benson believed the winning would take care of itself if he took care of the details.

He was a throwback in many respects. He wore a dress shirt and tie on the sidelines during games. His teams wore plain, Penn State–style uniforms. For years, Benson even resisted moving from black to white shoes.

Prior to each game, he would repeat what were known as Gen. Neyland's seven maxims. Those were the seven things said by

General Robert Neyland before every game during his three stints as the head football coach at the University of Tennessee. Benson, you see, had played for Bowden Wyatt at the University of Arkansas. Wyatt, in turn, had played for Neyland at Tennessee.

Benson's players were a reflection of their leader. They wore suits on road trips, they maintained a clean-cut appearance at all times and they played the game cleanly. His former players, who turned out by the hundreds for Tuesday's services, had a strong loyalty to the coach they called The Man. They realized that this tough taskmaster had shaped them into men.

Benson's 162-140-8 record at Ouachita is amazing when one considers how little money he had to spend on his program and how poor the facilities were. For much of his tenure, he had only two full-time assistant coaches. Most high school coaching staffs in Arkansas were larger than what he had at Ouachita. He produced 16 All-America and 208 all-conference players. Yet he considered his greatest accomplishment the fact that almost all of his players graduated. Former Tigers moved on to success in the worlds of business, medicine, law, education and other professions.

Dan Grant, who was Ouachita's president for 18 of Benson's 31 seasons as head coach, put it this way: "I taught for 22 years at Vanderbilt and the chancellor would have given his right arm to have a coach with Benson's record of accomplishments."

"I never thought of Buddy Benson as working for me or, for that matter, for Ouachita," said Ben Elrod, who replaced Grant as president. "He had his own inner compass that he consulted for his sense of direction as a coach and as a man, and the results verified the accuracy of the compass. We were friends who respected each other."

Like so many Southern males, I absolutely love college football. While I enjoy attending one or two Southeastern Conference games each season and have attended more than 20 Cotton Bowls through the years, my Saturdays generally are spent at NCAA Division II games. The competition is fierce, but there's something more pure about the game. These really are student-athletes. Few of them will ever move on to play professional football.

Jim Tressel may dress on game days like Buddy Benson once did with his tie and his sweater, but The Man never would have tolerated players trading memorabilia for cash. And tattoos? Heck, Benson didn't even allow long hair.

Here's how Fred Morrow put it in a 1975 *Arkansas Democrat* column: "His athletes are going to go to class. They're not going to abuse (or even get caught using) tobacco or alcohol, and they're going to keep their hair nice and neat, and they're going to say yes sir and no sir. Oh, they're also going to receive degrees."

Following his example, dozens of Benson's former players became high school and college coaches. Let's hope they're teaching this generation of young men the things he stood for during those 31 seasons.

May 18, 2011
Mr. Jack

It's likely that Jack Stephens never thought about golf while growing up in Prattsville during the Great Depression. As people tried to scratch out a living from that red clay soil in the pine woods of Grant County, there wasn't much time for such pursuits.

Stephens, of course, would go on to be one of the most successful business figures in Arkansas during the 20th century, joining his older brother Witt in earning Stephens Inc. of Little Rock a spot among the nation's largest investment banks. Along the way, Jack Stephens also would become an icon in the world of golf. Largely because of his legacy—Stephens died in July 2005 at age 81—former president George W. Bush will be in Little Rock on Friday of next week to celebrate the 10th anniversary of The First Tee of Central Arkansas, a youth golf program.

Bush is following in the footsteps of his father by coming to Little Rock to talk about golf. I was at The First Tee complex—the former Rock Creek Golf Course in south Little Rock—on that spring day in

2001 when the guest list consisted of former president George H. W. Bush, Arnold Palmer, Byron Nelson and PGA Tour commissioner Tim Finchem. They came to honor Stephens for the $5 million contribution that helped start The First Tee program nationally in an effort to get more children involved in the sport. Stephens then kicked in additional money to make The First Tee of Central Arkansas the model program for the country.

Stephens didn't even begin playing golf seriously until he was 35. Because of his many business connections, though, he was invited to join the famed Augusta National Golf Club in Georgia in 1962. I had the honor of working closely with Stephens for a year after I moved back to Arkansas from Washington, D.C., in 1989. I learned then that he wasn't one for social gatherings, small talk and society climbers. So I don't doubt the story his son Warren told on the night Jack Stephens was inducted into the Arkansas Sports Hall of Fame in 2000.

According to Warren Stephens, his father had left a boring social gathering early at Augusta and was walking alone along the course when someone spoke to him. The man who spoke was sitting on the porch of a cabin overlooking the course, and a conversation began. That conversation led to a friendship between Jack Stephens and Augusta National founder Bobby Jones.

In 1975, Stephens became a member of the executive committee at Augusta. In 1991, he became only the fourth chairman in the history of the club, the home of the Masters. He served in that role until 1998. After turning over the duties of chairman to Hootie Johnson, Stephens was named chairman emeritus.

Las Vegas–based writer Jack Sheehan once wrote, "Most golfers recognize Stephens as the soft-spoken gentleman with a buttery Southern drawl who presided over Butler cabin ceremonies from 1992-98, including Tiger Woods' historic 12-stroke win in 1997, the Nick Faldo-Greg Norman drama of '96 and Ben Crenshaw's emotional 'win it for Harvey Penick' triumph in 1995. One of the few structures allowed on the grounds at Augusta is the Stephens Cabin, a naming privilege that put Jack in company with Bobby Jones, Cliff Roberts and President Dwight Eisenhower. When Tiger shot 270 to win by 12 strokes, the word spread quickly that the members would try to Tiger-proof the course. Stephens didn't seem in a particular rush. When someone asked what he'd do if Tiger were to shoot even lower scores in coming years, Jack replied, 'I suppose we'll anoint him.'"

Finchem remembers approaching Stephens about The First Tee.

"We initially went to Jack for advice on the startup," he says. "We weren't asking for money. But Jack's grant really got us started in a big way....Jack Stephens was more important than any other individual in moving this program forward."

At the time of the 2001 dedication, Byron Nelson was 89. The winner of an unprecedented 11th consecutive PGA tournament in 1945, he had lived a lot of golf history. Yet Nelson didn't hesitate on that day to say, "I don't know anybody who has done for golf what Jack Stephens has."

The younger Bush now serves as the honorary chairman of The First Tee nationally. His father had been in that role since the 1997 inception of a program that has now reached more than 4.7 million children. In a sense, the event will be about fathers and sons— George H. W. Bush and George W. Bush; Jack Stephens and Warren Stephens.

Jack Stephens once told a reporter, "Golf is a great teacher in life. The same skills needed to master this game are the same skills needed to master life, a life full of unseen obstacles and excitement."

He also said, "There are only two pleasures associated with money—making it and giving it away." His gift to The First Tee bears fruit each day just off South University Avenue in Little Rock.

September 14, 2011
The Dove Opener

It's the Saturday before Labor Day, which means the start of dove season for thousands of people across the South. A dove shoot on the first day of the season is a tradition, dating back decades on many Southern farms.

Here's how Jonathan Miles once put it in *Field and Stream*: "More than the reappearance of school buses on the roads, it's the dove opener that signals a summer's passing in the Deep South, which is perhaps why dove shoots—big, communal events with dozens of hunters scattered throughout a field—have so long been paired with celebrations, barbecues, grand revels. In northern climes, the hunting of mourning doves—which some consider songbirds— is a controversy-scarred topic.

"In the South, however, dove hunting is a venerable tradition, older than bourbon and as beloved as college football. Dove hunting offers challenging pass shooting, it's true, but here it's about much more than that: Kids, wives, dogs, camaraderie, post-hunt cocktails, grilled dove breasts and pork barbecue, old customs and the changing of the seasons."

Growing up, Labor Day weekend meant three things in my family—food, football and dove hunting. My father absolutely loved to hunt doves. If the season opened on a Saturday, we often would hunt in the morning and again in the afternoon. We also would hunt on Sunday afternoon. Sunday morning, of course, was reserved for church. On Labor Day, we once more would hunt during both the morning and afternoon.

My dad was a superb shot. He had been raised in Saline County in a poor family during the Great Depression. Being able to shoot well at rabbits, squirrels, ducks, doves and quail could sometimes mean the difference between a supper with meat on the table and one with only biscuits and gravy.

The Labor Day morning hunt was often with my father's college roommate from the 1940s at Ouachita, O. J. "Buddy" Harris, and Buddy's two sons, Cliff and Tommy. Cliff went on to be a pretty decent football player for Ouachita Baptist University and the Dallas Cowboys. And Tommy was a good college football player for the Arkansas Razorbacks.

If my September 2 birthday fell at the start of dove season, I often requested fried dove breasts, rice and gravy for my birthday dinner. My mother always obliged.

My dad delighted in telling the story each Labor Day of how he and some friends once gave dozens of dove breasts to a man who loved both moonshine and wild game.

Dad asked the man several weeks later, "How were those dove breasts?"

"I don't want you to ever give me another dove," the man replied. "I've never been as sick in my life as I was for two days. I either got some bad doves or some bad whiskey. I would like to think it was the doves."

Autumn officially arrives next week. Some of us welcome the fall on the first Saturday in September, though. Here's the irony for someone who has such fond memories of past dove hunts: If I go at all these days, it's just on opening day.

Most Southern dove hunters are that way. They go into the fields on opening morning and they don't go again. College football takes up the other fall Saturdays for Southern males.

When I go to an opening morning hunt, it's usually at the Meacham family farm on the Monroe-Lee county line. Other obligations kept me away this month. I missed seeing friends such as Wiley, Steve, Don, Mickey, Rex and Tom. Yes, there's another Rex who hunts there. We also duck hunt together on occasion.

They call Rex Johnson the Rex Who Cooks since he's a talented breakfast cook. I, on the other hand, have been nicknamed the Rex Who Eats. The brunch, you see, is as much a part of the trip to the farm as the duck and dove hunts. There are usually pork chops, bacon, sausage, scrambled eggs, biscuits, muscadine jelly and fried potatoes. A nap is the order of the day after brunch.

Heading east on Interstate 40 through the darkness on that first morning of dove season, it's easy to spot the fellow pilgrims. Some of them have dog boxes in the back of their pickup trucks. Other pickups carry four-wheelers. When the weather is hot, as it often is on the first Saturday of September, you find yourself sweating and swatting mosquitoes prior to daylight. You look forward to the rising sun, not only because it means the start of shooting but also because it drives off the mosquitoes.

I usually maintain my title as the world's worst shot, though I can make myself useful cleaning the doves. While my dad never succeeded in teaching me to shoot like he could, he did teach me how to pop out a dove breast. When the other Rex is hard at work in the kitchen, I help clean the game. The number of birds killed isn't a major deal. The first morning of dove season in the South is more about the friendships, the jokes and the tall tales. It's about getting outside and watching the sun come up over the rural landscape. It's about being able to sense that our long, hot summer is ending.

"Southern dove hunting is a cultural social function; it is about camaraderie and, more importantly, tradition," R. Michael Diullo writes at www.gundogsonline.com. "It is a community event, and it is quite common to see three or more generations of family members heading out together to the dove fields. Dove hunting's history and traditions can be traced far back into the culture—traditions which have been handed down through generations of Southern hunters, some of whose lineage can be traced to the original settlers of the very land on which they hunt.

Indeed, I hunt on a farm that has been in the same family for almost 100 years. Each time I'm there, I feel as if I'm playing my part in sustaining a great Southern tradition.

December 7, 2011
Championship Games

It has become a tradition in our home. I head to Little Rock's War Memorial Stadium the first two weekends each December to witness the six high school state championship football games.

The Arkansas Activities Association holds three games the first weekend of December—one on Friday night, one on Saturday afternoon and one on Saturday night. There are another three games

the second weekend of December that follow the same schedule—
one game on Friday and two on Saturday.

This past weekend, the old stadium played host to two of the
best high school football games I've seen. On Friday night, a senior
cornerback from El Dorado named Deandre Williams intercepted a
pass near the goal line in the closing seconds as El Dorado held on for
a 24-20 victory over Lake Hamilton for the Class 6A championship.
It was the third consecutive state championship for El Dorado, a
town that loves high school football as much as any city in Arkansas.
Lake Hamilton and El Dorado have played seven times the past four
seasons, and the three most recent games have been decided by a
total of 12 points. Lake Hamilton had won the regular season game
this fall.

On Saturday afternoon, Bentonville came into the Class 7A
championship game as a heavy favorite against Fayetteville.
Bentonville entered with a record of 12-0, having routed Fayetteville
by a score of 41-6 on September 23. Bentonville had a 25-game
winning streak, an offense averaging 44 points per game and a
defense allowing an average of only 8.9 points per game.

Fayetteville trailed 21-7 at the end of the third quarter but fought
back, scoring touchdowns with 11:27 and 4:39 remaining to tie the
game. In fact, the Bulldogs had a chance to win with 27 seconds left,
but Max Coffin's 40-yard field goal attempt was wide to the right.
In overtime, Bentonville got the ball first and scored in three plays.
It looked as if a team that had not lost since the second round of the
2009 playoffs would hold on.

Fayetteville was down to its final play, a fourth-and-goal from
three yards away. Quarterback Austin Allen passed to wide receiver
Reid Holmes for a touchdown to bring the Bulldogs within a point,
28-27. Fayetteville coach Daryl Patton could have called for an extra
point to send the game to a second overtime. Instead, he decided to
do something else. He made the call to go for two—to win or lose the
state championship on the next play.

It was like a scene from one of those corny sports movies. Allen rolled to his right and then looked back to his left. He threw to tight end Tyler Tuck, who cradled the football, setting off a wild celebration on the field and in the east stands. Fayetteville, a 35-point loser to Bentonville in September, had done the seemingly impossible. The Bulldogs had won the state championship.

It reminded me why I love high school football. I thought back to 1976, when an entire town's emotions seemed to rise and fall with the fortunes of the high school team on which I was the starting center. No one picked the Arkadelphia Badgers to make it to the state championship game that year (the team had been 5-5 the preceding season), but once we got rolling, we were hard to stop. We upset a highly rated Camden Panther team early in the season and soon moved to the top of the rankings in our classification. Our tailback, Trent Bryant, captured the attention of major college coaches. He would go on to play at the University of Arkansas and play for a time in the NFL for the Kansas City Chiefs.

On a miserable homecoming night during which the wind blew and the rain fell, we tied Hot Springs Lakeside on a muddy field. We finished the regular season 9-0-1. In the first round of the playoffs at Star City, we scored on our first three possessions and rolled to an easy victory. Cabot posed a threat in the semifinal game, which was played at War Memorial Stadium. In a defensive struggle, Cabot fumbled a punt and Arkadelphia recovered and later scored the winning touchdown.

In those days, the championship games were not all played at War Memorial Stadium. The decision was made to hold the title game in Arkadelphia at Henderson State University's stadium. The week before that game was like this week has been weather-wise in much of Arkansas, as several inches of rain fell. The field was a quagmire, slowing our running game and leading to mistakes.

Trailing late, the Badgers drove the length of the field. Twice in the final minute, we appeared to score, but each time the officials marked the football short. The game ended with the favored Badgers inches from the end zone, upset by Mena. It has been 35 years, and I still think about those final plays. The team has never held a reunion of any type.

Perhaps with the passage of time, the boys of 1976, now men in their 50s, will manage to get together one of these days and discuss that season.

Our quarterback, Darren O'Quinn, is now a Little Rock lawyer.

"Everyone was so deeply hurt by the game that we all just never talked about it again," he says. "It's kind of like the 1969 Razorbacks who lost to Texas with Frank Broyles never wanting to watch the film or talk about it. It's a shame because we had everything to be proud of. There were a lot of great competitors on that 1976 team. It was a magical and life-changing year for me.

"I remember we had basketball practice the day after the loss, and I was too sad to go. But Daddy made me. The thing I learned eventually is life is not always fair, but you have to keep getting up, putting your feet on the floor and competing."

It's a lesson the now heartbroken players from Lake Hamilton and Bentonville will learn in time.

December 28, 2011
The Jockey

Alonzo "Lonnie" Clayton reached sports stardom at an early age. In 1892, at age 15, he became the youngest jockey to win the Kentucky Derby. It's safe to say, however, that most Arkansans have never heard of Clayton.

The Arkansas Sports Hall of Fame will attempt to remedy that situation February 3 when Clayton is among the 11 individual inductees. Clayton is one of two inductees from the posthumous category.

Born in Kansas City, Kansas, in 1876, Clayton moved with his parents to what's now North Little Rock when he was 10. There were nine children in the family, and finances were tight even though his father had steady work as a carpenter. Clayton worked as a hotel errand boy and shoeshine boy to earn extra income for his family. It was noted in an 1896 story in the *Thoroughbred Record* that Clayton had attended school as a boy and was considered "exceptionally bright."

Clayton was only 12 when he left home to join his brother, Albertus, a jockey who was riding at the time for the legendary E. J. "Lucky" Baldwin. Alonzo Clayton soon found work as an exercise rider for Baldwin's stables. His first race as a jockey came in 1890 at Clifton, New Jersey. He had his first victory later that year.

Thoroughbred racing had become one of the top sports in America by that time, and it didn't take long for those on the East Coast to recognize Clayton as a rising star. He won the Jerome Stakes aboard Picknicker and the Champagne Stakes aboard Azra at Morris Park in Westchester County, New York, in 1891. On May 11, 1892, Clayton was aboard Azra as his mount came from behind in the stretch to win the Kentucky Derby by a nose. Clayton became one of only two 15-year-old jockeys to win America's most famous race.

Clayton would be in the money in the Kentucky Derby three more times, finishing second in 1893, third in 1895 and second in 1897. Clayton's best year was 1895 when he had 144 wins and finished in the money in almost 60 percent of his races. He won the Arkansas Derby that year at the Little Rock Jockey Club's Clinton Park. In 1896, he became one of the few black jockeys ever to compete in the Preakness Stakes at Baltimore, where he finished third.

Racing historian Ed Hotaling said Clayton "became one of the great riders of the New York circuit all through the 1890s, but he rode all over the country."

"While spending most of his time on the road, Clayton, who never married, came back to North Little Rock regularly to visit family," Cary Bradburn wrote in the online Encyclopedia of Arkansas History & Culture. "He bought his parents a farm in 1894 in what is now Sherwood and had a Queen Anne–style house built in North Little Rock in 1895."

Bradburn wrote that while the reason for Clayton's departure from Arkansas isn't clear, "in a larger context racism did contribute.

In the early 1900s, bigotry drove black jockeys out of the sport they had dominated in America since the mid-1600s. Most stable owners stopped hiring them when sanctions, and even physical threats against black jockeys, increased. Some went overseas, as Clayton may have done."

Indeed, black jockeys once ruled the sport. Hotaling told the *Baltimore Sun* that they were "the first great American athletes, white or black, and they were written out of the history books. The saddest part is that they weren't and haven't been brought back into the sport."

Black jockeys won at least 15 of the first 28 runnings of the Kentucky Derby. As racing gained prominence following the Civil War, many horse owners used their former slaves as jockeys. Former slaves tended to gravitate toward the sport because they were comfortable working with horses. Jim Crow laws changed that. The majority of black jockeys were gone by 1910, though some continued to race in more dangerous steeplechase events.

"Once economics—big money—came into racing, the black jockey was pushed out," Inez Chapel of the group African-Americans in Horse Racing told the *Sun.* "And racism is still alive. There are black jockeys out there, but they do what they have to do. They claim to be Jamaican or something else. If you speak in an unknown tongue, then the color of your skin doesn't bother people."

The last black jockey to ride in the Preakness Stakes was Willie Simms in 1898, and the last black jockey to compete in the Belmont Stakes was Jimmy Lee in 1908. The last black jockey to compete in the Kentucky Derby was Henry King aboard Planet in 1921.

"That was a rarity," Hotaling said. "If people see that and think black jockeys competed into the 1920s alongside white riders, that's just not true. By 1910, they were all but gone."

Clayton and his family lived in what later would be known as the Engelberger House in North Little Rock from 1895 to 1899. His earnings had enabled him to build a home the *Arkansas Gazette* described in 1895 as the "finest house on the North Side." The home at 2105 Maple St. was purchased by Swiss immigrant Joseph Engelberger in 1912 and was listed in 1990 on the National Register of Historic Places.

In April 1901, Clayton was arrested at Aqueduct in New York for allegedly fixing a race. The charge later was dismissed, but his career was over for all practical purposes. He made short comeback attempts in Montana in 1902 and Memphis in 1904. Clayton died in March 1917 in California of tuberculosis. He's buried in Los Angeles.

January 2, 2012
Piney Creek

The rain was coming down hard when my alarm sounded at 3:30 a.m. It wasn't cold enough for ice, but it wasn't warm either. The Weather Channel said it was 39 degrees in Little Rock.

There are very few things that will motivate me to get up at that hour. A trip to hunt ducks with Wiley Meacham at the Piney Creek Duck Club at Monroe is one of them. I've written about Wiley before. He's 80 now, still getting up in the middle of the night and making the drive from his home in Brinkley to his farm office under the large pecan trees on the land where he was born and raised.

The date had been marked on my calendar for weeks. Steve "Wild Man" Wilson of the Arkansas Game & Fish Commission had called to inform me that he would film the Christmas edition of his "Talkin' Outdoors" television show at Piney Creek. Those watching on Christmas Day witnessed grown men standing in cold water, wearing camouflage Santa caps and singing Christmas songs.

"Why would adults get up in the middle of the night and then act like that?" my wife asked.

Unless you've experienced the mallard madness in the flooded green timber of east Arkansas, you can't answer that question. It goes far beyond shooting ducks. It's watching the sun rise, listening to the owls and geese, exchanging stories and giving friends a hard time after bad shots.

It's listening to Steve Meacham and Don Thompson call the ducks. It's sharing a bench with Rex Johnson.

Back where we parked the boats, Joe Weiss was busy cooking that Friday morning. Yes, cooking. You see, these flooded woods have a kitchen. In 1987, a grocery store owner named Lattimore Michael opened the first Back Yard Burgers restaurant in Cleveland, Mississippi. A year later, Weiss, a native of nearby Clarksdale, became a franchisee and was instrumental in the expansion of the chain.

Weiss now owns the Blue & White Restaurant, a roadside classic that has been in business along U.S. Highway 61 in Tunica, Miss., since 1937. On this gray morning, though, he was playing chef in the flooded timber of the Arkansas Delta—grilling slices of teal while putting out crackers and Mickle's Pickles from Picayune, Miss., truly among the best pickles I've ever had.

Standing there eating slices of grilled teal on a cracker, I thought about the storied tradition of Arkansas duck hunting. It has become a family custom to have wild Arkansas ducks for dinner in the days leading up to Christmas. I brought two mallard drakes back with me, stopping at McSwain's Sports Center on U.S. Highway 165 in North Little Rock to have the ladies in the back room clean them. With dozens of ducks in the room, it was obvious that others had been hunting that rainy Friday morning. They said they could clean my ducks while I waited, so I watched them work their magic.

I later walked by the Peabody Hotel's lobby fountain in Little Rock to pay homage to the four mallard hens and one mallard drake that swim there. Even the famous Peabody ducks have their genesis in an east Arkansas duck hunt. In 1932, Frank Schutt, general manager of the original Peabody Hotel at Memphis, accompanied a friend on an Arkansas duck hunting trip.

The hotel website tells what happened after that: "The men had a little too much Jack Daniel's Tennessee sippin' whiskey and thought it would be funny to place some of their live duck decoys (it was legal then for hunters to use live decoys) in the beautiful Peabody fountain. Three small English call ducks were selected as 'guinea pigs,' and the reaction was nothing short of enthusiastic. Soon, five North American mallard ducks would replace the original ducks."

I've long enjoyed reading the outdoors stories of Nash Buckingham, a Tennessean who died in 1971 at age 90. Buckingham wrote nine books and hundreds of magazine articles. He preferred hunting for ducks and bobwhite quail, the two types of hunting my father most enjoyed. Dad always considered duck and quail hunting to be gentlemen's sports. Arkansas duck hunting figured prominently in much of what Buckingham wrote.

On December 1, 1948, Buckingham was hunting near Clarendon with a friend named Clifford Green. At Green's car, they met a game warden, who recognized Buckingham and asked to see his famous 12-gauge shotgun that had been nicknamed Bo Whoop after the deep sound it made upon discharge. The warden laid the gun on the car's back fender. Buckingham and Green later drove off without retrieving the shotgun. Upon realizing their mistake, they turned around and slowly retraced their route. They never found the gun. Buckingham wrote often about the loss of Bo Whoop. Like Elvis sightings, there were regular Bo Whoop sightings, all of which proved false.

In 2005, a man brought a gun to a South Carolina gunsmith for repair. The gunsmith, Jim Kelly, was a student of hunting history. He saw an inscription that read "made for Nash Buckingham." He had found Bo Whoop. The owner later auctioned the gun to pay for medical expenses for his sick father. In March 2010, 84-year-old Hal Howard Jr. learned of the upcoming auction. Howard, a former executive at the investment banking firm T. Rowe Price, had been raised in Memphis. His father was Buckingham's best friend and hunting partner. Hal Howard Jr., in fact, was Buckingham's godson.

Howard shelled out $201,250 for Bo Whoop, the third-highest amount ever paid for an American shotgun. A month later, it was announced that Howard was donating Bo Whoop to the Ducks Unlimited national headquarters at Memphis. What has never been clear is how Bo Whoop got from the woods near Clarendon to

Savannah, Georgia, where a sawmill foreman bought it for $50 in the 1950s, not knowing its significance. It's just another part of the mystique of that fine Arkansas duck hunting tradition.

February 22, 2012
The *Original* Original

A man representing the tiny *Times-Herald* in Forrest City once was among the best-known sportswriters in America—at least among other sportswriters, coaches and athletes. Readers outside St. Francis County might not have known who Raoul H. Carlisle was, but those in the sports world knew him well. Carlisle made sure of that.

He seemingly was everywhere—the Triple Crown races, championship fights and always the Sugar Bowl. He had a special place in his heart for New Orleans.

His grandson, Craig Carlisle Morledge, says he had four great loves in his life: "My grandmother, Martha Louise Carlisle; Southeastern Conference football; watching the ponies run; and killing his limit in the L'Anguille River bottoms every morning the duck season was in."

Brett Norsworthy of Forrest City, who co-hosts a daily sports talk radio show in Memphis, describes Carlisle as "the *original* original."

Carlisle came to mind earlier this month while reading an online column by Peter King of *Sports Illustrated* about King's trip to the Super Bowl in Indianapolis.

"Interesting being with Randy Moss (the announcer, not the pass-catcher) Sunday for NBC on the pregame show," King wrote. "Told me a great story. Moss, of course, is a big horse guy."

Moss, a Hot Springs native, covered Oaklawn Park for the *Arkansas Gazette* and then moved to the *Arkansas Democrat* following the 1982 Arkansas Derby in one of the first high-profile *Gazette* defections in the newspaper war.

Here's what Moss told King: "I've been to 31 of the last 32 Kentucky Derbies. The first one was amazing. They have a seniority system in the press box, and I knew one of the veteran writers, a guy from Arkansas, who was going to watch it off the TV monitor because he couldn't see that well. So he told me I could use his seat, which was No. 2 in the press box. But he said, 'I better take you down and introduce you to the two guys next to you so they don't think you're stealing the seat.'

"He takes me down, and I meet the two guys. He says, 'This is Dick Young.' Then, 'This is Red Smith.' Wow. I was 21. They were the two guys who'd covered the Derby the longest. I've been to every Derby since then but one, and I've never had a seat quite that good."

So Red Smith of the *New York Times*, a legend in American journalism, had seat No. 1. Who was this Arkansan with seat No. 2? It was Raoul Carlisle.

Four years earlier in 1976, the folks at Pimlico in Baltimore began the Old Hilltop Award. The award was designed to pay tribute to members of the media who covered thoroughbred racing "with excellence and distinction." The first two honorees were Red Smith and Raoul Carlisle.

On November 22, 1980, less than seven months after giving up his Kentucky Derby seat to Moss, Carlisle was killed while returning home from a Ducks Unlimited banquet in Forrest City when his vehicle was struck by a train. He died a month short of his 83rd birthday. Carlisle was famous in his older years for approaching young sportswriters like me in the Oaklawn press box and telling story after story. He would carry a scrapbook to verify that he actually had done all the things he talked about.

Arkansas sportswriter Jim Bailey once described Carlisle as a "fellow who isn't very easy to explain in a few words."

Carlisle began attending sports events across the country as a young man, getting credentials through his work at the *Times-Herald*. In the 1920s, it wasn't as difficult to obtain credentials to major events as it is these days. Carlisle spent a lot of time on trains attending games, fights and races.

"By the time media requirements began to tighten, Raoul had

been grandfathered in," says Moss, who now lives in Minnesota and works for the NFL Network in addition to NBC.

Steve Cady of the *New York Times* mentioned Carlisle in a 1975 article, noting that he was covering his 57th Kentucky Derby. That means Carlisle would have seen Sir Barton and every other Triple Crown winner. With Carlisle having died in November 1980, there was no one to sit between Smith and Young at the Kentucky Derby on the first Saturday in May 1981.

"With their eccentric but gentlemanly buffer gone, Young was moved into the No. 2 seat at the Derby next to Mr. Smith, his archrival who Young had actually criticized in print," Moss says.

On January 1, 1980—the day Alabama played Arkansas in the Sugar Bowl (the Crimson Tide won its second consecutive national title that day)—the *Tuscaloosa News* had a front-page blurb promoting an inside story. The blurb read: "Raoul Carlisle has seen his share of Sugar Bowls—all 46, in fact—and can keep you entertained talking about them."

I was in New Orleans covering the Sugar Bowl that year. Carlisle had bragged about his "dear friend" Paul "Bear" Bryant, the Alabama coach. Some of us were betting he didn't even know Bryant. Just before a joint news conference with Arkansas head coach Lou Holtz, Bryant walked into the room. To our amazement, he strolled over to Carlisle and gave him a hug.

The *original* original from Forrest City really did know everyone in the world of sports, it seemed.

March 14, 2012
Coach Tate

If you're one of the lucky ones, you had at least one teacher who inspired you to be all you could be, a person who pushed you further than you thought you could go. For a lot of athletes, that person was a coach rather than a classroom teacher.

For a lot of boys in the South, to be even more specific, that person was a football coach. For me, that person was Coach Willie Tate of

Arkadelphia, who died last week at age 69 following a lengthy battle with Alzheimer's disease. It's hard to believe he was only 17 years older than me. He was a giant of my youth, a man a whole town could look up to.

Raised in a large family at Gum Springs in Clark County, Tate attended college at what's now the University of Arkansas at Pine Bluff and became a star football and baseball player. He began his coaching career at Hope, moving later to Arkadelphia. He would spend the rest of his career there, working first at Goza Junior High School, later at Arkadelphia High School and finally at Henderson State University.

He was my coach for four of my final five years of football. He was the head coach in the eighth and ninth grades. In the 11th grade, after I had earned the job of starting center, he moved up to the high school level as our offensive line coach. I'm constantly quoting Tate more than 35 years later. He had that kind of effect on me. There are, no doubt, a lot of men across Arkansas who could tell similar stories about the football coaches who helped mold them.

He would warn us about "season women," those girls who would date you during the fall if you were a football player and then drop you for a basketball player in the winter.

He would preach self-esteem and then tell us, "If you ever read that Willie Tate committed suicide, you better call the police. Somebody has murdered me and made it appear to be a suicide. I would never do that because I love Willie Tate."

He would say "let me show you how to block," and we would all back up. Yes, we were in full pads. Yes, he was in shorts and a T-shirt. But no one wanted to be on the business end of Tate's forearm. He was a gifted athlete who had earned All-Southwestern Athletic Conference honors in both football and basketball in college.

We loved the man off the field as much as we feared him when we were on the field. Arkadelphia had experienced severe racial tensions in the spring of 1972. By the fall of 1973, I was playing for Tate. He was black, I am white, but color mattered to none of us when we were under his guidance. He convinced us we were all Goza Junior High Beaver red and white and later Arkadelphia High Badger red and blue.

As a junior starter on a team filled with seniors, I was determined not to disappoint my offensive line coach. If you missed an assignment or happened to be called for holding, you would go 20 yards out of your way when coming off the field to avoid running directly by Tate. He wouldn't scream at you. Instead, he would put his hands on his hips while giving you a stare that burned all the way to your soul.

He would spend weekends watching the film of Friday's game while grading each of his linemen. The grades would be passed out on Monday. A positive word on that sheet was enough to put an extra bounce in your step during the Monday afternoon practice. The humidity always seemed to hang heavier than in other parts of town at our practice field. As the sweat poured out of us, the coach would laugh and sing about it being a "blue Monday."

In the state semifinal game of 1976, our undefeated Badgers took on a talented Cabot team at Little Rock's War Memorial Stadium. The Cabot defense had shut out the majority of its opponents and was touted as one of the best high school defenses ever in Arkansas. I had upper body strength in those days and didn't mind blocking large defensive linemen. The small, quick ones were the ones who bothered me. Cabot had the quickest nose guard I had ever come up against.

At halftime, as I sat in our dressing room, the coach walked over to me and said, "If you will block your man, we will be in the state championship game." We recovered a fumbled punt late, drove the ball into the end zone and won 7-6 to advance to the state title game.

The next week, we were upset by Mena. The game ended with the ball just inches away from what would have been the winning touchdown. I was the deep snapper in addition to being the regular center. The playing conditions on the muddy field were the worst I had ever experienced. I had made a bad snap on a punt and was blaming myself for the loss. More than anything, I believed I had let Willie Tate down.

I had my face buried in my hands when I felt that strong arm reach around me and give me a hug. It was Tate. He whispered in my ear that it would be okay and told me to take my muddy uniform off and go shower. With the tears still coming down my cheeks, I said, "Yes sir." I still have my muddy mouthpiece from that game.

We lost a large number of seniors to graduation. Our quarterback was hurt early in the 1977 campaign, and my senior season was a disappointment. What kept me going was the chance to have another practice under Tate's guidance.

Following that senior season, I was chosen by a Hope radio station for something called the KXAR Dream Team. It was meant to honor the top high school football players in southwest Arkansas.

Tate said he would take me to Hope for the banquet. We rode in his Ford, just the two of us cruising down Interstate 30. With my football career at an end, he discussed things with me not as he would with a player but instead as a friend.

As we drove back to Arkadelphia that night, it hit me somewhere around Prescott. I was no longer being treated as a boy. Under Willie Tate's tutelage, I had become a man.

November 21, 2012
Dunklin's Ducks

Saturday was a high holy day for many Arkansans, since it marked the start of duck season. As usual, the lodge was full at George Dunklin Jr.'s Five Oaks in Arkansas County, which annually attracts hunters from across the country.

"We had a great morning," Dunklin said. "There was an unusual amount of mallards for this early in the season. It was an absolutely gorgeous morning."

On June 30, Dunklin's seven-year term on the Arkansas Game and Fish Commission ended. He was the commission's chairman during his final year and a leading proponent for finding innovative

There's a mystique to hunting ducks in the flooded green timber of east Arkansas.

ways to attract migrating ducks to Arkansas. In May, Dunklin will become president of Ducks Unlimited, the world's most famous waterfowl conservation organization. He will be the 42nd president in DU history and only the second from Arkansas. E. L. McHaney of Little Rock became the DU president in 1948.

DU began in 1937 during the Dust Bowl era as waterfowl numbers dropped due to drought. The organization was formed to preserve breeding areas in the Canadian prairies. From 1937 to 1983, all funds raised were spent in Canada. Since 1983, money has been spent for waterfowl conservation efforts in the United States and Mexico in addition to Canada.

DU now has almost 550,000 adult members and about 46,000 youth members. Local chapters host more than 4,400 fundraising events each year, meaning that Dunklin will spend a lot of time away from his beloved Five Oaks during his two years as president. Since its founding, DU has helped conserve 6.3 million acres in Canada, 4.5 million acres in the United States and 1.8 million acres in Mexico. The United States has lost more than half its original wetlands and continues to lose an average of 80,000 wetland acres each year. When soybean prices soared in the 1970s, thousands of acres of wetlands in east Arkansas were drained for row-crop agriculture. Much of that was marginal farmland at best.

In an attempt to reverse the trend, Dunklin has planted thousands of hardwood trees. I spent a day at Five Oaks earlier this fall. As I rode with Dunklin, he talked at length about how one area had been cutover timberland when he took over the farm in 1980. Dunklin eventually leveled the fields and then created small sloughs 18 inches below the grade of the rest of the land. He also built mounds that are 18 inches above grade. Years from now, when the hardwoods are mature, this area will provide duck hunting in flooded timber. For now, it's a waterfowl rest area. Between these hardwoods and a small lake is a 15-acre corn plot that provides additional food.

"We do everything we can to make it easy on ducks," Dunklin said. "It takes less energy for them to stand on those 18-inch mounds. We come in here and mow the field before the season. Again, that's designed to make it easy on the ducks. If a duck is expending more energy than he's consuming, he will go somewhere else. We don't want those ducks expending too much energy. Our goal is to provide them with everything they need from the moment they arrive in November until the day they leave in January."

At the height of the duck season, Dunklin will have 3,000 acres of timber flooded. Back at the Five Oaks lodge on the day of my visit, his chef was planning menus for the coming hunting season. Five Oaks specializes in two-day corporate hunts. The lodge is available for business meetings and corporate retreats the remainder of the year. Dunklin's home is just down the road.

When he took over the farm, which long had been in his mother's family, Dunklin lived at DeWitt. He moved into a room in the lodge after buying it in 1983 and built a house when he got married in 1987. Dunklin's wife, Livia, spent her early years in New York City. She moved to Memphis at age 13 when her father, a cardiologist, took a job there. The two met when Dunklin was working at the Memphis Racquet Club. The couple has three daughters. Dunklin says that though his wife was raised a city girl, there would be no way to get her out of the country now.

These days, Dunklin has his own full-time biologist, Jody Pagan, whom he hired away from the U.S. Department of Agriculture in October 2005. The two men formed Five Oaks Wildlife Services, which now advises landowners across the country.

"We can share everything we've learned and help ensure they don't make the mistakes we've made," Dunklin says. "I love going around the country and looking at various places and the habitat they offer."

In 2002, Dunklin developed a type of golden millet that can be used to improve waterfowl habitat while also providing forage for quail, dove and turkey. He sells the millet seeds nationwide. Dunklin and Pagan also operate a nursery where they grow bottomland hardwoods that are used for wetlands restoration. They even sell a full line of water-control structures to regulate water levels.

Their literature reads: "Remember there are no magic bullets in waterfowl management, but there are certain practices you can implement to improve habitat quality. You can't control the weather, nor can you control the hatch, but you can control your habitat quality."

Dunklin grew up in Pine Bluff with tennis as a passion. Duck hunting also became a passion after he and a cousin, Bill Dunklin, came up on thousands of ducks in the 1970s at a flooded spot near Reydell in Jefferson County. What's known as the "Reydell hole" is reserved for family and friends. Through the years, Dunklin has become even more interested in the science—or is it an art?—of attracting and holding ducks. Rarely has anyone been as qualified to serve as the Ducks Unlimited president.

January 9, 2013
Big Lake Baptism

I stepped down from the elevated duck blind, anxious to get in the boat for a tour of Pulaski County's Big Lake. Unfortunately, with my left leg in the boat and my right leg still in the blind, the boat moved away from me. I wound up in the water on a cold Saturday morning. Here's the good news: The water wasn't deep, and my waders had no leaks. Amazingly, I didn't have any wet clothes.

The other hunters called it my Big Lake baptism and vowed to name the spot just behind the blind the Rex Hole. I, in turn, explained to them that I was doing in-depth research for a newspaper column and wanted to determine the lake's depth. I'm sure they'll embellish the story in the months and years to come at the Big Lake Hunting Club. After all, what's a hunting club for if not to make memories and turn them into tall tales?

Located just a few miles from the southern border of the state's largest city, Big Lake is one of this state's historic and natural treasures. Even though it's in the state's most populous county, most people don't know it's there. About 1,100 acres are covered in water. There's some open water, but much of Big Lake is filled with thick stands of cypress and tupelo.

The club has a history that dates back to 1886 when it was incorporated as the Big Lake Club by several of Little Rock's most prominent citizens. Later documents list it as the Big Lake Hunting Club, the Big Lake Sportsman's Club and the Big Lake Sportsmen's Club. Among the familiar last names on the list of founders are Worthen, Kavanaugh, Penick and Geyer. Future governor Carl Bailey was an early member of the club.

Big Lake and almost 4,000 surrounding acres now are owned by Arkadelphia banker Ross Whipple. That's good news since Whipple is among the state's foremost conservationists. Despite its proximity to Little Rock, there's virtually no chance the land will be developed under Whipple's ownership.

The story of how the original Big Lake Club disbanded reads like something out of a Southern Gothic novel. In 1943, someone began putting arsenic in the sugar at the Big Lake clubhouse. It couldn't be determined who the culprit was and who was the intended victim. No one would talk. So the members decided to disband the club. The problems were exacerbated by the fact that the country's focus on winning World War II left little time or disposable income for such a club.

Shortly after the end of the war, south Arkansas timber magnate Hugh Ross learned that the land was for sale. Each week, Ross would take a Missouri Pacific train from Arkadelphia to Little Rock for a Wednesday night poker game at downtown Little Rock's Marion Hotel, an event that attracted many of the state's top business leaders. Knowing of Ross' desire to purchase timberland, Little Rock investment banker W. R. "Witt" Stephens made him aware of Big Lake's availability. The sale was completed in 1946.

Hugh Ross' father-in-law, J .G. Clark, had begun amassing thousands of acres of timberland in southwest Arkansas in the 1880s. Ross' daughter, Jane Ross, became a leading Arkansas philanthropist. Jane Ross died in July 1999, but the Ross Foundation still manages more than 60,000 acres of timberland with the proceeds used for charitable purposes. The Ross family occasionally used the Big Lake clubhouse for family fishing outings, but it was no longer operated as a club.

In 1951, Hugh Ross tore down the original clubhouse and used some of the cypress timber to build a house on Lake Hamilton.

"They would come up here to fish from time to time, but after the house on Lake Hamilton was built, there wasn't much reason to come to Big Lake," Whipple says. "The land was more of an investment than a club at that point."

What Whipple describes as "a group of Cajuns with pirogues" was hired by the Ross family to clear cypress trees from the lake. The valuable timber was processed on the site at a small sawmill. Jane Ross' first love was photography, and she took photographs of the operation. Whipple still has those photos in a scrapbook. Whipple, who began running the Ross Foundation in the late 1970s, first came to Big Lake more than three decades ago. In 1996, he bought Big Lake from Jane Ross and has been adding acreage ever since. He moved a mobile home onto the property in 1997 to use for occasional duck hunts. In 2004, he built a plush lodge on the site of the original 1886 structure.

Several years ago, a central Arkansas construction executive named David Gatzke approached Whipple with a box that was filled with records from the early years of the Big Lake Club. Knowing that Gatzke often hunted in the area, a descendant of J. W. Mons (who was once an officer in the club) had given Gatzke the files. Gatzke gave them to Whipple, who had the files restored. Many of the photos, maps and letters now line the walls of the lodge, making it as much a museum of Arkansas history as it is a duck club.

Honorary memberships in the Big Lake Club were given to governors, U.S. senators, judges, county officials and others. Whipple has dozens of thank-you letters from those officials. He jokes that the honorary memberships were especially popular during Prohibition. The 1886 articles of incorporation, bylaws and rules are in a bound book, all handwritten in beautiful calligraphy.

It's hard to imagine that there are many hunting clubs in the country with such a rich history and so many intact records. It's even harder to imagine that an ecological wonder such as Big Lake sits on Little Rock's doorstep, hidden in plain sight. My Big Lake baptism was memorable in more ways than one.

November 27, 2013
The Football Doctor

For more than a quarter of a century, Jeff Root and I have spent fall Saturdays in press boxes from Alabama to Oklahoma broadcasting small college football games on the radio. If you had asked me 20 years ago, I would have told you that we would have given up our hobby of calling Ouachita Baptist University football games by now, leaving the lengthy drives to younger men with more energy and fewer family obligations. But a funny thing happened along the way. The older we get, the more important these fall Saturdays together become.

Jeff now serves as the dean of the School of Humanities at

Ouachita. When he received his doctorate a number of years ago, I began referring to him on the air as the Football Doctor, a takeoff on Dr. Ferdie Pacheco, the former personal physician for Muhammad Ali. Pacheco became a television boxing analyst in the 1970s and was known as the Fight Doctor. Jeff also has been the voice of the Arkadelphia High School football team for more than a quarter of a century. On the third Saturday in November, we had the honor of broadcasting one of the greatest football games either of us had ever witnessed.

The Battle of the Ravine in Arkadelphia is always special since it's the only college football game in the country that sees the visiting team walk to a road game. It was even more special this year because the Reddies of Henderson State University were seeking a second consecutive undefeated regular season. At 10-0, Henderson was ranked fourth nationally in NCAA Division II coming into the game. Standing in the way of the Reddies' undefeated regular season was a 7-2 Ouachita team that was just a few plays away from being undefeated. To fully understand what this series means to Jeff and me, you must know that we grew up a block from Ouachita's A. U. Williams Field and have attended most of the games between the two Arkadelphia schools since the rivalry resumed in 1963.

With about five minutes left in the fourth quarter, Ouachita went ahead of the heavily favored Reddies by a score of 35-31 following a long punt return for a touchdown. With just more than a minute on the clock, Henderson scored a touchdown to go back ahead, 38-35. On the final play of regulation, Ouachita kicked a field goal to tie the score. The first overtime ended with the score tied at 45-45. Ouachita went ahead 52-45 in the second overtime. Henderson was down to possibly its final play twice in that second overtime but converted both fourth-down plays and sent the game to a third overtime. The battle lasted almost four hours with players so tired they could barely stand at the end. After three overtimes, Henderson had won, 60-52, in what has to be ranked among the most exciting college football games ever played in the state of Arkansas.

Counting the pregame and postgame radio shows, Jeff and I were on the air for six hours that day. Evan, my 16-year-old son, was in the broadcast booth with us as we experienced exhilaration, heartbreak and exhaustion all in the same afternoon. It reminded me again why I so love college football, especially at the small college level where the athletes play for the love of the game. This isn't a column about college football as much as it is one about family, friends, a sense of place and great passions in life.

Evan and I left Little Rock early that Saturday morning and made the drive to Arkadelphia, parking as we always do in the driveway of the home in which I was raised. We then walked down Carter Road to Ouachita's A. U. Williams Field. It's a walk I've been making to Ouachita home games for half a century now. Ouachita and Henderson first played each other in football in 1895. The series was suspended in 1951 due to excessive vandalism. When they started playing again in 1963, I was 4 years old and at the game. Half a century. That's hard for me to fathom. It doesn't seem that long. I always feel like a boy again—giddy with excitement—on the day of the Battle of the Ravine.

Neither Jeff nor I had ever seen as many people packed into A. U. Williams Field as were there for this year's game. It felt good to have thousands of visitors in our Ouachita Hills neighborhood, especially on a day when the color of the leaves had never seemed more beautiful. Even though it has been more than three decades since I lived there full-time, that neighborhood is still home.

It's almost Thanksgiving, a time when we count our blessings and then give thanks for those blessings. I'm blessed with a loving wife and two fine sons. I'm blessed with a number of lifelong friends such as Jeff. I'm blessed to have passions in life such as my love of Ouachita football. They are things that make me look forward to getting out of bed each morning and tackling another day. I'm also blessed to have a strong sense of place. I know where home is. I don't have to search. Neither does Jeff.

"When I was 6 years old, I went to the concession stand with my brother during a Battle of the Ravine and got separated from him on my way back," Jeff told me last week. "My parents could see me and knew I was safe, but I couldn't locate them. It didn't bother me. I just sat down with some other Ouachita fans and watched the game. I felt that anyone on our side of the stadium was family. I still feel that way."

Long after the crowd had left, Jeff, Evan and I walked out of the stadium and down Carter Road. After an afternoon filled with cheers and marching band music, it was eerily quiet. Evan and I told Jeff goodbye as we reached the driveway that leads up a steep hill to his house. We then walked a few hundred yards to our car, ready to make the drive back to Little Rock through the mid-November darkness as a steady rain began to fall. As we completed our walk to the car, I thought about what we had experienced that day. I also thought about my hopes for my son. I hope he has lifelong friends like I have in Jeff. I hope he has passions past the age of 50 that make him feel like a boy again. I hope he has a sense of history, a sense of continuity, a sense of place.

Wherever it is, I hope he has a place that's for him what Ouachita Hills is for me: A place you can always come and know you're home.

January 8, 2014
The King of Augusta

In the days leading up to this week's college football national championship game, thousands of words were written about the fact that Auburn University head coach Gus Malzahn once worked at the high school level in Arkansas. High school coaches are an important part of the fabric of this state. I talk to many Arkansans who are quick to note that outside of their parents, the people who had the most influence on them were high school coaches.

My father spent most of his career traveling the state selling athletic goods. At one point, he knew about every high school coach in Arkansas. My best days were those when I would travel with him. My birthday is September 2. Rather than starting the first grade just as I turned age 6, I waited until I turned 7. My father decided it would be better if I were one of the oldest students in my grade rather than one of the youngest. "I redshirted him," he would say. I had attended a private kindergarten the previous year—there were no public kindergartens in those days—and my father determined that I would learn more crisscrossing the state with him than I would learn by repeating kindergarten.

Even though it has been 48 years, I have clear memories of those months on the road with my father. I can remember sitting on a couch next to a potbelly stove with the coaches in the old gym at Shirley on a cold winter day; taking off my shoes and wading in the Caddo River at Caddo Gap on a warm spring afternoon; waiting in line to buy a hamburger in a small café at Delight; watching deer run across the parking lot of the high school at Magazine. My favorite thing to do was simply sit and listen to my dad, who once had been a high school coach himself, and some of this state's veteran coaches trade stories.

I thought about all of that while reading articles last week about Malzahn's high school coaching days. And I thought about Augusta's Curtis King, perhaps the most famous high school football coach of them all. During the annual coaches' clinic early each August, King would come to our motel room and tell stories late into the night as he and my father smoked their pipes. He was funny. I recall him looking at me one night, smiling and asking: "How long has it been since you were whipped by an old man with bad teeth?"

His son, Jerry King, is writing a book about the coach. Jerry was lucky because, like me, his dad took him everywhere. "I remember all the bus rides to and from games," Jerry King says. "Dad drove the bus, washed and dried all the uniforms, lined the field, maintained the bleachers, you name it. He also taught two classes of algebra and one of geometry. One student, at the first of a school year, leaned into his classroom and asked, 'Coach, is this plane geometry?' He replied, 'Yes, but it will never be plain to you.'"

The younger King relates another story that's well known among those of a certain age at Augusta: "Dad was always out of money. One time, he had no lime to put on the field. During practice, the players began to complain about the smell. They stopped practice and looked around the edge of the fence that surrounded the field for a dead animal. As it turned out, Dad had taken powdered milk from the cafeteria and used it on the field. It had rained, the milk had soured and the whole south end of Augusta stunk."

It's duck season, so Jerry King couldn't resist telling the story of the time Curtis King took his two sons duck hunting: "We were in the blind, and Dad said, 'OK, boys, these ducks are circling. When I count to three, let's shoot them.' Well, on the count of two, he shot and then began laughing. He said, 'Don't you boys ever trust a duck hunter.'"

Curtis King was raised in the Ozark Mountains at Mountain View, but he made a name for himself in the Arkansas Delta. He began his coaching and teaching career in his hometown. During a retirement banquet in 1973, he said: "I had a brand new Model A, a pretty young wife, six foxhounds and $17.50 in my pocket. Tonight, 44 years later, I return with a secondhand car and a worn-out woman. My dogs are dead, and I'm overdrawn at the bank."

King was only 5' 7 and weighed 160 pounds. A writer once described him as a combination of Popeye and Superman. There was no football team at Mountain View when King was growing up so he played basketball and baseball. He was an assistant coach at Beebe from 1937 to 1940 for another legendary coach, Des Arc native Ambrose "Bro" Erwin. Erwin recommended King, who was working construction jobs in Tennessee at the time, to members of the Augusta School Board in 1944. King was the Augusta coach from 1944 to 1973, compiling a 182-105-12 record in football despite consistently playing larger schools such as Searcy, Newport and Batesville. He also coached boys' basketball, girls' basketball and track.

"I never had enough sense to do anything else," he once said. "Any idiot can coach. You only have to do three things to be able to coach: Drive a bus, clean out a commode and repair equipment."

King was inducted into the Arkansas Sports Hall of Fame in 1980, and the Curtis King Award was established by the Arkansas High School Coaches Association. King died in October 1980. Services were held at Augusta in the football stadium that bears his name. The stands were packed that day. Gus Malzahn often tells interviewers that he comes from the high school coaching tree in Arkansas. For years, Augusta's Curtis King was the base of that tree.

January 22, 2014
Swede

A column about Curtis King, a coach who worked at Augusta High School from 1944 to 1973, led to numerous comments from King's former players. That's what happens when you write about teachers and coaches who influenced the lives of hundreds of people. The impetus for the column had been the many stories being written in advance of the national college football championship game about Auburn University head football coach Gus Malzahn and the fact that he had spent much of his career as a high school coach in Arkansas.

King never received national publicity—he was more of an Arkansas phenomenon—but other Arkansas high school football coaches have. In September 2009, *Sports Illustrated* devoted a story to Pulaski Academy head coach Kevin Kelley, whose teams don't punt and usually go with the onside kick. A number of Arkansans remember the story on Kelley. But only those of a certain age will remember 1973 when *Sports Illustrated* focused not once but twice on an Arkansas high school coach. He was Robert E. "Swede" Lee, who led the high school Razorbacks at Texarkana to three consecutive state championships.

Here's what *Sports Illustrated* had to say in its April 23, 1973, edition: "Texarkana straddles the Texas-Arkansas state line, and the football rivalry between the local high schools on either side of the line is fierce, although usually one-sided in the direction of Texas. In 1964, under Coach Robert E. "Swede" Lee, the Arkansas high school beat Texas for the first time in 23 years. After Lee left to become an assistant at Texas A&M, the hard times returned. Now, Arkansas has hired Lee back from A&M, which cheered everybody until the school board said his salary would be $20,000. His predecessor made $12,200 and the proposed salary is higher than that of any other member of the faculty, including the school superintendent."

The Texarkana School Board's vote to hire Lee was 7-1. The lone dissenter was Bill Warner. He told the magazine: "I don't object to the man but to the salary. I think it's excessive. It will cost too much to bring our other people into line with it. The teachers are unhappy, and I think there are a lot of concerned citizens in the town, too."

The national magazine concluded its story this way: "As they say in Texas, there are only three sports: football, spring football and recruiting. Arkansas seems to have the same fever."

The previous season had been marked by racial tension as black players boycotted the team. It was a turbulent time in southwest Arkansas. In my hometown of Arkadelphia, there was a riot at the high school in the spring of 1972 that closed the school for a few days and resulted in armed guards in the halls for the remainder of the school year. At Texarkana, a group of business leaders believed Lee could help quell racial tensions. Ten of them agreed to contribute $500 each to add an extra $5,000 to the $20,000 that the school board was paying Lee. That $5,000 would be billed as compensation for a television show that aired on KTAL-TV at Texarkana.

Lee had played high school football for crosstown rival Texas High and then played for the University of Texas Longhorns. He was on the Longhorn team following the 1956 season when Darrell Royal made the decision to leave the University of Washington to coach at Texas. Longtime State Capitol lobbyist Earl Jones, who grew up at Texarkana, remembers obtaining tickets from Lee to attend the 1964 Arkansas-Texas football game at Austin.

"The tickets were right behind the Texas bench, and Swede warned us not to let on that we were rooting for Arkansas," Jones says. "But when Ken Hatfield returned that punt for a touchdown, we couldn't contain ourselves."

Arkansas would go on to win several versions of the national championship that season. Back in Texarkana, Lee was leading his team to that momentous victory over its rival from the other side of the state line. Jones—whose father, Earl Jones Sr., had moved to Texarkana from North Carolina in October 1947 to open the Belk-Jones Department Store—was among the businessmen who contributed money in 1973. Led by players such as Graylon Wyatt, Robert Williams, Mike Trammell and Earnest Cheatham, the 1973 squad completed the season with a 42-21 victory over Fort Smith Southside in the state championship game. Lee's team recorded the first perfect season in school history with a 13-0 record.

Sports Illustrated came back in its December 10, 1973, edition with this report: "Texarkana High School decided last spring to pay a $20,000 salary to lure Coach Swede Lee back from Texas A&M, where he was an assistant. Lee had been a big success at Texarkana before going off to A&M, but the high school's football fortunes plummeted during his absence. A minority of citizens objected to the salary....Now, however, the returns are in, and the opposition would have a rough time rousing any anti-Lee sentiment. The Arkansas high school had not defeated its state-line rival since Lee's last previous year of tenure in 1964. This year it not only beat the Texas high school, it won 13 straight games and the Arkansas Class AAA championship. If that isn't worth $20,000, what is?"

Texarkana captured the 1974 state championship with a 21-0 shutout of West Memphis and the 1975 state title with a 31-14 victory over Forrest City. After leaving coaching, Lee was the chief executive officer of the Texarkana Chamber of Commerce. He raised $100,000 in 1992 and entered the race for Congress as a Republican against Representative Jim Chapman Jr., a Democrat of Texas' 1st District. After winning the GOP primary, Lee dropped out of the race, leaving Chapman unopposed. Around Texarkana, Lee will never be best remembered as a chamber executive or a political candidate. He'll always be remembered as the high school football coach who made it into *Sports Illustrated* twice in 1973.

November 26, 2014
Tears at 10-0

As the game clock ticked down on a cold, gray Saturday afternoon, I tried to describe the scene at Carpenter-Haygood Stadium in Arkadelphia to those listening to my broadcast of the 88th Battle of the Ravine. For the previous 30 minutes—ever since it had become evident that Ouachita Baptist University would beat Henderson State University to go to 10-0 for the first time in school history—the messages had been flooding my phone. They came from ecstatic Ouachita graduates across the country who were listening online.

I painted a verbal picture as the Ouachita stands emptied, students and even some adults storming the field in the wake of one of the most historic victories in the annals of a football program that dates back to 1895. Henderson had become the Goliath among NCAA Division II football programs in the state, going undefeated during the 2012 and 2013 regular seasons and winning the four previous Battles of the Ravine. The Reddies were 30-1 in regular-season games since the start of the 2012 campaign, having lost only to a talented Harding University squad in the final minute of play earlier this season. Ouachita trailed 17-7 in the first quarter, and it appeared the Reddies were poised to blow the Tigers out. I thought about something the late Buddy Benson, the head coach at Ouachita for 31 seasons, would tell his team before each game: "If at first the game or breaks go against you, don't get shook or rattled. Put on more steam."

Benson had played for Bowden Wyatt at the University of Arkansas. Wyatt had played for General Robert Neyland at the University of Tennessee. Wyatt would repeat Neyland's pregame maxims before games, and Benson continued that tradition at Ouachita. The Tigers indeed put on more steam, outscoring the powerful Reddies 34-3 the rest of the way to win 41-20. I counted down the final seconds on the radio and looked at the Ouachita fans pouring from the stands.

That's when the tears came. Silly, you say, for a 55-year-old man to cry at the end of an athletic contest. It's only a game, you say. I'm sorry, but it's more than a game for me. Ouachita football has been one of my passions since birth.

I grew up a block from Ouachita's football stadium in Arkadelphia, the son of a former Tiger quarterback and a former Ouachitonian beauty (I still have the yearbook in which my mother was featured as such). Like most boys who grew up in Arkansas, I rooted for the Razorbacks. Unlike most boys, Arkansas was never my main team. Ouachita was. We didn't often go to Hog games in Fayetteville or Little Rock. We were too busy following the Tigers. My fondest childhood memories are of trips back from places like Searcy, Conway, Russellville, Magnolia and Monticello in the back of my father's Oldsmobile after Ouachita games.

From age six through high school, I walked the Ouachita sidelines during games along with a group of friends. Benson allowed us to work as ball boys and water boys. My father, who died in March 2011, would have enjoyed this undefeated season. He had been raised poor during the Great Depression at Benton. Following his high school graduation in 1942, he took a job with the Chicago Bridge & Iron Co., which was building an aluminum plant in Saline County. The United States had entered World War II in December 1941, and there was a rush to get the plant operating. Dad was paid union wages and found himself making more than his father. He told his parents that he would stay with the company rather than go to college.

My father was offered a football scholarship to Ouachita, and my grandmother was insistent that he attend college, something neither she nor my grandfather had done. She called Ouachita head coach Bill Walton and ordered him not to let my father come home. The 1942 Ouachita team went 9-1, losing only to Union University in Jackson, Tennessee. Dad joined the Army Air Corps the following spring and served for two years. He returned to Ouachita after the war and played on the 1945-47 teams. He met a pretty young lady named Carolyn Caskey from Des Arc and married her prior to graduation.

My sister recently was cleaning out the house we grew up in and found the program from the Battle of the Ravine that was played Thanksgiving Day 1947. My father is listed as starting quarterback. She gave me the program, which is now among my most cherished possessions.

I also thought of Benson, a childhood hero. He had been one of the nation's most highly recruited players coming out of high school at De Queen. He threw the famous Powder River pass when the Razorbacks beat nationally ranked Ole Miss at War Memorial Stadium in 1954. Benson died on Good Friday in 2011, just weeks after I lost my dad. And I thought of a Crossett native named Mac Sisson, the longtime Ouachita sports information director who gave me the chance as an untested freshman in 1978 to begin broadcasting Ouachita games. Mac is also gone.

My wish for you this Thanksgiving is that you also have one or more great passions in life. It might be a passion for music, acting or writing. It need not have anything to do with sports. It has to do with finding something you care about deeply throughout your life. It's even more special if you've suffered setbacks along the way so you can more fully appreciate the high points. I know defeat. Ouachita didn't have a winning season from 1991 until 2008, and yet I continued to broadcast games all those years. The fact that it's now the only college program in the state with seven consecutive winning seasons makes the accomplishment sweeter.

As the tears rolled down my cheeks, my mind wandered. On this cold November day, I was transported back in time. I was a kid again, marveling at my good fortune: the good fortune of one who grew up in a small town in the South and attended a small college where people call you by your name and care about you; a place where people give you opportunities. After all, who has ever heard of a 19-year-old college play-by-play announcer? Once again, I was in the back seat of the Oldsmobile, fighting to keep my eyes open as Dad drove us through the autumn Arkansas night after a Ouachita game. Once again, Buddy Benson was on the sideline in his starched shirt and tie, and Mac Sisson was in the press box. Once again, my beloved Tigers were on top and the future was limitless. I'm blessed; blessed beyond description as another Thanksgiving arrives.

December 3, 2014
You're the Best

Emogene Nutt of Little Rock stays busy this time of year watching two of her four sons coach basketball. Dickey is the head coach at Southeast Missouri State University, and Dennis is the head coach at Ouachita Baptist University. Then there are the 13 grandchildren, including two sets of twins and one set of triplets. There also are the two well-known sons who coached football, Houston Dale and Danny. Somehow she found time to write a book about her late husband, Houston Nutt Sr., and it's a fascinating read.

The book is titled *You're the Best! Reflections on the Life of Houston Nutt*. It's the story of a man who was born during the Great Depression in the pine woods of south Arkansas and later became an icon in the deaf community. Houston Sr., who died in April 2005 at age 74, often used the phrase "you're the best" when encouraging his students.

"I guess I knew one day I would write a book about Houston," Emogene says. "It's more than being born to deaf parents and raised in a deaf environment where all of his siblings were either totally or partially deaf. It's even more than having played for two legendary coaches. It's about the American dream. Things in Houston's life that could have been a detriment to some people were handled with ease. Houston set high goals for himself in athletics. His dream was to grow up and make life better for deaf people. In addition to this dream, he had an unbelievable passion for basketball. Because of Houston's dedication and hard work, he earned a college education and lived out his dream of coaching basketball and working with the deaf."

Houston and Emogene Nutt moved onto the campus of the Arkansas School for the Deaf at Little Rock in 1956. Emogene says conversations in the deaf community can be "very blunt, straightforward and to the point." She hopes the book will help explain the complexities of the deaf culture. One such complexity, she says, is that "being deaf doesn't mean you are part of the deaf culture. For example, people who lose their hearing from illnesses or deaf children who are born to hearing parents often haven't been privileged to sign language or the knowledge that makes up the deaf culture. Most do acquire the language and culture later in life. However, their acceptance in deaf culture partially depends on their skill in the language. Then there are people like Houston, who are born into deaf culture, inherit the language and take pride in it."

Emogene Nutt wasn't born into that culture, but she learned it while living in a dormitory at the School for the Deaf. When the Nutts arrived in Little Rock as newlyweds, most of the staff members at the school were deaf people who once had been students. It was a steep learning curve, but soon she was like a second mother to the deaf students her husband mentored.

Houston Nutt Sr. graduated from Fordyce High School in 1951 and earned a basketball scholarship to play for Adolph Rupp at the University of Kentucky. Rupp had been coaching at Kentucky since the fall of 1930 and would remain the head coach there until the spring of 1972, compiling an 876-190 record. The head football coach at Kentucky just happened to be from Fordyce. You might have heard of him. Yes, it was Paul "Bear" Bryant, who told Rupp about Houston Nutt Sr.

Nutt later hitchhiked from Fordyce to Lexington, Kentucky, to enroll. The Wildcats were the defending national champions. Kentucky went 29-3 during Nutt's freshman season and made it to the NCAA Elite Eight.

In October 1951, three former Kentucky players were arrested for having taken bribes from gamblers to shave points in a National Invitation Tournament game during the 1948-49 season. The Southeastern Conference voted to ban Kentucky from competing during the 1952-53 season due to that point-shaving scandal, and the

NCAA advised nonconference teams not to schedule the Wildcats. The season was scrapped. Houston Sr. enrolled at Little Rock Junior College with the idea of going back to Kentucky after a year. Instead, he wound up transferring to Oklahoma A&M (now Oklahoma State University) in 1953 to play for another legend, Henry Iba.

How many people could say they played for Rupp and Iba while having Bryant as a family friend? Just one.

"While I was a student at Oklahoma A&M, a tall, thin, handsome guy came strolling through the library with a friend and just happened to sit down at my table," Emogene writes. "He got my attention and said, 'Do you know me?' My reply was, 'No, I don't know you.' In so many words, he explained he had played basketball for Adolph Rupp at Kentucky and was now playing for Coach Iba. I wasn't impressed. I knew absolutely nothing about basketball. Furthermore, I wasn't at all interested. After this introduction, I would occasionally see Houston on campus. He stood out because he was at least a head taller than most everyone else."

She found herself impressed not with his basketball ability but by his smile, his personality and the fact that he didn't drink, smoke or use bad language. During his senior year, Houston Sr. persuaded Emogene to attend a basketball game. After graduation, he had the chance to be a graduate assistant for Iba or play basketball for the Phillips 66 Oilers, an AAU powerhouse in those days. He turned down both offers. He believed his calling was to work with deaf children back home in Arkansas. Emogene went to Fordyce to meet the Nutt family. Marriage soon followed along with a new life in Little Rock.

"Houston whisked me off my feet, and I landed at the Arkansas School for the Deaf," Emogene writes. Hundreds of deaf children would be the beneficiaries of that decision.

November 11, 2015
The Battle of the Ravine

If fellow columnist Paul Greenberg can wax poetic about the

Bradley County pink tomato each summer, I figure I'm allowed to pay tribute each fall to the Battle of the Ravine. After all, it's my favorite day of the year.

When the teams from Ouachita Baptist University and Henderson State University meet Saturday afternoon at Ouachita's Cliff Harris Stadium, it will mark the 89th time the two Arkadelphia colleges have played each other in football. It's a unique rivalry—the only college football game in America in which the road team doesn't fly or bus to a game. It walks. The two stadiums are separated only by two-lane U.S. Highway 67. And the ravine, which is filled with kudzu, still runs between the two main campuses less than a mile to the north.

How close are the schools to each other? Consider the 1999 incident that became known as Trashcam. A Henderson graduate assistant coach took a video camera into Arkadelphia's Central Park, which overlooks the Ouachita practice fields. As he was taping the Tiger practice, the graduate assistant was seen by a Ouachita player. The cameraman, realizing he had been spotted, sped away in his car, leaving the camera in a nearby trash can. When the camera was found with a Henderson identification tag on it, Ouachita athletic director David Sharp removed the video and returned the camera to Henderson. It was the proper thing to do. Though the rivalry is intense, these folks have to live with each other all year. They sit in the same pews at church and find themselves next to each other in the waiting room at the doctor's office.

Having grown up a block from Ouachita's stadium, I realize that I have a hometown bias. But people from outside Arkansas who've experienced the Battle of the Ravine tell me it's indeed among the great rivalries in college football. It might not receive the attention of Auburn-Alabama or Michigan-Ohio State, but those who've played in these games, coached in them, covered them as journalists or simply watched from the stands understand. This is a battle that divides families. If your team wins, you can crow about it for the next 364 days. If your team loses, you feel the pain for a year. No wonder this game was promoted decades ago as the Biggest Little Football

Game in America, a moniker initially used on the East Coast for the NCAA Division III rivalry between Williams College and Amherst College, who first played in 1884.

Ouachita and Henderson, who compete at the NCAA Division II level, first played in 1895. The pranks between students at the two schools got so out of hand that the series was suspended following the 1950 game and not resumed until 1963. The November 10, 2007, game between Williams and Amherst in Williamstown, Massachusetts was selected as the location for ESPN's popular "College Game Day" program. One of these days, the folks at ESPN will make the wise decision to bring that show to Arkadelphia. With Ouachita and Henderson both fielding good teams in recent years—the last four Great American Conference titles have gone to Arkadelphia, two at Ouachita and two at Henderson—the Battle of the Ravine has received national publicity. Last month, *Champion*, the official magazine of the NCAA, featured the rivalry in a story titled "The Short Walk."

"One college's water turned purple," Jared Thompson wrote. "Across the road, red marshmallows rained from the sky. A future state governor set the other school's party ablaze. One time, a homecoming queen was kidnapped for three nights. And no one recalls where the drag queens buried the tiger's tail....The pranks defining Division II's oldest football series have been legendary. The football games have been extraordinary, too. The ancestries supporting either side are entwined tighter than the kudzu that suffocates the nearby ravine from which the rivalry's namesake was found. In Arkadelphia, you grow up cheering either for red or for purple. Yet credits transfer freely between the two schools, and students from one often take classes at the other. Where else might you see the starting quarterback sit next to an opposing lineman in biology class?"

To illustrate how families are divided, I give you Cliff Harris, the former Dallas Cowboy star for whom Ouachita's new stadium is named. Harris and his father played for Ouachita. But his mother was a graduate of Henderson. Sharp, the Ouachita athletic director, also has deep family ties to this series. He and his older brother, Paul, played in the Battle of the Ravine and later coached in the series as Ouachita assistants. Their father, Ike, kicked three successful onside kicks in the final seven minutes of the 1949 Battle of the Ravine as Ouachita overcame a 14-0 deficit. Otis "Magic Toe" Turner, who later was appointed as an associate justice on the Arkansas Supreme Court, kicked the winning field goal for a 17-14 Ouachita victory.

The lights are turned on at both stadiums the week of the game to discourage pranks. Signs on the campuses are covered. Ouachita students guard the Tiger statue in the middle of their campus to keep it from being painted red, and Henderson officials turn off the fountain at the entrance to the campus to keep it from being filled with purple suds. In my family, the day Ouachita played Henderson in football was as big as Christmas. We could walk to both stadiums from our house. When the rivalry resumed in 1963, I was four years old. You can bet I was at the game. Even though I'm in my 33rd season of doing the play-by-play on radio of Ouachita games, this rivalry never gets old. The butterflies in my stomach Saturday afternoon will be such that I'll be almost ill when we sign on. I hope that never changes— that sense of anticipation, that realization of just how much this series has been a part of my life and the life of my family (my father played football at Ouachita in the 1940s and met my mother there).

Early Saturday afternoon, state troopers will stop traffic on the highway, and the Reddies will walk across to play after having put on their uniforms in their own dressing room. Shortly after 4 p.m., the troopers will stop traffic again, and the Reddies will trudge back across the highway. They've played 88 times through the years. Henderson has won 42 times, and Ouachita has won 40. There have been six ties. Of those 88 battles, the game has been decided by a touchdown or less 39 times with Ouachita holding a 19-14-6 advantage in those games. I look at the clock and count the hours until Saturday's kickoff. I love this rivalry, its traditions and its colorful history. I do love it so.

Family
& Home

March 12, 2011

Going Home

It was warm on that first Thursday night in March when the phone call came. The call was dreaded but not unexpected. As I drove to west Little Rock, the memories came flooding back.

I remembered the late nights in his big Oldsmobile as we returned home from watching high school and college football and basketball games.

I remembered the early Saturday mornings when he would roust me from bed before daylight in order to go quail or duck hunting.

I remembered him teaching me how to put a worm on a hook and later how to tie on an artificial lure. I remembered him teaching me how to clean bream, catfish, crappie and bass.

I remembered him teaching me how to swing a baseball bat and catch a fly ball.

I also became proficient under his tutelage at breasting out a bunch of doves and cleaning a limit of quail, though I remained a terrible shot while he was the best wing shot I've ever known.

He saw to it that "sir" and "ma'am" and "please" and "thank you" were regular parts of my vocabulary.

They really were the Greatest Generation, weren't they? They were men who were raised poor, served their country during World War II and then worked hard to care for their families, build businesses and improve their communities.

After three years of coaching at the high school level in Newport, my dad joined his older brother at Southwest Sporting Goods Co. in Arkadelphia. The Nelson brothers built that business into one of the largest retailers of team athletic supplies in the South. It didn't happen without a lot of what my dad called "elbow grease."

Dad spent long days on the road calling on high school and college coaches. As a boy, there was nothing I loved better than being on the road with him. He was truly my hero. He knew virtually every coach in the state on a first-name basis.

When he wasn't selling team supplies, he was officiating football

229

and basketball games. He also was a baseball umpire and for many years was the state's premier track starter. I suspect that shooting that starting pistol next to his right ear all those years was one reason he was hard of hearing.

I remember coming home from a particularly harsh football loss one Friday night when I was the starting center at Arkadelphia High School. Dad, who almost never criticized me, said as I walked through the den: "That nose guard whipped you tonight."

He was right, of course. It hadn't been one of my better games. But I was crushed by the comment. I went to my room, shut the door and crawled into bed. In the hall outside, I could hear my mom gently chastise him.

The door to the bedroom opened. Dad knelt beside my bed and said, "I'm sorry I said that. I didn't mean it. Get some sleep. We'll go duck hunting in the morning and have our limit by 8 a.m."

I slept well after that.

It was painful to watch his health deteriorate. In September 2008, we moved him from the home where he had lived for almost 50 years to a nursing home in Little Rock. The question he asked most often as the dementia worsened the past two years was, "When am I going to go home?"

On that first Thursday night in March, Red Nelson went home.

I spent more than an hour alone in his room that evening, waiting for the funeral home personnel to make the drive from Arkadelphia to Little Rock. I thought back on all of the time we had spent together.

How I wish I could turn back the clock for one last quail hunt in the cutovers of south Arkansas, one last duck hunt in the Ouachita River bottoms, one last fishing trip on the Caddo River, one last drive home following a Ouachita Tiger football game. But we're not allowed to turn back that clock, are we?

I watched the hearse as it slowly pulled out of the front gates of Parkway Village in Little Rock. My hunting companion, my fishing companion, my adviser, my best friend, my hero—my dad— was headed toward the southwest, home to Arkadelphia where the jonquils, the wild plum trees, the tulip magnolias and the Bradford pears were already in full bloom.

Our long, cold winter had ended. Spring had arrived.

December 25, 2013
An Arkansas Christmas

The first Christmas I remember was 50 years ago today. Those memories of December 25, 1963, are vivid because it was my brother's last Christmas.

We shared a room at our family home on Carter Road in Arkadelphia. There are some fleeting memories from late 1963, when I was four and my brother was nine. I remember lifting weights on one of the beds, only to have the barbell slip and leave a hole in the wall. I remember listening to the radio one night as the Beatles sang "I Want to Hold Your Hand," which was written by John Lennon and Paul McCartney, recorded in October 1963 and released on November 29 of that year. We were supposed to be asleep rather than listening to the radio. We tried to reach between our two beds to hold hands, giggling loudly enough to attract our mother's attention. She turned off the radio, but we continued to giggle.

My most enduring memory of 1963 occurred in the wee hours of Dec. 25. I recall my brother shaking me and saying, "Let's go see what Santa Claus brought." I remember sneaking through the darkness to the living room, flipping on a light and seeing the gifts from Santa. Santa didn't wrap his gifts. My parents wrapped theirs. Bob had a bicycle. I had a red toy fire truck big enough for me to fit inside, along with a fire hat. Acting on my brother's dare, I pedaled the fire truck down the hall that connected our home's three bedrooms, waking our older sister and our parents. We were ordered back to bed.

There's a framed photo at our Little Rock home of me in that fire truck, wearing the chief's hat. My wife is the daughter of a career fireman, which is one reason she likes the photo. I like it because it reminds me of my last Christmas with Bob. He was killed just more than nine weeks later in an accident. Though there would be a huge void on Christmas mornings (the stocking with his name on it is still at our family home), Dec. 25 remained a big day. My father wasn't one to sing carols or buy expensive gifts, but he loved the Christmas season and was determined that my sister and I would enjoy it as well. His primary weekend activity this time of year was quail hunting. I always knew Christmas was approaching when he would carry a saw along with his 20-gauge Browning shotgun. While hunting on the Pennington farm in the Ouachita River bottoms near the Clark-Dallas county line, we would saw down a cedar tree and bring it home. Like most Arkansans, we now buy our Christmas tree at a lot. The tree was grown commercially, likely in a state far away. But an Arkansas cedar still smells like Christmas to me.

Cutting the cedar tree wasn't the only extra activity on those early December bird hunts. We would use our shotguns to shoot mistletoe from oak trees and use the saw to remove branches from holly trees that had plenty of red berries on them. All of that would be hauled back into town and used to decorate the house. A few days later, the ladder would be brought out of the storage room so my father could put colored lights on the big cedar tree in the front yard. I remember coming home from school one year and being greeted with the disturbing news that one of our beagles had torn up a Frosty the Snowman yard decoration of which I was particularly fond. We always had at least two bird dogs for quail hunting, but they were more work dogs than pets since my dad took bird hunting so seriously. The beagles were the house pets and mainly excelled at getting fat on table scraps and tearing up things such as Frosty.

My mom would be busy in the kitchen on Christmas morning, while my dad made sure there were fires burning in both fireplaces if it were cold. After stoking the fires, he delighted in sitting in a chair in the living room, smoking a pipe filled with Sir Walter Raleigh tobacco and surveying the scene—the cedar tree, the mistletoe, the holly branches, the gifts wrapped under the tree, his children (and later grandchildren) in their pajamas. After opening the gifts, if we were lucky, breakfast would consist of fried quail, grits, biscuits and preserves made from the wild blackberries my dad had picked the previous summer.

I was blessed to have all four of my grandparents live into their 90s. Ernest and Leanna Nelson lived on Olive Street in Benton. W. J. and Bess Caskey lived on Erwin Street in Des Arc. We often would pile into the car after breakfast and go to Benton, where we would open gifts and have Christmas dinner (always a baked hen). At about 3 p.m., we would head to Des Arc. There would be even more gift opening and a big supper. Tired from all of the activity and full from all of the food, I never had a problem falling asleep in one of the old upstairs beds above the kitchen.

Sometimes we would wait until Dec. 26 to go to Benton and Des Arc. On those Christmas afternoons, my dad would ask, "Want to get out of the house for a couple of hours and get the bird dogs some exercise?" We would cross the Ouachita River, seeing children in front of country houses playing with their new toys as we made our way east toward Dalark on Arkansas Highway 7. The Christmas afternoon bird hunt would continue until dark as we walked the edges of soybean and cotton fields. After getting home, we would put the dogs in their pen, clean any birds we had killed and shower.

Then, my father would end the day just as he had started it. He would make sure the fire in the fireplace was burning brightly before sitting down, lighting his pipe and cracking some pecans.

Each family has its Christmas traditions. For me, an Arkansas Christmas is the smell of a freshly cut cedar, wet bird dogs, pipe smoke and the smoke from a wood-burning fireplace. It's the taste of fried quail and blackberry preserves. It's the sound of a 20-gauge Browning firing and a saw bringing down a holly branch. And, a half century later, it's the memory of a bright red fire truck that belonged to me. Though no one would ever classify it as a Christmas carol, it's also the sound of "I Want to Hold Your Hand." My Christmas wish for you is that you hold someone's hand who is dear to you today and experience your own uniquely Arkansas Christmas.

July 29, 2015
Farewell to a House

I knew the day was coming, but that didn't make it any easier. As my sister and I sat in the offices of a title company across the street from the Clark County Courthouse at Arkadelphia on a Monday morning, I looked through the papers showing that my parents had purchased the house in the Ouachita Hills neighborhood in the spring of 1961. I was not yet two years old. In other words, it was the only house I knew as a boy.

What's now Ouachita Baptist University began developing the wooded hills near the Ouachita River in the late 1950s for faculty housing. Most of the houses when I was young were occupied by Ouachita faculty members, coaches and administrators. My father and mother were Ouachita graduates, but they didn't work at the school. They ran a business downtown. I didn't realize it as a child, of course, but I was living in a special place. My neighbors included a noted musician, a talented playwright, a famous basketball coach, a philosopher, a writer, a theologian and even the state's lieutenant governor. It was the kind of neighborhood that could only be found in a college town.

It was just a short walk to the Ouachita River and Mill Creek, where I could wade, throw rocks and fish. There was a pond across the street to fish in and an old barn to hide in. Ouachita had cattle and horses in the pasture across the street from our house in those days. So even though we were inside the city limits, it was like living in the country. It was the best of both worlds. In the winter, the abundant hills in the neighborhood provided the perfect venue for sledding when there was the occasional south Arkansas snow. In the spring, floods on the Ouachita River provided opportunities to look for turtles and snakes in places we might not otherwise find them. In the summer, the Little League baseball field was an easy bicycle ride away. In the fall, the huge pecan trees along the river provided the nuts we would use at Thanksgiving and Christmas. If I would pick them up, my dad would shell them. The practice field for my beloved

Ouachita Tiger football team was just down the street, giving me a place to hang out after school as a water boy until I had my own football practices once I became a teenager.

It's human nature to look back on things with rose-colored glasses, but there really was a Mayberry element to that neighborhood where everyone knew each other and socialized together. Most of us even attended the same church, the First Baptist Church of Arkadelphia. I lived in a dorm the entire time I was a student at Ouachita, but I could come home each afternoon to check my mail, deliver dirty laundry and wind down for a few minutes before returning to my job as sports editor of the local newspaper. As my father's dementia and other ailments took hold, we were forced to move my parents to a facility in Little Rock. Even though neither of us lived in Arkadelphia, my sister and I hung on to the house.

After all, there was more than 50 years' worth of stuff to clean out. For the longest time, we had neither the time nor the will to take on the task.

We left the water and electricity on, and I occasionally would spend nights there after broadcasting Ouachita football games on the radio. I held out the hope that I could renovate the house as a weekend writing retreat. Finally, my wife convinced me how impractical that plan would be. Last spring, my sister retired following a career in public education and began what turned out to be a new full-time job, cleaning out the house in Ouachita Hills. I'm not sure I would have been able to do it. I would have wanted to read every old newspaper clipping and save those things that really aren't worth saving.

I was at home in Little Rock on the Sunday morning prior to the real estate closing with the television tuned to one of the few programs I watch, *CBS Sunday Morning*. Steve Hartman, the network's modern-day Charles Karalt, had a piece about moving his father out of a house in Toledo, Ohio, that had been in the family since the 1950s. I don't remember Hartman's exact words, but his ending to the story went something like this: "A house with no one in it is no longer a home. It's just a house. What endures are the memories and the lives that were touched by those who once lived there."

I departed my home in Little Rock early on a Monday morning for the trip to Arkadelphia. As I made the one-hour drive, I thought of Steve Hartman's words. I thought of my father, who has been gone for four years now. I thought of my mother, who will turn 90 in August. I thought of my older brother. He got to grow up in that house for less than three years before leaving this earth in 1964 when he was nine and I was four. I met my sister at 7 a.m. for breakfast at the Cracker Barrel in Caddo Valley. We sipped our coffee after the meal and didn't say much. Neither of us looked forward to the real estate closing, though we knew it was something that had to be done. We signed the papers shortly after 8:30 a.m.

My sister stayed to visit with the real estate agent, and I made one last trip to the house. I walked through the kitchen where I ate most of my meals, the den where I spent so many nights in front of the fireplace watching sports events on television, the living room where we would open gifts on Christmas morning. I walked for the final time into the recreation room my father had added to the house, the one that had the pool table and hosted hundreds of Ouachita students and others through the years. I walked into my parents' bedroom, my sister's bedroom and finally the bedroom I had shared with my brother for too short a time. Then, I took the key off the chain, laid it on the kitchen counter, took a long look and shut the door before the memories could totally consume me. It was time to say so long to 648 Carter Road.

I stepped into the carport where my dad once had parked his big Oldsmobile, started my car, drove slowly around the circle and then headed for U.S. Highway 67, Interstate 30 and the office in downtown Little Rock. The tears didn't clear until somewhere east of Malvern.

December 2, 2015
Mom

I knew immediately what the news would be when the telephone rang shortly before 6 a.m. on the first truly cold Sunday morning of fall. My wife told me it was Parkway Village calling. My mom, who had been going downhill since a fall earlier this year resulted in her hip being broken in three places, had died at age 90.

I drove quickly to the facility off Chenal Parkway in west Little Rock, called my sister and then sat with the body while waiting for the funeral home personnel to arrive from Arkadelphia. During that quiet period of reflection, I thought about her journey and the changes she had seen in this state through the decades. I inherited my love of Arkansas from her. She was born August 21, 1925, to Bess Rex Caskey and W. J. Caskey in the old White River town of Des Arc, a place filled with colorful characters. Her father owned the funeral home and hardware store on Main Street, and she was raised in a big house a couple of blocks away on Erwin Street. My grandfather was also a county elected official, and Mom took trips with him to communities with names like Tollville, Ulm and Beulah.

The Caskeys were staunch Baptists, and Mom would laugh decades later at the memory of the elderly Catholic lady at Slovak who pointed at her and asked in her thick eastern European accent: "Would the child like some wine?" Mom soaked up the traditions and culture of the lower White River region. The First Baptist Church of Des Arc was just across the street from the Caskey home, and my mother would spend hours there. She was at the church practicing with the youth choir for an upcoming Christmas concert when word came on that fateful Sunday afternoon in December 1941 that the Japanese had bombed Pearl Harbor. Soon, her three older brothers— Bill, Mike and Joe—were out of the country, serving in the armed forces. There were three blue stars in the front window of the Caskey home. It was just my grandparents, my mother and her older sister Ellen Bess, listening to the radio each evening for war news and saying a nightly prayer for those who were far from home.

237

Her brothers were still gone on May 27, 1943, when my mother spoke at her high school graduation. One of my most treasured possessions is a typed copy of her graduation address that my sister found while cleaning out our family home. My mom said that day: "Most of us have grown up in a period of world-sweeping events. Most of us are being impressed each day with the fact that we are coming out of school in the most critical period of American history. The far-reaching effect of the present great struggle for renewal of the rights of man is an inspiration for anyone. Deep in the heart of every boy or girl lives an ambition to become great. To study the noble deeds and great advancements of others is to long to do something equally as grand ourselves, and we are inspired with a burning desire for some opportunity for the display of heroism or strength of character. We see how far short we are of what seems necessary to do those things."

Her three brothers (all of whom would return home safely from the war and live to ripe old ages) graduated from Arkansas Tech. But W. J. Caskey, the Baptist deacon, wanted his girls to go to the Baptist school in Arkadelphia. Mom enrolled at what's now Ouachita Baptist University in the fall of 1943. She excelled in school and after the war met Robert L. "Red" Nelson of Benton, who was returning to Ouachita following service in the U.S. Army Air Forces as a bombardier on a B-17. He was a sports star at Ouachita, excelling in football, basketball and baseball. He even set what was then a school basketball record for most points in a game and quarterbacked the football team his senior year.

Mom, meanwhile, was named the campus beauty. The quarterback and the beauty queen were married on August 11, 1946, at the Caskey home in Des Arc.

Mom graduated from college in the spring of 1947 and worked for two Arkadelphia businessmen while my dad finished his senior year. Following Dad's graduation, he was offered the job of head football coach at Newport High School. He accepted the offer, and the young couple headed off to Jackson County, where my mom taught elementary school while Dad coached the Greyhounds. Their first child, a daughter named Lynda, was born in 1950. After three years at Newport, my father joined his older brother in business at Arkadelphia. The Nelson brothers built Southwest Sporting Goods Co. into one of the region's largest providers of athletic supplies to high school and college teams, and my mom served for many years as the company's business manager. Her contributions to the business were as vital as my father's.

Dad would spend days at a time on the road, calling on high school and college coaches. Mom stayed behind in Arkadelphia to oversee the business and raise her family. A son named Bob was born in 1954. I came along in 1959. The ultimate test of my mother's faith and strength came on February 29, 1964, and in the days, months and years that followed. My parents and Bob were in Pine Bluff to watch a Ouachita basketball game when my brother was run over by a delivery truck. My mother held him as they rushed to the hospital, where he died at age nine. As the father of two sons, I cannot imagine how one could go on after watching a nine-year-old child die. But Mom had my father, my sister and me to care for so she persevered, leaning on her strong Christian faith.

Mom and Dad celebrated their 64th wedding anniversary in 2010. They were a couple in the truest sense of the word. She was never quite the same after my father died on March 3, 2011. Mom would have been embarrassed by a column devoted to her. She was never one to draw attention to herself. We buried Carolyn Caskey Nelson next to my father and my brother on the morning before Thanksgiving. The next day, with the turkey and dressing on the table, we gave thanks for the life she lived and the example she set. She was a proud daughter of the Arkansas Grand Prairie. I was proud to call her my mom.

EPILOGUE

As I write this, the front page of the *Arkansas Democrat-Gazette* contains a story noting that 49 Arkansas counties lost population in 2015 and only 26 counties gained population. The state gained population overall—about 11,400 additional residents—with most of that growth fueled by the economic boom in northwest Arkansas.

The urbanization of Arkansas continues.

Between the 2000 census and the 2010 census, 39 counties gained population and 36 lost population. As you might guess, the counties that gained population tended to be in the northwest, west, central and north-central parts of the state. The counties that lost population tended to be in east and south Arkansas. There were exceptions. The Jonesboro area, for example, has grown at a rapid rate since the turn of the century, fueling growth in Craighead and Greene counties in northeast Arkansas.

In general, though, large parts of the Delta of east Arkansas and the pine woods of south Arkansas are emptying out. The population shift from east and south to north and west has been occurring in Arkansas since at least the 1950 census, when the widespread mechanization of agriculture meant that tens of thousands of tenant farmers and sharecroppers no longer were needed in the state's rural areas. That trend, however, has accelerated since the turn of the century.

I don't consider it my job to make a value judgment on whether this is a good thing or a bad thing. It doesn't matter what I think. People are going to do what's best for their families and go where the jobs are.

What cannot be denied is that Arkansas is a far different place now than it was a decade ago and will be an even more different place a decade from now. Part of what I've tried to do through the years is capture the essence of the independently owned restaurants, the swimming holes, the hunting grounds, the colorful characters, the local festivals and the sports events that were such an important part of the Arkansas in which I was raised in the 1960s and '70s.

Those who know me realize that I'm fiercely proud of being from Arkansas. When the *Arkansas Democrat* sent me to Washington, D.C., in 1986, I knew it would be a temporary stay. It was a wonderful opportunity for a young man in his 20s, but I had no desire to spend the rest of my career in the nation's capital. By the end of the decade, I was home. I brought along a new bride who was a south Texas native. She soon fell in love with this place they had called the Wonder State when I was a boy. Our two sons were born here, raised here and chose to attend college here.

I know this sounds provincial, but here goes: Arkansas is such a unique, quirky place that I believe it takes someone who grew up here and traveled its rural highways as a child to really explain what makes us tick. We welcome those who move to Arkansas from elsewhere and hope they soon will consider themselves Arkansans. Please understand that we don't brag like Texans or brand ourselves as different from the rest of the world like Mississippians. We know what we've got going for us here. And despite our many problems, it still remains a fine place to call home.

I hope you've enjoyed the journey on these pages.

Rex Nelson, who is senior vice president and director of corporate community relations at Simmons First National Corp., has had a long career in government, journalism and public affairs. He writes a regular column for the *Arkansas Democrat-Gazette*, appears often on various radio shows and is the author of the popular Southern Fried blog at www.rexnelsonsouthernfried.com. A native of Arkadelphia, he lives in Little Rock with his wife and two sons.

9 781935 106982